The Recognition of H. P. Lovecraft

The Hippocampus Press Library of Criticism

S. T. Joshi, *Primal Sources: Essays on H. P. Lovecraft* (2003)
S. T. Joshi, *The Evolution of the Weird Tale* (2004)
Robert H. Waugh, *The Monster in the Mirror: Looking for H. P. Lovecraft* (2006)
Scott Connors, ed., *The Freedom of Fantastic Things: Selected Criticism on Clark Ashton Smith* (2006)
Ben Szumskyj, ed., *Two-Gun Bob: A Centennial Study of Robert E. Howard* (2006)
S. T. Joshi and Rosemary Pardoe, ed., *Warnings to the Curious: A Sheaf of Criticism on M. R. James* (2007)
S. T. Joshi, *Classics and Contemporaries: Some Notes on Horror Fiction* (2009)
Kenneth W. Faig, Jr., *The Unknown Lovecraft* (2009)
Massimo Berruti, *Dim-Remembered Stories: A Critical Study of R. H. Barlow* (2010)
Gary William Crawford, Jim Rockhill, and Brian J. Showers, ed., *Reflections in a Glass Darkly: Essays on J. Sheridan Le Fanu* (2011)
Robert H. Waugh, *A Monster of Voices: Speaking for H. P. Lovecraft* (2011)
Donald Sidney-Fryer, *The Golden State Phantasticks: The California Romantics and Related Subjects* (2012)
William F. Nolan, *Nolan on Bradbury: Sixty Years of Writing about the Master of Science Fiction* (2013)
Steven J. Mariconda, *H. P. Lovecraft: Art, Artifact, and Reality* (2013)
S. T. Joshi, *Unutterable Horror: A History of Supernatural Fiction* (2014)
Massimo Berruti, S. T. Joshi, and Sam Gafford, ed., *William Hope Hodgson: Voices from the Borderland* (2014)
Robert H. Waugh, *The Tragic Thread in Science Fiction: Essays on David Lindsay, Olaf Stapledon, et al.* (2019)
Charles Hoffman and Marc Cerasini, *Robert E. Howard: A Closer Look* (2020)
Robert H. Waugh, *A Monster for Many: Talking with H. P. Lovecraft* (2021)

Lovecraft Annual (2007–)
Dead Reckonings (2007–)

The Recognition of H. P. Lovecraft

His Rise from Obscurity to World Renown

S. T. Joshi

Hippocampus Press

New York

Published by Hippocampus Press
P.O. Box 641, New York, NY 10156.
www.hippocampuspress.com

Cover illustration and design by Jason Van Hollander
Hippocampus Press logo designed by Anastasia Damianakos.

First Edition
1 3 5 7 9 8 6 4 2

ISBN 978-1-61498-345-3 (paperback)
ISBN 978-1-61498-346-0 (ebook)

Contents

Preface

This book seeks to chart both the dissemination of H. P. Lovecraft's work during and after his lifetime and to identify and assess the discussions of his life, work, and thought among academicians, critics, reviewers, and (where possible) general readers in that same period. The materials that are available for this undertaking are of such a radically differing sort, depending on the era that is being discussed, as to engender a kind of cognitive dissonance in the historian. During Lovecraft's lifetime, as well as in the first three or four decades following his death (i.e., roughly the period 1905 to 1971), his work was so minimally distributed, and the criticism of that work so vanishingly small, that we are obliged to point to citations of Lovecraft in the letter columns of magazines or to random mentions in books or magazines to convey the notion that Lovecraft was still a matter of interest to either the weird fiction community or the literary community at large; but in the decades following 1971, the amount of relevant material is so immense that one can scarcely do more than write a few sentences about any given biography, treatise, scholarly or popular article, or edition of Lovecraft's work here or abroad. As a result, the earlier portions of this book may seem excessively detailed, whereas in the later portions both primary and secondary texts of undeniable importance might be thought to be cited with almost insulting brevity. But there seems to be no alternative to the plan I have adopted, if it is not to result in a treatise many times the size of this one.

There is good reason to question whether I am the right person to write a book of this sort, given my own intimate involvement in the propagation of Lovecraft's texts and in the critical analysis of his life and work over the past four decades. Given that I have already discussed some facets of the earlier portions of this book in my biography (*I Am Providence,* 2010), and have in a personal way ruminated on my work as a Lovecraft scholar in my memoirs (*What Is Anything? Memoirs of a Life in Lovecraft,* 2018), it could well be asked (a) whether I have anything new to say on this subject, and (b) whether I can gauge my own contributions with the objectivity that I seek to bring to other sections of this work. I shall have to leave it to readers to determine how well I have accomplished either of these goals.

Especially in the earlier chapters of this book, I use certain texts repeatedly, and so I have seen fit to cite them directly in the text by the following abbreviations:

AV Joshi & Schultz, *Ave atque Vale* (2018)
CE Lovecraft, *Collected Essays* (2004–06; 5 vols.)
CF Lovecraft, *Collected Fiction: A Variorum Edition* (2015–17; 4 vols.)
HPL H. P. Lovecraft
WW Joshi, *A Weird Writer in our Midst* (2010)

Full bibliographical information on these and other works can be found in the bibliography at the end of the book. That bibliography of course lists only those works I have cited here, and does not pretend to be a comprehensive listing of works by and about Lovecraft; even a skeletonic list of such works would take many pages.

I am grateful to Stefan Dziemianowicz and Steven J. Mariconda for their assistance and expertise in providing information and commentary for this book.

I. Beginnings (1905–1922)

It is one of the many anomalies in the recognition of H. P. Lovecraft that the first discussion of him occurred before his work even appeared in print. In 1905, a column in a New York newspaper took account of Lovecraft's boast that he had all manner of meteorological equipment:

> H. P. Lovecraft, who says he forecasts for Rhode Island, writes to say that he thinks his predictions will reach over into New York and New England.
>
> "It may interest you to know," he writes, "that I have one mercurial thermometer by Spooner, six maximum and minimum thermomemeters [*sic*] by Casella, one psychometrical apparatus, one rain, one hair hygrometer and a wind vane." He spells the name of the thermometer a syllable longer than usual to indicate a superior length of column.[1]

Lovecraft had established a meteorological station in his house as an adjunct to his astronomical studies. This interest had initially developed toward the end of 1903, as notices in the *Scientific Gazette* suggest. The issue of January 24, 1904, announced a new "Climatological Station" that "belongs to the publishers [*sic*] of this paper"; it had "6 circular windows with shutters, in case of severe storm. The instruments have not all arrived yet . . . Although the station is not, as yet, fully equipped, it *can* do much practice-work, for the storm glass is very accurate, and the wet-bulb thermometer, which was made by the ob-

---

1. [Unsigned], "Long Distance Predictions," *Amsterdam* [NY] *Evening Recorder* (6 September 1905): 1.

server works to perfection." We can probably connect this with another surviving juvenile item, a "Providence Observatory Forecast" for April 5, 1904, made on the 4th. This is a single sheet giving a prediction of the weather for the next day ("no clouds will cross the sky—excepting a few sunset strata").

This interest led to Lovecraft's participation in a contest sponsored by a New York lawyer, Frederick R. Fast, for the best weather forecasts. The article in the *Amsterdam Evening Recorder* states that Fast "offered $100 for the most successful forecast," and that the *New York Herald* reported on the matter. So it appears that the article is quoting a letter that Lovecraft wrote to Fast, which was then quoted in the *Herald*. (The *Herald* article has not been located.)

Lovecraft had written smugly in the *Rhode Island Journal of Astronomy* of 3 September 1905 that his "forecasts have been right 1/3 more times than the local weather station since October [1904?]." Even so, Lovecraft apparently did not win the contest.[2]

As stated, this whole incident occurred before Lovecraft's first official appearance in print—a letter to the editor of the *Providence Sunday Journal* (3 June 1906) on a point of astronomy. Soon thereafter, two different sets of astronomy columns began to be published: one in the *Pawtuxet Valley Gleaner* (beginning on 27 July and appearing with some regularity in every weekly issue of the paper at least down to the end of 1906, and possibly as late as 1908),[3] and a monthly column in the Provi-

2. For more on this issue, see Richard Bleiler, "H. P. Lovecraft's First Appearance in Print," *Lovecraft Annual* No. 14 (2020): 26–36. In spite of the title of the essay, this discussion of HPL does not constitute, in the bibliographical sense, an "appearance in print," because it is not a self-standing item printed under HPL's byline.

3. No issues of the *Gleaner* have been found subsequent to 28 December 1906, although evidence exists that the paper continued at least through 1907.

dence *Tribune* (morning, evening, and Sunday editions), beginning on 1 August and proceeding till 1 June 1908. Scattered letters to the editor also appeared down to the end of 1909, most famously in the *Scientific American* of 25 August 1906—one of the most prominent publications of any work by Lovecraft for many decades.

This was, of course, the time when Lovecraft was attending Hope Street High School, albeit somewhat irregularly and with many absences. He had attended for the 1904–05 school year, then sat out nearly the entirety of the 1905–06 term, then returned for two years (1906–08) before dropping out in June 1908. If he had completed the 1905–06 term, he would have graduated in 1908; but in the event, he was many credits short of graduation before he experienced the "nervous breakdown" that sidelined him for the next five years.

During this "blank" period Lovecraft did little except read books from his family library (and, very likely, the Providence Public Library), dabble in correspondence courses in chemistry, attend (probably briefly) the First Universalist Church (or, at least, the "Men's Club" there), and write a few poems, one of which—"Providence in 2000 A.D."—did appear in print, in the *Providence Evening Bulletin,* 4 March 1912. Lovecraft does not report on whether this poem (satirically suggesting that in ninety years' time the largely Anglo-Saxon names of locales in Providence would be replaced by names pertaining to the city's ethnic minorities) elicited any commentary among readers.

What *did* provoke plenty of commentary—and, bizarrely enough, led to the gradual abandonment of Lovecraft's self-imposed hermitry and in effect made the rest of his career possible—was the letters and poems that Lovecraft published in the *Argosy* and *All-Story* in 1913–14. These flagship periodicals of Frank A. Munsey's magazine chain were immensely popular venues for the publication of popular fiction of all sorts, including a modicum of weird fiction as well as the Tarzan and John Carter novels of Edgar Rice Burroughs. As with his *Scientific American* letter, the material that Lovecraft published here (amounting only to eight items, five letters and three poems) were among the most widely distributed works appearing under his name during and well after his lifetime.

His first letter, signed only "H. P. L., of Providence, Rhode Island,"[4] appeared in the *Argosy* for November 1911 and is, surprisingly enough, a paean of praise to the serialised historical novels of Albert Payson Terhune, whom Lovecraft singles out for his "surpassing merit, in selection of historical period, development of plot, and purity of English" (8).[5] The amusing thing is that Terhune (1872–1942), aside from writing historical novels, later became famous for writing dog stories (notably the short story collection *Lad: A Dog* [1919] and its many successors), a species that the ailurophile Lovecraft held in low esteem.[6] In any event, Lovecraft's letter announces that he has been a "Reader since 1905" (8).

But it was in the fall of 1913 that Lovecraft's comments in the *Argosy* became truly controversial. The September 1913 issue published a letter that ran to well over 1000 words condemning the work of the romance writer Fred Jackson (1886–1953). Jackson certainly enjoyed far more success (if widespread publi-

4. Joshi, *H. P. Lovecraft in the Argosy* 8. All subsequent material from the *Argosy* and *All-Story* are taken from this publication and will be cited in the text by page number.

5. HPL also wrote a poem, "To Mr. Terhune, on His Historical Fiction," which presumably dates to this period; but it remained unpublished during his lifetime.

6. Terhune's stories about Lad were not the basis for the film and television show *Lassie*. Lassie was created by Eric Knight in a story published in the *Saturday Evening Post* in 1938.

cation and income made from writing count as "success") than Lovecraft, as he wrote screenplays for at least fifty films and had numerous plays produced on Broadway, all apart from his serialised novels in *Argosy* and elsewhere—but, amusingly enough, he now seems largely known today precisely because of Lovecraft's attacks on him.

Lovecraft's letter is full of pungent jabs at Jackson: his work is "trivial, effeminate, and, in places, coarse"; it is full of grammatical errors; and, in general, Jackson belongs to the "saccharine, gelatinous school of literature" (9). Lovecraft is of course taking issue with the numerous sentimental romances published under Jackson's name at this time—material that the reclusive dreamer from Providence, who even years later admitted was "unfamiliar with amatory phenomena save through cursory reading,"[7] was not inclined to favour.

It is unlikely that either Lovecraft or the editors of the *Argosy* expected that this letter—somewhat stiff in diction and drawn from his readings of eighteenth-century prose writers (it is headed by a poetic epigraph by Thomas Tickell on Addison's *Cato*)—would have elicited the response that it did. In the November 1913 issue two letters supported Lovecraft, but two others did not. One, by T. P. Crean, states: "I am still puzzling over H. P. Lovecraft's letter. . . . Mr. Lovecraft, from his letter, should be able to tell a good story when he reads one. I am personally of the opinion that his letter was merely to display to THE ARGOSY world his vocabulary, or he may be a less successful author" (11). Without becoming over-analytical, these comments—which might be classified as hostile biographical criticism designed to impugn Lovecraft's *motives* in writing his letter without addressing the substance of his remarks—are representative of the kind

---

7. HPL to Rheinhart Kleiner, 27 September 1919; *Letters to Rheinhart Kleiner and Others* 143.

of "criticism" Lovecraft received over the next year or so in the *Argosy*.

Consider Elizabeth E. Loop in the December 1913 issue: "If he would use a few less adjectives and more words which the general public are more familiar with than labyrinthine, laureled, luminary, lucubrations, and many others" (12; yes, this alliterative comment is a sentence fragment). Or F. W. Saunders in the same issue, who finds that a number of words used in Lovecraft's letter are "not in my little 8 x 10 dictionary" (13). H. C. Doyle in the February 1914 issue puts forth the more daring hypothesis that Lovecraft is "very likely to be a person with a chronic grouch against all humanity" (17). To Ira B. Forrest (April 1914), Lovecraft is "a grouchy old bachelor and dislikes sentiment in any form" (19). The accidental soundness of this judgment is purely adventitious, as of course Forrest could have known nothing about Lovecraft as a person.

I have bypassed the other letter attacking Lovecraft in the November 1913 issue: this was by John Russell, and it was *in verse*. The first stanza runs as follows:

> Does Mr. Lovecraft think it wise
> With such long words to criticize
> An author whom we greatly prize?
> That's Freddie Jackson. (10)

Russell was a Scottish-born writer then living in Tampa, Florida, and his poetic squib directly incited Lovecraft to reply in kind, with the four-part "Ad Criticos" (To [my] critics), written in magnificent heroic couplets reminiscent of Pope's *Dunciad*. But only two parts appeared in the *Argosy:* "Liber Primus" in the January 1914 issue and "Liber Secundus" in the February 1914 issue. The publication of these two segments in consecutive issues suggests that Lovecraft had in fact sent all four parts to the editor of the letters column, Matthew White, Jr., but that White for some reason did not publish the remaining two. He did deign to publish a prose letter ("Correction for Lovecraft") in the March 1914 issue, in which Lovecraft somewhat pedantically objects to the typographical alteration whereby the *Argosy* inexplicably retained the British spelling variant "shew" but altered the rhyme in the next line, "know," to "knew." This, in fact, was Lovecraft's final published document in the *Argosy* until the editor compelled Russell and Lovecraft to end the feud in the October 1914 issue.

Lovecraft's poetic lambasting of some of his opponents did not sit well either with them or with other readers. F. W. Saunders attempted to reply in kind with a rather incoherent poem of his own, "Ruat Caelum," in the April 1914 issue. But it was Russell who replied most pungently in verse. His poem in the May 1914 issue begins:

> Lovecraft has dropped from rime to prose,
> To shew that what he knew, he knows.
> I say that really to my view
> 'Twas little that he ever knew. (22)

This is actually much more malicious than anything Lovecraft ever wrote, in prose or in verse.

But others came forward, suggesting (lightheartedly, one imagines) that actual violence should be done to Lovecraft. Jack E. Brown states, "I get sore at people like H. P. L.," then adds: "I am a cow-puncher, and certainly would like to loosen up my .44-six on that man Lovecraft" (23). One K. Morris writes that "you might pass the word to the authorities that there are places for people like Mr. H. P. Lovecraft with brain-storms" (23). I imagine Morris is recommending that Lovecraft be locked up in a lunatic asylum. Then there is C. M. Turner, whose letter is titled "Lovecraft in Irons" and actually states that very thing with an extended metaphor relating to imprisonment on a ship: "So, please put Mr. Lovecraft in 'irons,' and place Mr. Fred Jackson in the position of first mate and let the good old ARGOSY sail on" (24). Very clever!

The overriding concern among many of the letters hostile to Lovecraft is the notion that any sort of criticism—which, in these letters, is articulated by such pejorative slang terms as "knock," "kick," and its analogues—is somehow off limits. This line of thought (if it can be called that) begins with a brief letter by A. F. B. in the January 1914 issue, although it is directed not toward Lovecraft but toward another writer hiding behind initials who had supported Lovecraft: "Mr. E. F. W. C., I consider you a knocker. Do you know a good story when you see one? Let common sense prevail and don't insult people" (14). T. P. Crean writes that Lovecraft's "extensive vocabulary and easily adapted rimes should be employed other than roasting an author, who, although he may have a few defects in a story, produces a tale that is interesting from start to finish, which is all that a reader of a fiction magazine can ask for" (16). Clifford D. Ennis believes that Lovecraft should use his extensive vocabulary in "praising, not criticizing" (17). Here again the very act of "criticizing" (i.e., of making censorious comments, no matter how justified or well argued) is condemned.

And yet, it is indeed unreasonable to expect a popular magazine to publish work of high literary calibre. But John Russell, in a poem in the April 1914 issue, falls into the fallacy of assuming that, since sentiment appears in the work of "Dickens and Fenny [i.e., James Fenimore Cooper], Shakespeare, Scott" (20), it is acceptable in Jackson's work. Is Russell really suggesting that Jackson can be compared to these classics? The very posing of the question is an adequate answer. And yet, H. Kendall states remarkably: "In my opinion Mr. Jackson's stories are too high grade for the people who are knocking him. Were he to put in a few more villains, some murders, a bunch of six-shooters, burglars, *et cetera,* he would appeal to the knockers" (31). It is safe to say that, in that case, Lovecraft would not be among those who suddenly transform their hostility of Jackson to praise.

There is little profit in studying the *Argosy/All-Story* controversy any further. It is striking that (a) a number of those who defended Jackson's sentimental romances were men, in contrast to today, where the overwhelming majority of readers of such material are women, and (b) that so many readers were unable to make a distinction between the stories that they personally found enjoyable and those that actually qualify as genuine literature. Comments such as R. McE.'s ("I think it is just the best magazine I ever read" [27]) or S. L.'s (the *Argosy* authors "are the best ever" [27]) suggest the yawning gulf in education and critical judgment between Lovecraft and his opponents. These latter were of course not trained literary critics or even truly educated readers, so their hostility to someone high-handedly attacking one of their favourites was only to be expected.

Indeed, Lovecraft received an unexpected attack in the *All-Story* after the publication of another long letter in the 7 March 1914 issue—a letter that was largely praiseworthy ("In the present age of vulgar taste and sordid realism it is a relief to peruse a publication such as THE ALL-STORY, which has ever been and still remains under the influence of the imaginative school of Poe and Verne" [34]), although it does offer some criticism of scientific and other errors in the work of Burroughs, who is otherwise lauded ("At or near the head of your list of writers Edgar Rice Burroughs undoubtedly stands" [34]) in a comment that would have mortified Lovecraft in later years.

This letter elicited a bitter response from one S. P. N., who blasted Lovecraft:

> In the ALL-STORY WEEKLY for March 7 I read a letter signed H. P. L., and dated at Providence, Rhode Island. I have become acquainted with that gentleman before. He seems to be a born knocker and an egotist of the worst type. His vanity is awful. His assumed eloquence and literary powers are disgusting.
>
> [. . .] let me give you a piece of advise [*sic*] about H. P. L., Editor. Watch him, he's dangerous. This letter of his didn't knock so much, but it will come with time.
>
> He can't help it. It's born in him to knock, and he can't possibly boost and do it gracefully. Wait till he starts firing some of his rotten poetry at you. Oh, my! (36)

This letter largely sums up the many threads of attack Lovecraft endured from readers of the *Argosy*.

But of course, the importance of this whole episode in Lovecraft's life was that he (and also John Russell) were invited by Edward F. Daas to join the United Amateur Press Association (UAPA). Daas had noted the ongoing controversy and assumed that Lovecraft would make a worthy member of the association. He could not possibly have known that this simple act allowed Lovecraft, in due course of time, to blossom into the writer who has now attained worldwide fame.

Lovecraft officially joined the UAPA on 6 April 1914; he was designated as member 1945c. For the better part of a year he did little but attempt to gain a sense of the nature and parameters of the organisation he had joined. In the six months following his entry, he published only a single article, "A Task for Amateur Journalists" (*New Member,* July 1914), and one poem, "On a Modern Lothario" (*Blarney Stone,* July–August 1914). His unexpected appointment as chairman of the Department of Public Criticism in the fall of 1914 led to his writing the "Department of Public Criticism" columns (official surveys of amateur publications) in the *United Amateur* for November 1914 and January and March 1915. He also published a few more poems and articles in other papers from late 1914 into early 1915.

But matters changed significantly in the spring of 1915, when Lovecraft published the first issue of his own paper, the *Conservative* (dated March 1915 but only printed and distributed in April). Lovecraft evidently made an effort to send it to most members of the UAPA. Its reaction can be gauged by a comment by Rheinhart Kleiner in a memoir of Lovecraft:

> . . . many were immediately aware that a brilliant new talent had made itself known. The entire contents of the issue, both prose and verse, were the work of the editor, who obviously knew exactly what he wished to say, and no less exactly how to say it. *The Conservative* took a unique place among the valuable publications of its time, and held that place with ease through the period of seven or eight years during which it made occasional pronouncements. Its critical pronouncements were relished by some and resented by others, but there was no doubt of the respect in which they were held by all.[8]

Lovecraft published thirteen issues of the *Conservative* over the next eight years; much of the contents was his own material—essays, poetry, and editorials. And of course Lovecraft contributed voluminously to other periodicals during the period 1914–25, when the UAPA largely became moribund. Lovecraft also quietly joined the rival National Amateur Press Association (NAPA) in 1917 and contributed to its journals also, notably the *Tryout,* edited by Charles W. Smith of Haverhill, Mass., which published a large proportion of Lovecraft's early poetry. The number of his contributions from 1914 to 1925 is staggering: 157 articles (including editorials, review columns, etc.), 159 poems, and 25 short stories.

I am not interested in pursuing the back-and-forth controversies that Lovecraft's articles and poems elicited, interesting as

---

8. "Howard Phillips Lovecraft," *Californian* 5, No. 1 (Summer 1937): 5.

these sometimes are. In particular, James F. Morton (years before he came into direct contact with Lovecraft) and Charles D. Isaacson lambasted Lovecraft for his political and literary opinions in two articles published in Isaacson's journal *In a Minor Key* (undated, but issued in the early summer of 1915). Lovecraft also engaged in disputes with such other amateurs as Anthony F. Moitoret and Ida C. Haughton. But these tempests in a teapot do not constitute literary criticism in any meaningful sense.[9]

The very few scraps of actual criticism—either biographical or critical—of Lovecraft in this initial phase of his amateur activity can virtually be counted on the fingers of one hand. Surprisingly, the first came almost less than a year and a half after Lovecraft's entry into the UAPA. Andrew F. Lockhart wrote a piece entitled "Little Journeys to the Homes of Prominent Amateurs" for the *United Amateur* of September 1915 that gave a broad outline of the twenty-five-year-old Lovecraft. This was the first instalment of a recurring column; the second, published in October 1915, was written by Lovecraft himself (under his "El Imparcial" pseudonym) and discussed Lockhart. Lovecraft wrote another instalment of the column (the fifth in the series), for the July 1917 *United Amateur,* on the amateur writer Eleanor J. Barnhart.

Lockhart's piece (*AV* 168–71) is of interest because it was obviously not based on any personal encounters with Lovecraft (he lived in Millbank, South Dakota) but purely on correspondence. It is a tad sentimental, but its chief importance is in exhib-

---

9. I similarly bypass the controversies in which HPL engaged with Orville L. Leach (*Providence Sunday Journal,* 1908) and J. F. Hartmann (Providence *Evening News,* 1914) over points of science and astronomy. The latter are of interest only because Hartmann was entirely unaware that the satires HPL wrote under the "Isaac Bickerstaffe, Jun." pseudonym were in fact by HPL.

iting how Lovecraft was already crafting an image of himself that would, with some modifications, serve to encapsulate his personality and literary work not only for the rest of his life but for decades after his death. We here see the image of the "recluse" (168) and "invalid" (169) surrounded by old books (Lovecraft had specified to Lockhart that he owned books dating to 1681 and 1702); Lockhart himself contributes an image that no doubt delighted his subject: "methinks I can see Lovecraft poring over these time-stained bits o' bookish lore as the monks of old followed the printed lines with quivering fingers in the taper's uncertain, flickering light" (169). It is, indeed, likely that at least some of the actual prose in the piece is taken directly or in a loose paraphrase from Lovecraft's letters.

As Lovecraft himself did in later years, Lockhart emphasises that the Providence writer informally and unwittingly began his association with amateur journalism by issuing his juvenile hectographed periodicals, the *Scientific Gazette* (1899f.) and the *Rhode Island Journal of Astronomy* (1903f.), to friends and family members. Lockhart also notes Lovecraft's astronomy columns in the Providence papers.

One would have supposed that Lovecraft's bountiful contributions to the amateur press, especially during the period 1915–19, would have elicited at least brief discussion in the "Department of Public Criticism" (or, perhaps, in the corresponding "Bureau of Critics" column in the *National Amateur*); but, at least as far as that first column is concerned, Lovecraft himself wrote the bulk of them for the period in question; even when Rheinhart Kleiner was appointed chairman for the 1917–18 term, health difficulties necessitated that Lovecraft take over his duties, and he wrote the columns for January, March, and May 1918. Some of Lovecraft's comments on his own work are of some minimal interest, but most are too obviously self-deprecatory to be of true value as self-criticism (on the poem "An American to the British Flag": "The metre is regular and the rhymes correct, though there is no very distinguished merit in the effusion" [*CE* 1.187]).

The first actual critical article on Lovecraft by someone other than himself is Rheinhart Kleiner's "A Note on Howard P. Lovecraft's Verse" (*United Amateur*, March 1919; *WW* 47–48). By this point, Lovecraft had flooded the amateur press with his poetical "effusions," chiefly written in imitation of the verse of John Dryden, Samuel Johnson, and Alexander Pope. It had proved markedly unpopular with readers, but that didn't deter Lovecraft from writing it, nor from some of his favourite editors (always in desperate need of "copy") from publishing it. Kleiner acknowledges the overall difficulty: "Certain critics have regarded his efforts as too obviously imitative of a style that has long been discredited" (47). ("Discredited" is an odd word to use in this context; Kleiner probably meant to say "outmoded.")

But Kleiner goes on to praise the one branch of Lovecraft's poetic output (aside from his weird poetry, relatively little of which had been written or published up to this point): his satirical verse. Satire had been a consistent strain in Lovecraft's temperament and literary work from childhood: one of the best works of his juvenile period (1897–1908) is the humorous poem "H. Lovecraft's Attempted Journey betwixt Providence & Fall River on the N.Y.N.H. & H.R.R." (1901); one of the poems of *Poemata Minora, Volume II* (1902), "On the Vanity of Human Ambition," is clearly modelled upon Samuel Johnson's satire *The Vanity of Human Wishes* (1749), itself an imitation of Juvenal's tenth satire. Lovecraft's own satire, in both prose and poetry, owes far more to the mordant Juvenal than to the milder Horace, as the vicious poem "Medusa: A Portrait" (1922)—a flaying of his amateur nemesis Ida C. Haughton—demonstrates.

Kleiner is on solid ground in stating:

> As a satirist along familiar lines, particularly those laid down by [Samuel] Butler, [Jonathan] Swift and [Alexander] Pope, he is most himself—paradoxical though it seems. In reading his satires one cannot help but feel the zest with which the author has composed them. They are admirable for the way in which they reveal the depth and intensity of Mr. Lovecraft's convictions, while the wit, irony, sarcasm and humour to be found in them serve as an indication of his powers as a controversialist. (48)

Kleiner here shows a keen understanding of the nature of influence: for a writer like Lovecraft, literary influence does not necessarily devolve into mechanical pastiche; he was able in many instances to absorb his influences—whether it be the poets Kleiner names or such fantaisistes as Poe, Dunsany, Machen, and others—and infuse his own imagination into works that might otherwise seem to rely too heavily on their models.

We are, of course, most interested in responses to Lovecraft's fiction. As is well known, he had written reams of fiction from the age of about seven to the age of eighteen; but following his "nervous breakdown" of 1908, he destroyed all but two of his tales of the previous five years, "The Beast in the Cave" (1905) and "The Alchemist" (1908). (His mother had saved some of his very early juvenile stories, such as "The Little Glass Bottle.") It is a little peculiar that "The Alchemist" did not appear in the *United Amateur* until November 1916: this was Lovecraft's "credential" (i.e., a work that is designed to establish a prospective member's abilities as a writer) and usually appeared almost immediately upon the member's joining of the association. Why it was delayed for more than two and a half years after Lovecraft's entry—by which point he had published dozens of articles and poems in the amateur press—is unclear.

It was W. Paul Cook who, reading this tale, urged Lovecraft to resume the writing of fiction. Lovecraft, always in need of external encouragement to bolster his fragile self-esteem, seemed to comply almost immediately, writing "The Tomb" and "Dagon" in the summer of 1917. No doubt Lovecraft sent the stories to Cook, but we are not privy to his response to them. Cook did go ahead and publish "The Beast in the Cave" in the *Vagrant* (June 1918). Otherwise, what we have is Cook's brief article, "Howard P. Lovecraft's Fiction" (*Vagrant,* November 1919; *WW* 48–49), a kind of elaborate preface to "Dagon," which appeared in that issue.

This article is notable merely for its existence; I know of nothing in the amateur press precisely analogous to it. Beginning by praising both of Lovecraft's juvenile tales ("The Alchemist" "was enough to stamp him as a pupil of Poe in its unnatural, mystical and actually morbid outlook"; the chief virtue of "The Beast in the Cave" was "the skill with which an atmosphere was created" [48]), he sings the praises of "Dagon":

> In "Dagon," [. . .] Mr. Lovecraft steps into his own as a writer of fiction. In reading this story, two or three names of short-story writers are immediately called to mind. First of all, of course, Poe; and Mr. Lovecraft would be the first to acknowledge his allegiance to our American master. Second, Maupassant, and I am quite sure that Mr. Lovecraft would deny any kinship with the great Frenchman. [. . .]
>
> I cannot fully appreciate Mr. Lovecraft as a poet [. . .] But I can and do appreciate him as a story-writer. He is at this day the only amateur story-writer worthy of more than a polite passing notice. (49)

There are some remarkable assertions here. I do not imagine that Cook is at all intending to declare Lovecraft the equal of Poe or Maupassant, merely that his work was either inspired by them or bears significant resemblances to them.[10] But the mere associa-

---

10. HPL at this time had probably not read Maupassant. He may have done so only in 1922, when he obtained Julian Hawthorne's *Lock and Key Library* [1909], where several Maupassant stories, including "The Horla," were included; at that same time he apparently obtained a six-volume edition of Maupassant (HPL to Maurice W. Moe, [August 1922]; *Letters to*

tion of an "amateur" writer with these august figures is noteworthy. And Cook's claim that Lovecraft is the only amateur fiction writer "worthy of more than a polite passing notice" might actually be considered a slap in the fact to such an author as Edith Miniter, who had published fiction professionally—notably the novel *Our Natupski Neighbors* (1916), which Lovecraft owned—as well as others such as Samuel Loveman and Alfred Galpin, whose tales were not markedly inferior to the stories Lovecraft was writing at this juncture.

Cook took his time publishing "The Tomb," perhaps because he felt it too reliant on Poe; it appeared in the *Vagrant* for March 1922. Cook also published "The Statement of Randolph Carter" (*Vagrant,* May 1920). But, as I have mentioned, two score of Lovecraft's early stories appeared in the amateur press from 1916 to 1925, and at least a few of them elicited some comment.

Let us first examine the stories from this period that were and were *not* published in the amateur press. I print these stories in chronological order by date of writing (as indicated by the centred headings) and provide publishing information in parentheses for those that were published.

1905

"The Beast in the Cave" (*Vagrant,* June 1918)

1908

"The Alchemist" (*United Amateur,* November 1916)

1917

"The Tomb" (*Vagrant,* March 1922)

"Dagon" (*Vagrant,* November 1919)

"A Reminiscence of Dr. Samuel Johnson" (*United Amateur,* November 1917; as by "Humphry Littlewit, Esq.")

Maurice W. Moe and Others 105).

1918

"Polaris" (*Philosopher,* December 1920; *National Amateur,* May 1926)

1919

"Beyond the Wall of Sleep" (*Pine Cones,* October 1919)
"Memory" (*United Co-operative,* June 1919)
"Old Bugs"
"The Transition of Juan Romero"
"The White Ship" (*United Amateur,* November 1919)
"The Street" (*Wolverine,* December 1920; *National Amateur,* January 1922)
"The Doom That Came to Sarnath" (*Scot,* June 1920)
"The Statement of Randolph Carter" (*Vagrant,* May 1920)

1920

"The Terrible Old Man" (*Tryout,* July 1921)
"The Tree" (*Tryout,* October 1921)
"The Cats of Ulthar" (*Tryout,* November 1920)
"The Temple"
"Facts concerning the Late Arthur Jermyn and His Family" (*Wolverine,* March & June 1921)
"Celephaïs" (*Rainbow,* May 1922)
"From Beyond"
"Nyarlathotep" (*United Amateur,* November 1920; *National Amateur,* July 1926)
"The Picture in the House" (*National Amateur,* July 1919)
"Ex Oblivione" (*United Amateur,* March 1921; as by "Ward Phillips")
"Sweet Ermengarde; or, The Heart of a Country Girl"[11]

1921

"The Nameless City" (*Wolverine,* November 1921)
"The Quest of Iranon"
"The Moon-Bog"
"The Outsider"

---

11. Date of writing unknown, but it probably dates to 1920–21.

"The Other Gods"
"The Music of Erich Zann" (*National Amateur,* March 1922)
"Herbert West—Reanimator"

1922

"Hypnos" (*National Amateur,* May 1923)
"What the Moon Brings" (*National Amateur,* May 1923)
"The Hound"
"The Lurking Fear"

1923

"The Rats in the Walls"
"The Unnamable"
"The Festival"

1924

"The Shunned House"

1925

"The Horror at Red Hook"
"He"
"In the Vault" (*Tryout,* November 1925)

In addition, three collaborated stories appeared:

"The Crawling Chaos" (with Winifred V. Jackson) (*United Co-operative,* April 1921; as by "Elizabeth Berkeley and Lewis Theobald, Jun.")
"Poetry and the Gods" (with Anna Helen Crofts) (*United Amateur,* September 1920)
"The Green Meadow" (with Winifred V. Jackson) (*Vagrant,* [Spring 1927]; as by "Elizabeth Neville Berkeley and Lewis Theobald, Jr.")

I am not sure that it is worth studying this list with painstaking minuteness, but some interesting patterns emerge. It is clear that Lovecraft was keen on putting his fictional work in front of the amateurs of both the UAPA and NAPA; indeed, it is a bit surprising, given Lovecraft's repeated claims that he was a devoted "United man," how many stories (seven—four of them reprints) appeared in the *National Amateur.* Only six appeared in the *United Amateur.* Others were bestowed upon friends: aside from Cook, these included Charles W. Smith, editor of the *Tryout* (four stories), Horace L. Lawson, editor of the *Wolverine* (three, one of them a two-part "serial"), Alfred Galpin, editor of the *Philosopher* (one), John Clinton Pryor, editor of *Pine Cones* (one), Gavin T. McColl, editor of the *Scot* (one), and Sonia H. Greene, editor of the *Rainbow* (one). It cannot, however, be said that Lawson, Pryor, or McColl were particularly close colleagues.

Of the stories that were *not* published, many of them were probably (or at least were considered by Lovecraft to be) too long for publication in the amateur press. Even during his revival of amateur activity in the 1930s, Lovecraft habitually lamented the fact that the brevity of most journals (a product of limitations in typesetting equipment, the cost of paper, the difficulty of securing submissions, and other factors) made it nearly impossible to publish stories of any significant length. This perhaps accounts for the lack of publication of "The Temple," although, at 5430 words, it is not markedly longer than "The Nameless City" (5070 words), which did get published. Lovecraft had sent "From Beyond" (3030 words) to Arthur Harris, the Welsh editor of *Interesting Items,* in the summer of 1921; but Harris kept Lovecraft dangling for months without ever printing the story.

And consider the four short stories of 1921, none of which are longer than 3400 words and several of which are considerably shorter; why did they not appear? "The Moon-Bog" was actually read out loud by Lovecraft at an amateur gathering in Boston near St. Patrick's Day of 1921. Perhaps he thought it an inferior work—as he almost certainly regarded "The Transition of Juan Romero." As for "The Outsider," Lovecraft appears to have made no attempt to place this tale anywhere for several years; in 1926 he let W. Paul Cook have it for the first issue of the *Recluse,* but was then persuaded by Farnsworth Wright to let *Weird Tales* publish it. It is more readily understandable why such humorous squibs as "Old Bugs" and "Sweet Ermengarde," clearly written for himself or for close colleagues, were not published.

The later stories of this period were written at a time when Lovecraft was transitioning into professional publication; "Herbert West—Reanimator" and "The Lurking Fear" were commissioned by George Julian Houtain, an amateur journalist who with his wife established the very poorly paying professional magazine *Home Brew,* for which Lovecraft was paid all of $5.00 per instalment. And Lovecraft clearly hoped that all the tales of 1923–25 would be professionally published and therefore bring in some much-needed income; that actually happened in the case of all the stories except "The Shunned House." Indeed, "In the Vault" is the anomaly here in the fact that it *did* appear in an amateur journal; but that was only an acknowledgement of Lovecraft's debt to Charles W. Smith, who provided the plot germ for the story.

As mentioned, a few of these stories did garner some actual criticism, albeit quite brief, in the amateur press. Perhaps the most notable item was an instalment of "The Vivisector" (*Wolverine,* November 1921; *WW* 50) written by Alfred Galpin under the column's "house name," "Zoilus" (a reference to a fourth century B.C.E. Greek critic who had the temerity to criticise the Homeric poems). Galpin, in the course of assessing recent issues of the *Wolverine* itself, devotes a lengthy paragraph to "Arthur Jermyn." There are some quite extravagant dollops of praise here:

> "Facts Concerning the Late Arthur Jermyn and His Family," by Mr. Lovecraft, shows another phase of that writer's gloomy but

> powerful genius. It is perfect in execution, restrained in manner, complete, and marked by Mr. Lovecraft's uniquely effective handling of introductory and concluding portions. [. . .] it is unquestionably original and does not derive from Poe, Dunsany, or any other of Mr. Lovecraft's favorites and predecessors. Its affiliations are rather closer with Ambrose Bierce, and I personally should place it beside much of Bierce's best work without fearing for the fame of the United's representative. [. . .] For the power and persuasion of his style, and for the gripping, unearthly cast of his imagination, he is as great as any living author in his field and in the range of my acquaintance. He certainly excels Lord Dunsany in directness of narration, and the whole realm of the horrible in imagination.

Lovecraft, from the beginning to the end of his career, scoffed at the assertion that any of his work was equivalent or superior to the work of what he considered "real" weird authors such as Bierce and Dunsany. The comparison to Bierce probably derives from the gloomy, misanthropic nature of the tale, especially its imperishable opening line: "Life is a hideous thing, and from the background behind what we know of it peer daemoniacal hints of truth which sometimes make it a thousandfold more hideous" (*CF* 1.171). The comparison to Dunsany is a bit less impressive than it may appear, since the great majority of Dunsany's work was in the realm of ethereal fantasy as opposed to "the horrible in imagination."

But Galpin astutely notes that Lovecraft "is singularly lacking in psychological perception, a thing which is essential to immortalize any tale except that of the sheerest and most Shelleyan fiber. As a consequence of this latter lack the plot of the Jermyn tale is a trifle obvious, and its principal character is wooden." Lovecraft would probably have acknowledged the soundness of this criticism, given that he himself had admitted earlier in 1921 that "I could not write about 'ordinary people' because I am not in the least interested in them. [. . .] Man's relations to man do not captivate my fancy. It is man's relations to the cosmos—to the unknown—which alone arouses in me the spark of creative imagination" ("The Defence Remains Open!"; *CE* 5.53). This principle would be unimpeachably sound in those tales embodying Lovecraft's "cosmic" perspective, but "Arthur Jermyn" does so only tangentially.

Galpin, of course, had been a close colleague of Lovecraft since 1918, and in his early years he dabbled in the weird. His poem "Selenaio-Phantasma" (*Conservative,* June 1918) is a close imitation (and in part perhaps a parody) of Lovecraft's "Nemesis" (written on Hallowe'en 1917). His brief story "Marsh-Mad: A Nightmare" (*Philosopher,* December 1920) so impressed Lovecraft that he held off writing "The Tree" for some months, believing Galpin's story to have anticipated the "living tree" idea embodied in his own tale.

In a "Bureau of Critics" column in the *National Amateur* (November 1921), Samuel Loveman also discusses "Arthur Jermyn." In this story, Loveman maintains, "we have what may well be called a singularly perfect specimen of his method of handling the subtle but hair-raising material." And the praise continues:

> Mr. Lovecraft conjures up an unholy atmosphere; the wind of "unguessed horrors" slowly revolves until with something akin to the Shakespearian activity of Macbeth, his characters, pure fiction no longer, but creatures satanically endowed to obey the minutest impulse of the gods of haschish, opium and mandragora, sustain and complete their doom to the darkening and inevitable end.[12]

Lovecraft himself was pleased by a passing comment by Pearl K. Merritt in the *American Amateur* (September 1920): "I recall that one night I let the moon shine in my eyes because I was

12. Samuel Loveman, "Official Criticism: Bureau of Critics," *National Amateur* (November 1921); rpt. in Loveman's *Out of the Immortal Night,* rev. ed. 285.

afraid to get up and pull down the shade after reading one of his stories—'Dagon,' I think it was."[13]

But if Galpin, Loveman, and a few others appreciated Lovecraft's tales, the majority of UAPA and NAPA members appear to have disliked them or found them incomprehensible, if we are to trust the veracity of Lovecraft's wry comment in "News Notes" (*United Amateur*, January 1922):

> Readers who noted Mr. Galpin's friendly review of "The Crawling Chaos" will be interested to know that the opinion of the learned often differ. A prominent politician with a taste for the "wild, weird tales" of H. P. Lovecraft mistakenly credited the whole narrative to him, and during a denunciation of Lovecraftian stories remarked: "We can hardly go them. That Crawling Chaos is the limit. His attempts at Poe-esque tales will land him— Did you know he was on the staff of 'The Houtain Home Brew' to furnish six of his worst—" Mr. Lovecraft awaits his landing with keen interest. (*CE* 1.308)

A somewhat less intemperate instantiation of this incomprehension is provided by the responses to Lovecraft's tales as found in the existing papers of the Transatlantic Circulator,[14] an Anglo-American group of amateurs who exchanged stories and poems in manuscript and critiqued them. Many facets of Lovecraft's involvement with the Circulator are unclear, such as who introduced him to the group (perhaps John Ravenor Bullen, a Canadian amateur with whom Lovecraft was associated in later years) and how long it existed prior to Lovecraft's involvement (roughly January–September 1921) and how long it endured after his departure.

But the surviving papers reveal a mix of admiration, criti-

13. HPL cites the comment in "The Defence Reopens!" (1921; *CF* 5.48).

14. The papers are extant at JHL. I quote some passages from them in my introduction to *In Defence of Dagon* (1984); now reprinted as "*In Defence of Dagon* and HPL's Philosophy" in my *Lovecraft and a World in Transition* 115–21.

cism, and bafflement that exhibit a readership considerably higher on the educational scale than the readers of the *Argosy* and *All-Story* and probably higher than the average run of American amateurs. Lovecraft circulated "Dagon," "The White Ship," "The Tree," and several poems through the group—and as a result of the group's criticisms, he was impelled to write three papers ("The Defence Reopens!" [January 1921], "The Defence Remains Open!" [April 1921], and "Final Words" [September 1921]) that are among the most scintillating and perspicacious pieces he had written up to this time.

One A. H. Brown had suggested that Lovecraft's tales should more fully reflect "the thoughts and actions of ordinary people," thereby allowing them "to appeal to a larger class." It was this comment that led Lovecraft to acknowledge his lack of interest in "ordinary people." That comment—along with John Munday's comment on "Dagon" ("Do you remember Kipling's little poem with the refrain 'But is it art'? So would I courteously ask: 'Is it wholesome' of Mr. Lovecraft's story")—may have been instrumental in the evolution of Lovecraft's view that weird fiction has a "keen potency over a very important, though not numerically great, minority of our species" (*CE* 2.83). Indeed, the resounding (and tartly cynical) opening paragraph of "Supernatural Horror in Literature" (1927) is, I contend, inspired by just such comments as these:

> Against it [the weird tale] are discharged all the shafts of a materialistic sophistication which clings to frequently felt emotions and external events, and of a naively insipid idealism which deprecates the aesthetic motive and calls for a didactic literature to uplift the reader toward a suitable degree of smirking optimism. But in spite of all this opposition the weird tale has survived, developed, and attained remarkable heights of perfection; founded as it is on a profound and elementary principle whose appeal, if not always universal, must necessarily be poignant and permanent to minds of the requisite sensitiveness. (*CE* 2.82–83)

Other comments by Circulator members did not cause Lovecraft to see red as much as the remarks quoted above. Some of them were, indeed, quite flattering, as when Bullen cited his work in the same breath as H. G. Wells and Maurice Maeterlinck. A Dr. John Munday wrote that Lovecraft's work "makes one *think*" and that "Mr Lovecraft does not write for lazy readers." Astoundingly (and perhaps not entirely as a compliment), Munday went on to say: "I suspect that [Lovecraft's] letters are more interesting than his stories."

Bullen was clearly the most acute critic among the Circulator writers, and his appraisal of "The White Ship" as an allegory is of interest. He states that it is "a powerful prose-poem in which the allegorist informs us somewhat sorrowfully that he was once an idealist but is now a materialist—that he once dwelt happily in the land of Sona-Nyl but foolishly forsook it and pushed on to explore forbidden territory—only to find the Cathuria of his hopes a hollow shell." The analysis may well be off the mark—there is no evidence that Lovecraft was ever an idealist—but the mere fact that Bullen takes the tale as a serious work of philosophical fiction rather than as an escapist fantasy is notable.

But such relatively sensitive reactions to Lovecraft's tales were rare during his early years as an amateur writer—and they did not greatly improve when he began writing for professional magazines. Their readers, he soon discovered, even when they praised Lovecraft's tales, were pretty much on the level of the *Argosy/All-Story* defenders of Fred Jackson.

II. The Pulp Era (1923–1937)

I have mentioned that Lovecraft's initial forays into professional fiction publication[1] were his two stories, "Herbert West—Reanimator" (1921–22), and "The Lurking Fear" (1922), in *Home Brew*. There is no need to rehearse Lovecraft's tongue-in-cheek whining at becoming a hack writer: George Julian Houtain had asked him to write the stories in instalments (six for the first story, four for the second), each instalment running to as close to 2000 words as possible and containing a mini-climax or "punch" at the end to stir reader interest. It should be noted that *Home Brew* was actually a humour magazine, with overtones of the risqué; and that may partially explain why the first tale, and perhaps even the second, are to some degree parodies of the over-the-top horror tales that were already making themselves notorious in some of the popular magazines of the day. *Home Brew* did not have a letter column, so it is impossible to gauge readers' responses to Lovecraft's stories.

It is well known that *Weird Tales* (1923–54) published the majority of Lovecraft's tales during the period 1923–37, including many revisions and collaborations during the later 1920s and 1930s. But there has been insufficient discussion of why Lovecraft submitted specifically to it (as well as to other pulps in the weird or science fiction field, such as *Strange Tales of Mystery and*

1. This was not his first venture into professional publication: several of his poems, beginning as early as 1917, had appeared in the professional *National Magazine* in 1917. Indeed, one can assume that he was paid at least a nominal sum for his astronomy columns going all the way back to 1906.

Terror, *Amazing Stories*, *Astounding Stories*, and even more obscure periodicals) rather than such mainstream venues as *Collier's* or *Cosmopolitan* (where Ambrose Bierce had worked as a columnist and contributor for the period 1905–09). Granted, it would have been difficult for Lovecraft to break into such high-paying markets as these or the *Saturday Evening Post*, given his lack of reputation; but would his work have been rejected merely on the basis of content as opposed to his relative obscurity as a professional writer? One gets the impression that it would—and this applied to weird work by other American writers as well.

But the question remains as to whether the pulp magazines—which, ultimately, initiated or concretised all "genre fiction," from weird fiction to science fiction to westerns to romance—came into existence because this kind of material was being systematically banned by mainstream magazines, or whether mainstream magazines began omitting genre fiction because of the existence of the pulps. I suspect the former, although the case is difficult to prove except anecdotally.

H. Warner Munn, in a letter to the editor of *Weird Tales* (March 1925), makes the intriguing comment: "You are doing a great work in publishing stories that the great ultraconservative magazines might refuse" (*WW* 65). Munn does not name these magazines, but one suspects he is referring to all the "slick" magazines as well as the more highbrow literary journals, not to mention such literary quarterlies as the *Virginia Quarterly Review*. Late in life Lovecraft commented:

> After all, a taste for fantasy in large doses is a rather unusual thing. Most readers like it only occasionally—relishing a Machen book now & then, or faintly appreciating the timid & insipid bits (like "The House of the Laburnums" [by Mollie Panter-Downes] in the Dec. *Harpers*) sparingly scattered through the conventional magazines, but becoming distinctly bored when confronted by a solid or frequent diet of shadow & bizarrerie.[2]

---

2. HPL to Jonquil Leiber, 20 December 1936; *Letters to C. L. Moore and*

I think a strong case could be made that the emergence of literary Modernism—and especially the dominance of social realism in the work of Sinclair Lewis (whose *Main Street* [1920] and *Babbitt* [1922] were both critical and popular successes), F. Scott Fitzgerald, Willa Cather, Ernest Hemingway, William Faulkner, and many others beginning in the 1920s caused the banishment of genre fiction of all sorts from the "conventional magazines." And, as Lovecraft suggests, such magazines could not possibly have published genre fiction in quantity, thereby necessitating the establishment of specialised magazines catering to this kind of material.

There is no need to review how Lovecraft came to submit to *Weird Tales.* Several colleagues, including James F. Morton and his recent correspondent Clark Ashton Smith, urged him to submit, and the magazine's first editor, Edwin Baird, accepted five stories—"Dagon," "Arthur Jermyn," "The Cats of Ulthar," "The Hound," and "The Statement of Randolph Carter"—almost at once, or at least as soon as Lovecraft took the trouble to double-space the typescripts.

Before proceeding, it is worth noting that these submissions were not in fact Lovecraft's first attempts to land his material with pulp or popular magazines. In the cover letter that he sent to Baird submitting those five stories (and which Baird, no doubt with tongue in cheek, published in the September 1923 issue, a month before the first story, "Dagon," appeared), Lovecraft pointedly notes that he had submitted "The Tomb" and "Dagon" to other magazines. Baird did not print the names of the magazines in question, and in later years Lovecraft got confused as to which story was submitted where; but it is now clear that "The Tomb" was submitted to the *Black Cat* (1895–1922) and "Dagon" to *Black Mask* (1920–51).

As for the former, Lovecraft states in 1920 that "at the re-

Others 314.

peated nagging of my aunt [presumably Lillian D. Clark] I sent 'The Tomb' to THE BLACK CAT, and received it back in a month with nothing but an insulting printed rejection slip."[3] It is not clear why Lovecraft should have been insulted; he was, as far as professional publication was concerned, an entirely unknown author. As for why Lovecraft chose this periodical, he noted many years later that "*The Black Cat* ran a high percentage of weird material around 1904 or so, when I first began to notice it."[4] The selection of *Black Mask* as a possible venue for such a cosmic weird tale as "Dagon" is even more peculiar. It had been founded by H. L. Mencken and George Jean Nathan (editors of the highbrow periodical the *Smart Set*) as a crassly money-making venture aimed at what Mencken deemed the "booboisie." And while its first issue (April 1920) did feature the subtitle "An Illustrated Magazine of Detective, Mystery, Adventure, Romance, and Spiritualism," the proportion of actually supernatural material was quite low. In the later 1920s, of course, it became the chief venue for the new subgenre of the hard-boiled detective story.

In any event, it is worth examining how long it took for Baird (and his successor, Farnsworth Wright, who took over the editorship in early 1924) to publish the five Lovecraft stories:

"Dagon" (October 1923)
"The Hound" (February 1924)
"Arthur Jermyn" (April 1924)
"The Statement of Randolph Carter" (February 1925)
"The Cats of Ulthar" (February 1926)

And in the meantime, a story submitted later, "The Picture in the House," appeared in the January 1924 issue, while the land-

---

3. HPL to the Gallomo, [April 1920]; *Letters to Alfred Galpin* 84.

4. HPL to R. H. Barlow, 18 April [1932]; *O Fortunate Floridian* 29.

mark "The Rats in the Walls" graced the March 1924 issue. It is well known that Lovecraft submitted the latter to Robert H. Davis of the *Argosy,* who rejected it on the grounds that (in Lovecraft's words) "it [was] too horrible for the tender sensibilities of a delicately nurtured publick."[5] If nothing else, these various submissions do indicate that Lovecraft was developing some minimal business sense: *Black Cat, Black Mask,* and *Argosy* were well-established and (more to the point) well-paying ventures, unlike the fledgling *Weird Tales.*

Lovecraft's first year of involvement with *Weird Tales* certainly had its moments of exhilaration. Soon after the publication of "Dagon" he remarked that Baird "not long ago writ me in a manner which elevates my inherent vanity to unbearable altitudes. He says, 'my work makes a peculiar appeal to his readers', as attested by numerous letters from them."[6] It does not appear, however, that Baird printed any of these letters at this time in the letter column ("The Eyrie"), as letters commenting on Lovecraft's stories only began to appear in earnest in 1925. It is unsurprising that Baird singled out Lovecraft's stories as meritorious, at least in private correspondence; the issues of the first year of *Weird Tales* were filled with woefully crude and amateurish material, as the leading writers (e.g., Hamlin Garland and Ben Hecht) who had apparently promised to submit to the magazine failed to do so, leaving Baird to rely on blind submissions from tyros and hacks.

Lovecraft was also in touch with the magazine's owner, J. C.

---

5. HPL to Frank Belknap Long, 8 November 1923; *SL* 1.259.

6. HPL to James F. Morton, 28 October 1923; *Letters to James F. Morton* 57. HPL probably did not think much of the encomium he received at the hands of George Julian Houtain, who prefaced the sixth and final instalment of "Herbert West—Reanimator" (published as "Grewsome Tales") with the puff: "The greatest horror stories since Edgar Allen [*sic*] Poe."

Henneberger, who commissioned his star author to collaborate on a tale with Harry Houdini. While quite a feather in Lovecraft's cap, this assignment (broached to Lovecraft toward the end of 1923) was in fact a testament to the magazine's perilous financial condition. Houdini, by this time an immensely popular escape artist and also a crusader against bogus spiritualism, was brought in to lend some "celebrity" status to the floundering pulp; he was the putative author of a column, "Ask Houdini," that appeared in the March 1924 issue and two subsequent issues, along with a two-part novelette, "The Spirit Fakers of Hermannstadt" (March and April 1924) and another story, "The Hoax of the Spirit Lover" (April 1924), along with the Lovecraft piece, "Under the Pyramids" (published as "Imprisoned with the Pharaohs" in the "anniversary" issue of May/June/July 1924). It does not appear that Houdini wrote any of these items, and to this day it is unclear who did. Lovecraft was robbed of a joint byline for his story because he wrote it in the first person, as if Houdini were telling the tale himself; and Henneberger couldn't wrap his mind around the idea that a first-person-singular narrative could be a collaborative work. But Lovecraft was mollified: he got an advance of $100 for the story in February 1924, then another $100 upon delivery. For a story of just over 10,000 words, this amounts to a rate of 2¢ a word—probably the highest rate he ever received for any story he published in the pulp magazines.

As for the offer that Henneberger made to appoint Lovecraft as successor to Baird as editor of *Weird Tales,* we similarly need not spend much time on the matter. The preposterous criticism that Lovecraft turned down the offer just because it would have entailed moving to Chicago (where the editorial offices were located), a place that had no colonial architecture, can be discounted at once. Lovecraft shrewdly recognised that *Weird Tales* and another journal published by Henneberger, *Detective Tales,* were deeply in debt; and if they failed, it might have stranded Lovecraft in an uncongenial environment with little opportunity to earn an income. Moreover, he had just married Sonia H. Greene on 3 March 1924 and made the laborious move into her Brooklyn apartment, and he was not inclined to move again so soon. Finally, Lovecraft's finical taste—his relentless assertion of the "genuineness and dignity of the weirdly horrible tale as a literary form" (*CE* 2.83) and his intolerance for hack writing and mediocrity—would have doomed him as editor of a magazine that simply didn't pay enough to attract top-flight talent, so that it is unlikely that the magazine would have lasted another thirty years as it did under the tenure of Farnsworth Wright and, later, Dorothy McIlwraith.

So Lovecraft was happy to remain a contributor.[7] But his relations with the new editor, Farnsworth Wright, got off to a rocky start. In October 1924 he wrote "The Shunned House"—the first story he had written after his move to Brooklyn and only one of five stories he wrote during his two-year stay in the metropolis. Samuel Loveman, who became enraptured by the tale, promised to submit it to the publisher Alfred A. Knopf[8]—although what Knopf, or any book publisher, could do with an 11,000-word short story is unclear. It took Lovecraft nearly a year to submit the story to Wright—and then only after it had been rejected by Edwin Baird, who was now editor of *Detective Tales.*[9] Lovecraft's report on Wright's rejection is relatively bland: "I have gathered together all the material I must copy for

7. For a complete list of HPL's contributions to *Weird Tales,* see S. T. Joshi, "Lovecraft in *Weird Tales,*" *New Lovecraft Collector* No. 10 (Spring 1995): 3–4.

8. HPL to Lillian D. Clark, 17–18 November 1924; *Letters to Family and Family Friends* 221.

9. HPL to Lillian D. Clark, 27 July 1925; *Letters to Family and Family Friends* 324.

Wright, (who has, by the way, rejected 'The Shunned House' as beginning too gradually, though he extends it high personal praise) & will try to get some of this beastly typing done in the next few days."[10] But this double whammy—a rejection by the editor (Baird) who, when editor of *Weird Tales,* had accepted everything Lovecraft had submitted, and a rejection by *Weird Tales'* new editor—could not have sat well with Lovecraft. Wright's assessment is, in fact, probably sound; but it already suggests that Lovecraft's tales were extending beyond the boundaries of conventional pulp fiction so that they were becoming perilously unsaleable. It would be a problem that would dog him for the rest of his career.

Meanwhile, Lovecraft could take heart that "The Eyrie," whenever it published letters discussing him, constituted an almost unwavering paean to his work. It is striking how many letters were by individuals who later became Lovecraft's colleagues, either as writers or merely as fans. Hence, H. Warner Munn—who was on the verge of breaking into *Weird Tales* with the novelette "The Werewolf of Ponkert" (July 1925), a story he maintained was inspired by Lovecraft[11]—wrote in the March 1925 issue: "I am indeed delighted that Lovecraft is to be a steady contributor. *Weird Tales* discovered him, I believe, and if it had never done anything else, that would be sufficient reason for its continued existence" (*WW* 65). This is a remarkably prescient comment. Munn would not get into direct contact with Lovecraft until 1927.

August Derleth, in the March 1926 issue, praised "The Tomb" and referred to Lovecraft as "a second Poe" (*WW* 65). The comment was repeated in reference to "The Outsider" in the

10. HPL to Lillian D. Clark, 23–24 September 1925; *Letters to Family and Family Friends* 406.

11. See "H.P.L.: A Reminiscence" (*AV* 279–80).

June 1926 issue: "The story is worthy of Poe, and, if I may say so, I believe it to be better than any work of Poe" (*WW* 66). These remarks bespeak Derleth's relatively conventional approach to weird fiction. At this time, of course, he was barely seventeen years old and two months shy of publishing his first story in *Weird Tales.* He wrote his first letter to Lovecraft on 30 July 1926; Lovecraft replied four days later, thereby initiating a correspondence that lasted until the latter's death.

In the April 1926 E. Hoffmann Price accorded Lovecraft extravagant praise ("To paraphrase the Moslem: *There is but one Lovecraft, and the unnamable is his God*" [*WW* 66]). But his encomiums didn't prevent him—in his role as informal editorial adviser to Farnsworth Wright—from recommending the rejection of "The Strange High House in the Mist" when that story was submitted to him in the summer of 1927.[12] Wright later accepted the story. Lovecraft would not come into contact with Price until 1932. Henry S. Whitehead, already established as a *Weird Tales* regular, liked "The White Ship" ("It is one of the finest things of its sort I have ever seen. It is literature" [May 1927; *WW* 67]). It would not be until 1931 that Lovecraft met Whitehead in Florida.

Established authors also chimed in with flattering letters. Ray Cummings, famous for *The Girl in the Golden Atom* (first published as a novelette in the *All-Story* [15 March 1919], then serialised in the same magazine [24 January–28 February 1920]; Lovecraft presumably read one or both versions), expressed amazement at the new *Weird Tales* luminary: "Who in blazes is H. P. Lovecraft? I never heard the name before. If he is a present-day writer—which I can not imagine he is—he deserves to be world-famous. I read 'The Outsider' and 'The Tomb'. No need

12. HPL to Donald Wandrei, [2 August 1927]; *Letters with Donald and Howard Wandrei and to Emil Petaja* 140.

of telling you they are masterful stories" (*WW* 66). Lovecraft did not return the compliment. In writing to Clark Ashton Smith, he notes: "I shall sooner or later get around to the interplanetary field myself—& you may depend upon it that I shall not choose Edmond Hamilton, Ray Cummings, or Edgar Rice Burroughs as my model!"[13] But at least he did not attack Cummings in print, as he had done in earlier letters of his own to Edwin Baird (which, apparently, he did not expect Baird to publish in "The Eyrie") twitting Vincent Starrett, George Sterling, and others.

Edmond Hamilton himself found much to admire in "The Outsider": "It is surely the best thing *Weird Tales* ever published. If some literary detective had found it among Poe's papers it would have been acclaimed as his greatest work, without a doubt" (January 1928; *WW* 67). Greater than "The Fall of the House of Usher"? It is not surprising that Lovecraft did not have much respect for the "'Eyrie'-bombarding proletariat,"[14] even when the bombarders were established authors.

Indeed, the flamboyant praise that Lovecraft received in *Weird Tales* was, in his mind, tempered by the flamboyant praise the magazine itself received at the hands of naïve or juvenile readers, such as J. Vernon Shea, who pointedly announced in the October 1926 letter that "I am just a boy of thirteen, but I am in the opinion that *Weird Tales* is the best magazine ever published." Shea goes on to praise such writers as "Eli Colter, Seabury Quinn, H. P. Lovecraft, Robert S. Carr and Edmond Hamilton" (*WW* 66–67). Shea, when of somewhat maturer years, came in touch with Lovecraft in 1931 and corresponded with him for the rest of the latter's life.

We now come to "The Call of Cthulhu." Lovecraft's ecstatic

---

13. HPL to Clark Ashton Smith, 3 December 1929; *Dawnward Spire* 187.

14. HPL to Farnsworth Wright, 21 November 1933; *Letters to Woodburn Harris and Others*.

return to Providence in April 1926 after two years in loathsome New York inspired an outpouring of creativity such as he never experienced before or since. Over the next year he wrote that seminal story, along with "Pickman's Model," "The Silver Key," "The Strange High House in the Mist," *The Dream-Quest of Unknown Kadath, The Case of Charles Dexter Ward,* and "The Colour out of Space." Those two short novels remained unpublished until after his death, but the others were hailed as landmark tales. It is well known that Farnsworth Wright rejected "The Call of Cthulhu" when it was first submitted to him in the late summer or fall of 1926; clearly, its cosmic scope and introduction of an entirely new pseudomythology were so far beyond Wright's conceptions of what the readers of his magazine would accept that he felt he had no choice but to turn the story down. And the tale was only accepted as a result of a certain amount of chicanery on the part of Lovecraft's new friend Donald Wandrei, who—in the course of a hitchhiking expedition from St. Paul, Minnesota, to Providence in the summer of 1927—stopped by the *Weird Tales* editorial office in Chicago and hinted that Lovecraft was planning to submit the tale to another magazine. Wandrei frankly states that this account was entirely false, but "I could see that my fanciful account took effect, in the way Wright began to fidget and show signs of agitation, for he rose and paced around his office."[15] Wright soon asked to see the story again, and this time he accepted it. It appeared in the February 1928 issue.

The response to it in "The Eyrie" was not exactly over-

---

15. Donald Wandrei, "Lovecraft in Providence" (1959), in Joshi and Schultz, *AV* 276. Wandrei was in error. In the spring of 1927 HPL had in fact submitted "The Call of Cthulhu" to an obscure pulp magazine called *Mystery Stories,* edited by Robert Sampson; it was rejected in May. It is not clear why HPL submitted his tale there; it did not, so far as I can tell, publish any weird fiction, but was a straight crime/detective magazine (it published a Dashiell Hammett story in 1928).

whelming, as only two letters addressed the story. But one of them was by "R. E. Howard," who had already debuted in *Weird Tales* in 1925. Howard declares that the story "will live as one of the highest achievements of literature," stating of Lovecraft's work in general: "His scope is unlimited and his range is cosmic" (May 1928; *WW* 67–68). It would be another two years before Lovecraft and Howard came into correspondence. The other letter was by Jack Snow, who had published his first story in *Weird Tales* in September 1927 (one of five he had in the magazine), but gained his greatest celebrity in the 1940s with some sequels to the Oz books and other tales of fantasy. Snow's comment is a trifle over-the-top, but is worth citing: "Such stories do not require an ordinary 'thank you'; they go through life with the reader, coloring and enhancing his world and raising it from its mundane sordidness to fantastic heights of beauty and poesy from which no man nor thing can topple it" (July 1928; *WW* 68).

Wandrei's comment about Lovecraft seeking out other markets does become relevant in regard to "The Colour out of Space." There is now definitive evidence (contrary to the assertions of Sam Moskowitz and others) that Lovecraft bypassed *Weird Tales* altogether and sent the story directly to *Amazing Stories* soon after writing it in March 1927. The very decision to submit to this magazine—now regarded as definitively establishing the genre of science fiction when it began publication with the April 1926 issue—may have come indirectly from August Derleth. Lovecraft reports to Derleth on 20 February 1927 that he had "dropped it [i.e., a subscription to *Amazing Stories*] last month after deciding that the standard reprints were getting too few to make it worth buying";[16] but Derleth encouraged him to

---

16. *Essential Solitude* 71.

re-subscribe, and Lovecraft evidently did so. Even though he found much of the original material to be less than inspired, he continued purchasing it through 1927 for the reprints. He must have submitted "The Colour out of Space" no later than May 1927, as he notes to Derleth on 24 June that the story had been accepted.[17] Now consider the wording of Lovecraft's celebrated letter to Farnsworth Wright of 5 July 1927 upon the re-submission of "The Call of Cthulhu": "this spring and summer I've been too busy with revisory and kindred activities to write more than one tale—which, oddly enough, was accepted at once by *Amazing Stories* despite its full possession of the non-terrestrial qualities so characteristic of my recent work."[18] This is clearly Lovecraft's first mention of the story to Wright—and I suspect that his boast that the story had already been accepted by another magazine was a not-so-subtle suggestion that he was indeed becoming annoyed with Wright's rejections and was looking for other markets for his work. (Alas, *Amazing Stories* proved not to be such a market, since it took three dunning letters by Lovecraft to editor Hugo Gernsback to receive payment; and when that payment came—all of $25.00—it amounted to a paltry 1/5 of a cent a word.)

The reaction to "The Colour out of Space" in *Amazing Stories* has never been chronicled. It was on the whole subdued—but, anomalously, extended for more than a year. Shortly after publication a few readers wrote in to the letter column (blandly titled "Discussions"); William H. Macpherson's comment in the November 1927 issue is representative: "It is one of the best I have read in your magazine for a long time." Gordon W. Richmond claims that "it was a good story, but it did not fit the standard of your magazine. It had more of a weird, ghostly

---

17 *Essential Solitude* 97.

18. *Letters to Woodburn Harris and Others*.

trend."[19] The remark anticipates both the vicious "Boiling Point" controversy in the *Fantasy Fan* (1933–34) over Clark Ashton Smith's "The Dweller in the Gulf" and Lovecraft's own two stories in *Astounding Stories* in 1936.

In March 1928, a full six months after the story appeared, M. William Guerin liked the tale but couldn't remember the author's name: "'The Colour Out of Space' which I do not know who wrote was, to me, the best story printed in Amazing Stories."[20] The most curious letter appeared in July 1928, when a reader, D. E. Chichester, went on for several hundred words claiming that "In regard to my first choice in the September issue, 'The Colour Out of Space,' I did not see the colour, but there *is* a spot somewhere in New England like that described as the blasted heath, for I saw such a place when I was a boy about ten years old, when traveling with my parents." Chichester couldn't remember the exact location, but thought it was Connecticut or Massachusetts. The one critical comment that was published was by Jack Reid in this issue, who thought the tale was "a very poor story and made a bad showing in AMAZING STORIES."[21]

None of these writers, or the few others I have not quoted, were friends or correspondents of Lovecraft; and, in general, I find their comments lacking even the rudimentary critical acumen of *Weird Tales* readers. But perhaps the most memorable comment was made decades later by Fritz Leiber, who noted: "I read 'The Colour out of Space' when it first appeared in *Amazing Stories* and its dismal gray horror chilled my dreams for weeks."[22]

Lovecraft continued to receive fairly unmitigated praise in *Weird Tales*. This in part may be a function of Wright's disincli-

---

19. *Amazing Stories* 2, No. 8 (November 1927): 816, 817.

20. *Amazing Stories* 2, No. 12 (March 1928): 1212.

21. *Amazing Stories* 3, No. 4 (July 1928): 370, 376.

22. "My Correspondence with Lovecraft" (1958; *AV* 427).

nation to publish censorious letters in general, and in particular those directed at one of his star writers, whom he clearly held in high esteem, however capriciously he acted when actual submissions came to him. Lovecraft notes that "The Silver Key" was not only rejected when first submitted around July 1927, but, when re-submitted and accepted a year later and published in the January 1929 issue, "readers violently disliked" the story.[23] But Wright published none of these hostile letters.

It was, indeed, around this time—late 1927—that Wright proposed to publish a volume of Lovecraft's stories under the imprint of the corporation that issued the magazine, the Popular Fiction Publishing Company. The specifics of the volume need not concern us, although it is of some interest to note the title Lovecraft wished for the volume: "As for a *title*—my choice is 'The Outsider and Other Stories'. This is because I consider the touch of cosmic *outsideness*—of dim, shadowy *non-terrestrial* hints—to be the characteristic feature of my writing."[24] Since Lovecraft had by this time written mostly short stories ranging between 2000 and 4000 words, what he called "the *indispensable* nucleus of any book purporting to represent the *popular* side of my fiction" came to only 32,400 words. He then suggested augmenting this total with one of three longer stories ("The Horror at Red Hook," "The Call of Cthulhu," "The Colour out of Space"), which would add about 10,000 words, along with some "fillers" to reach what Lovecraft called "your 45 or 6 thousand words"—presumably the length that Wright had specified.

This seems like a very small volume, but standards of book publishing were very different at that time. Ralph Adams Cram's

---

23. HPL to August Derleth, [2 August 1929]; *Essential Solitude* 206.

24. HPL to Farnsworth Wright, 22 December 1927; *Letters to Woodburn Harris and Others*. The other quotations in this paragraph are taken from this letter.

volume of ghost stories, *Black Spirits and White* (1895), is only 27,000 words. Lord Dunsany's first volume, *The Gods of Pegāna* (1905), is barely 20,000 words. Fitzgerald's *The Great Gatsby* (1925) is only 50,000 words. A volume of political fantasies that Ambrose Bierce attempted to market earlier in the century would have come to only 25,000 words.

But the project came to nothing. Earlier in 1927 the company had published A. G. Birch's novella *The Moon Terror* (along with stories by Anthony M. Rud and Vincent Starrett[25]), but the book sold so poorly that plans for other books along the same line fell by the wayside.

Another book venture, on an even smaller scale, also came to nothing, frustrating Lovecraft almost to the end of his life. W. Paul Cook wished to establish a line of slim books and, in 1926, had published Samuel Loveman's long poem *The Hermaphrodite* and Frank Belknap Long's poetry collection *The Man from Genoa.* Lovecraft's long short story "The Shunned House" was to be a part of this line, and the booklet—all of 59 pages—was printed in the summer of 1928; but just then Cook suffered both personal and financial difficulties, and the book was never bound or distributed, beyond a handful of copies bound in 1934 by R. H. Barlow. Lovecraft sometimes sent colleagues a set of the unbound sheets.

The booklet contained a one-page preface by Frank Belknap Long, although Lovecraft considered it ridiculous for a short story to have a preface. The piece is a typical "puff" of the sort expected of such an item. A comment toward the beginning—"It

25. Starrett's story, "Penelope" (*Weird Tales,* May 1923), was the very one that HPL had criticized harshly in a letter to Edwin Baird published in the October 1923 issue. Rud's story was "Ooze" (*Weird Tales,* March 1923). Possibly HPL re-read the story in *The Moon Terror* (a book he owned), as it seems to have influenced "The Dunwich Horror," written in the summer of 1928.

is so far removed in theme from our familiar world of radios and politicians and adding machines that it does not touch, at any point, the ancillary stream of modern writing" (*WW* 51)—curiously anticipates a line of reasoning propounded decades later by Michel Houellebecq and others.

But Lovecraft was receiving recognition from somewhat more prestigious venues. Cook had published the first (and only) issue of the *Recluse* (1927), for which he had commissioned Lovecraft to write the treatise "Supernatural Horror in Literature," which took up a substantial proportion of the issue (37 out of 77 pages). Cook, noting that Lovecraft discussed numerous living writers of weird fiction—notably the four "modern masters," Arthur Machen, Algernon Blackwood, Lord Dunsany, and M. R. James—made a concerted effort to send a copy of the issue to these luminaries. We have assessments of Lovecraft's essay from two of them.

M. R. James, in a letter to Nicholas Llewelyn Davies (12 January 1928), takes umbrage at Lovecraft's style, saying that it "is of the most offensive"; his criticism evidently focused on the fact that "He uses the word cosmic about 24 times." A little more charitably he remarks: "But he has taken pains to search about & treat the subject from its beginning to MRJ, to whom he devotes several columns."[26] There is a certain arrogance in the remark, as if James axiomatically assumes that the history of weird fiction should conclude with him. (In fact, Lovecraft later dismissed James as "the earthiest member of the 'big four,'"[27] and elsewhere concluded that Walter de la Mare would have been a more appropriate figure to include among the "modern masters.") Arthur Machen's response can only be gauged from Donald Wandrei's

26. "An M. R. James Letter," *Ghosts & Scholars* 8 (1986): 28–33.

27. HPL to J. Vernon Shea, 5 February 1932; *Letters to J. Vernon Shea, Carl F. Strauch, and Lee McBride White* 90.

comment to Lovecraft: "I received a letter to-day from Machen, in which he mentioned your article and its hold on him."[28]

Still more significantly, Lovecraft's tales began to be noted in the two leading "best short stories" series then being published. By far the more prestigious was Edward J. O'Brien's *Best Short Stories* (1915f.). O'Brien was a highly regarded critic and editor; Lovecraft relished his searing treatise on the decline of the short story in the machine age, *The Dance of the Machines* (1929), a book he owned. O'Brien had earlier written a less polemical volume on approximately the same subject, *The Advance of the American Short Story* (1923). In the *Best Short Stories* series, aside from reprinting a score of stories in each volume, O'Brien has an extensive appendix ranking stories published in a wide array of magazines as 1-star, 2-star, and 3-star; the 3-star stories are the highest ranking, and these constitute a "Roll of Honor," the authors of whom have their "Biographical Notices" appearing elsewhere in the volume.

O'Brien had already taken note of "The Picture in the House" (*Weird Tales,* January 1924) in the 1924 volume, giving it a 1-star ranking. Then, in the 1928 volume, he gave "The Colour out of Space" a 3-star ranking. Lovecraft was overwhelmed by this notice, as he should have been—it is indeed a signal honour. For a time he believed that the story itself would actually be reprinted, but that was not to be the case. He provided O'Brien with what proved by far to be the lengthiest "Biographical Notice" in that volume. In 1929 O'Brien gave "The Dunwich Horror" (*Weird Tales,* April 1929) a three-star ranking, and "The Silver Key" (*Weird Tales,* January 1929) a 1-star ranking. Because Lovecraft's "Biographical Notice" had already appeared in the preceding volume, it did not appear again in this one.

---

28. Donald Wandrei to HPL, 27 September 1928; *Letters with Donald and Howard Wandrei and to Emil Petaja* 218.

The *O. Henry Memorial Award Prize Stories* (1919f.), edited by Blanche Colton Williams, was considerably less prestigious. Lovecraft recognised that it singled out stories that were quite a bit more conventional in outlook and execution—stories of the *Saturday Evening Post* sort. Interestingly, Williams cited "Pickman's Model" (*Weird Tales,* October 1927) in the 1928 volume (in "Stories Ranking Third"), bypassing "The Colour out of Space," a far superior story. In 1929 she cited "The Silver Key" ("Stories Ranking Second"); in 1932 "The Strange High House in the Mist" ("Stories Ranking Highest") and, regrettably, "In the Vault" (*Weird Tales,* April 1932) ("Stories Ranking Second"). Even so, it is of interest that two of these stories had been initially rejected by Wright, whose views on the short story—or, rather, the acceptability of a given tale to his readership—were in many ways even more conventional than that of Blanche Colton Williams.

The fact that both O'Brien and Williams even considered stories from *Weird Tales* and other pulps is something of a counterargument to the belief that pulp or genre fiction was stringently banned from mainstream publications or mainstream critical attention. But in fact, only a tiny proportion of tales from the pulp magazines were cited in these publications; and the actual reprinting of any such stories in the volumes themselves was an event of vanishing rarity.

Where Lovecraft's were, now, getting reprinted was in anthologies of weird fiction, some tolerably prestigious, some very much otherwise. Among the latter were the *Not at Night* anthologies edited by British editor Christine Campbell Thomson, many of them taken largely or exclusively from *Weird Tales.* The first such event—and the first time Lovecraft's fiction had appeared in a hardcover book—occurred in 1927, when "The Horror at Red Hook" was reprinted in *You'll Need a Night Light.*

"Pickman's Model" was reprinted in *By Daylight Only* (1929); "The Curse of Yig" (ghostwritten for Zealia Bishop) and "The Rats in the Walls" in *Switch On the Light* (1931); and "The Horror in the Museum" (ghostwritten for Hazel Heald) in *Terror by Night* (1934). Three of these stories appeared in *The "Not at Night" Omnibus* (1937), an extensive selection from the eleven preceding Thomson anthologies, reprinting those tales that the editor regarded as her particular favourites. The publisher of these volumes (Selwyn & Blount) was a frankly inferior company, as the poor printing and binding of the volumes suggest. Lovecraft himself is correct in stating of the first volume in the series: "As for that 'Not at Night'—that's a mere lowbrow hash of absolutely no taste or significance. Aesthetically speaking, it doesn't exist."[29]

Somewhat higher on the aesthetic scale is T. Everett Harré's *Beware After Dark!* (1929), which reprinted "The Call of Cthulhu." Lovecraft is in very good company here, cheek by jowl with stories by E. F. Benson, Irvin S. Cobb, Lafcadio Hearn, Ellen Glasgow, Edward Lucas White, Leonid Andreyev, Arthur Machen, Robert Louis Stevenson, E. Phillips Oppenheim, M. P. Shiel, and other popular or critically acclaimed writers. In his introduction Harré devotes more space to Lovecraft than to most other writers in the book: "H. P. Lovecraft, one of the newer fantasy writers, has done some of the best things in such fiction; only limited editions of his tales have been published. His 'The Call of Cthulhu,'" in its cumulative awesomeness and building of effect to its appalling finale, is reminiscent of Poe."[30]

29. HPL to Donald Wandrei, [20 January 1928]; *Letters with Donald and Howard Wandrei* . . . 196. We need not here discuss Herbert Asbury's *Not at Night!* (Macy-Macius, 1928), which reprinted "The Horror at Red Hook." This volume was an unlicenced selection of several of the Thomson anthologies published up to that time. Subsequent litigation caused the volume to be withdrawn from circulation.

30. T. Everett Harré, *Beware After Dark!* (New York: Macaulay, 1929), 11.

The book was reprinted later that year in a "cheap" edition by Gold Label Books, and reprinted again in 1942 and 1945 by Emerson Books. Lovecraft became acquainted with Harré in the 1930s, meeting him several times in New York.

One of the most significant publications in Lovecraft's lifetime was the appearance of "The Music of Erich Zann" in Dashiell Hammett's *Creeps by Night* (1931). It does not appear that Hammett—who had by this time published four of his five hard-boiled detective novels, along with dozens of short stories (mostly in *Black Mask*)—did much hands-on editing of the book. Lovecraft reports that numerous colleagues, including Frank Belknap Long and August Derleth, had made suggestions to Hammett for stories from *Weird Tales* to reprint. In the end, six stories from the magazine were included. The most notable inclusion in the volume overall, of course, was William Faulkner's "A Rose for Emily" (*Forum,* 30 April 1930), a classic of psychological terror. Hammett's brief introduction has no discussion of the individual tales in the book.

Even this volume, however, did not rank all that high in the realm of publishing. The John Day Co. was by no means an elite publisher, along the lines of Knopf, Scribner's. E. P. Dutton, and others. Still, the book did get widely reviewed; and at least one review briefly singled out Lovecraft (and also Frank Belknap Long) as among the notable authors in the book. This reviewer, Will Cuppy, mentioned "a variety of promising items by such professors as . . ."[31] Cuppy, as we will see, wrote admiringly of Lovecraft at a later date as well.

Creeps by Night was reprinted by Blue Ribbon Books later in 1931, and was reprinted again (with the omission of two stories, although "The Music of Erich Zann" was retained) in England

---

31. Will Cuppy, "Mystery and Adventure," *New York Herald Tribune Books* (1 November 1931): 14.

(Gollancz, 1932) under the title *Modern Tales of Terror.*[32] This latter edition likely led to the reprint of Lovecraft's story in the London *Evening Standard* (24 October 1932), where it took up an entire page of the paper (with a large illustration in the centre) and extended on to a second page. The anthology was reprinted again by the World Publishing Co. (1944), on extremely poor-quality paper, evidently because of war restrictions.

Otherwise, Lovecraft could bask in noteworthy but ephemeral praise from various sources. During his trip to Vermont in 1928, he and his friends were written up in the *Brattleboro Reformer* on two occasions. One was a brief unsigned article.[33] The other was a contribution to the "Pendrifter" column, run by Charles Crane (the column is mentioned in "The Whisperer in Darkness," although Crane is not), by Vrest Orton, a late member of the Kalem Club whom Lovecraft had first met in 1925. This article, "A Weird Writer Is in Our Midst," is really a remarkably astute and prescient piece on Lovecraft's unique status in literature. Orton confessed to an inability to appreciate weird fiction but nonetheless recognised Lovecraft as a pioneering contributor to the field. "Lovecraft is a very great writer . . . perhaps so great that he will never be appreciated" (*WW* 52). Orton stresses Lovecraft's New England roots and his non-commercial approach to writing. He concludes: "I do not say he is a greater writer than Poe, for in some departments he is not. But I do say that as a scholar and research worker in the one subject of the weird from his point of view, and a writer on that subject exclusively, H. P. Lovecraft is the greatest this century has ever seen or maybe ever will see" (*WW* 54).

---

32. It would be nearly two decades before Gollancz published its first volume of HPL's stories.

33. "Literary Persons Meet in Guilford," *Brattleboro Daily Reformer* (18 June 1928): 1.

Then there was Bertrand K. Hart, the literary editor of the *Providence Journal,* who ran a "Sideshow" column that ran almost daily. In mid-November 1929 Hart initiated a discussion of the most terrifying tale in literature, providing several examples. Lovecraft found this list so tame and conventional that, in spite of his professed distaste for bombarding the local press with letters,[34] he sent in his own list of favourites, which was duly published in the column for 23 November. Then his colleagues got into the act. Lists by Frank Belknap Long and August Derleth appeared in the columns for 25 and 30 November.

Then the discussion took an unexpected turn. Hart picked up a copy of *Beware After Dark!* and found to his amusement that the home of the artist Henry Anthony Wilcox (the Fleur-de-Lys building at 7 Thomas Street) was a residence he had once occupied. He professed to take umbrage and send "at least one large and abiding ghost by way of reprisal upon [Lovecraft's] own doorstep in Barnes Street" (29 November) at 3 A.M.[35] Lovecraft, taking up the challenge, replied with the magnificent sonnet "The Messenger" (written at 3:07 A.M.), which was duly published in the column of 3 December. Over the next several years Hart mentioned Lovecraft (and even printed two entire letters by him) in his columns.

Last, but by no means least, was William Bolitho, a South African–born journalist who began writing for the *New York World* in 1923 and emigrated to the United States in 1928. Bolitho mentioned Lovecraft at the very end of a column on "Pulp

34. After 1911 he published no letters in the *Journal* except a plea to preserve 18th-century buildings in Providence (10 October 1926) and a poignant defence of the historic and architectural value of "Old Brick Row" (24 March 1929). He also ghostwrote a letter on the same subject and had James F. Morton send it in, where it appeared in the issue for 22 December 1929.

35. See S. T. Joshi, "H. P. Lovecraft in 'The Sideshow,'" *Lovecraft Annual* No. 11 (2017): 60.

Magazines": "In this world there are chiefs, evidently. I am inclined to think they must be pretty good. There is Otis Adelbert Kline and H. P. Lovecraft, whom I am sure I would rather read than many fashionable lady novelists they give teas to; and poets too."[36] This is very ambiguous praise indeed; aside from the dubious comparison with the hack Kline, it is unclear whether Bolitho even read Lovecraft or Kline. But Lovecraft was tickled by the comment. The entire column was reprinted in *Weird Tales* for April 1930.

A minuscule augmentation of Lovecraft's self-esteem occurred when his friend Maurice W. Moe, then assisting in the preparation of a high school textbook, excerpted a small portion of the travel essay "Observations on Several Parts of America" (1928) in the volume. The book, *Junior Literature: Book Two* (1930), was officially edited by Sterling Leonard and Harold Y. Moffett, and the Lovecraft selection—designed to illuminate Washington Irving's "The Legend of Sleepy Hollow"—was printed in an appendix under the title "Sleepy Hollow To-day." Lovecraft waxed eloquent (probably in a self-parodic manner) about his enshrinement in a standard textbook: "Ah, me! Wright may reject my stuff, but at least, my name will achieve a mild & grudging kind of immortality on the reluctant lips of the young."[37] Although this was in fact the first time that Lovecraft's work appeared under the imprint of a major publisher (Macmillan), and although the book was reprinted in 1935, it thereafter disappeared and is now not easily located.

But Lovecraft suffered several setbacks during this time, some of which were so devastating that they may have prematurely curtailed his entire literary career. Always sensitive to re-

36. William Bolitho, "Pulp Magazines," *New York World* (4 January 1930): 11.
37. HPL to August Derleth, 21 November [1930]; *Essential Solitude* 290.

jection, Lovecraft was repeatedly frustrated by his inability to have a book of his stories published, especially when in most cases it was the publishers themselves who solicited his work for consideration. The *Weird Tales* project had died almost as soon as it was born in late 1927. Then, about a year and a half after Lovecraft received his first three-star rating in the O'Brien *Best Short Stories,* he received a letter from Clifton P. Fadiman of Simon & Schuster, which read in part:

> It is probable that your labours this far have been devoted mainly to the field of the short story. If you are contemplating any longer work of fiction, or if you would care to let me know anything of your literary plans in general, it will be a pleasure to hear from you.
>
> Any manuscript with which you favour us is assured an interested reading.[38]

In his naïveté, Lovecraft was unaware that this was in fact a form letter sent out by Fadiman to all writers appearing on the "Honor Roll" of recent volumes of the *Best Short Stories.* Lovecraft replied that he had no novel to submit (he regarded *The Dream-Quest of Unknown Kadath* as a "practice" work and didn't think *The Case of Charles Dexter Ward* was good enough—a tragically shortsighted evaluation), but offered to send some short stories. Fadiman's response was not encouraging:

> Thank you very much for your letter of the 21st. I am afraid that you are right in that our interest in a collection of short stories would not be very vivid.
>
> I hope, however, that you will buckle down & do that novel you speak of. If it is good, its subject matter [the weird] will be a help rather than a hindrance.[39]

---

38. Quoted in HPL's letter to Lillian D. Clark, 20–21 May 1930; *Letters to Family and Family Friends* 840.

39. Quoted in HPL's letter to Lillian D. Clark, 24–25 May 1930; *Letters to Family and Family Friends* 850.

Nothing of course came of this. The only point of interest here is that the prejudice against weird short stories, as opposed to novels, seems already well established at this time—a prejudice that would continue all the way to the present day.

Then came a double (or even triple) whammy in the summer of 1931, when Lovecraft was crushed by the nearly simultaneous rejection of *At the Mountains of Madness*—his most ambitious work to date—by *Weird Tales* and of a collection of his stories by G. P. Putnam's Sons. In regard to the first: Lovecraft knew that the story was quite long (about 41,000 words), but wrote to one correspondent that the work was "capable of a major serial division in the exact middle."[40] This is not to suggest that Lovecraft wrote the novel with magazine serialisation in mind; it was simply a matter of practicality to contemplate serialisation of such a long story as a way of realising some (indeed, a significant amount of) revenue from the arduous task of writing the text. But Wright turned the story down altogether:

> Yes—Wright "explained" his rejection of the "Mountains of Madness" in almost the same language as that with which he "explained" other recent rejections to Long & Derleth. It was "too long", "not easily divisible into parts", "not convincing"—& so on. Just what he has said of other things of mine (except for length)—some of which he has ultimately accepted after many hesitations.[41]

There may be more to be said for Wright's decision than what Lovecraft suggests here. In fact, the earlier chapters of *At the Mountains of Madness* are pretty heavy going, filled with dense scientific jargon and failing to have easily identifiable characters. Lovecraft was of course not aiming for these effects, but he should have known (and, in other contexts, he *did* know) that the *Weird Tales* serials were often the poorest contributions to

40. HPL to August Derleth, 24 March [1931]; *Essential Solitude* 325.
41. HPL to J. Vernon Shea, 7 August 1931; *Letters to J. Vernon Shea* . . . 29.

the magazines from a purely aesthetic perspective.

Lovecraft was essentially trying to have his cake and eat it too. He wished, in this instance, that Wright would ignore his known rationale for accepting serials, even though as a purely business decision the result might have been disastrous. On the other hand, Lovecraft *was* a popular writer for *Weird Tales,* and many readers yearned to have his work appear more frequently (in the late 1920s and 1930s, Wright was compelled to reprint Lovecraft's earlier stories in the "Weird Tales Reprints" section, in the absence of original work), so that it is likely that *At the Mountains of Madness,* no matter how slow-moving—and, more significantly, how far in advance of conventional pulp standards—it was, would have at least met with a modicum of praise, at least from Lovecraft's friends and colleagues, who regularly wrote in to "The Eyrie" to express their appreciation.

This rejection might have been slightly less painful if it had not come just around the time when G. P. Putnam's Sons turned down a collection of his tales. In late March 1931 Lovecraft reports that an editor at that firm, Winfield Shiras, had asked to see some of Lovecraft's stories for a potential collection. Lovecraft sent in a whopping thirty stories, then heard nothing from Shiras for months. In mid-July Lovecraft at least got the word—not an explicit rejection, but it amounted to the same thing: "Shiras . . . hems & haws & talks of changes he would like to see & plans he would like to make after the lapse of a few months."[42] He elaborates on the point to J. Vernon Shea:

> The grounds for rejection were twofold—first, that some of the tales are not subtle enough . . . too obvious & well-explained—(admitted! That ass Wright got me into the habit of obvious writing with his never-ending complaints against the indefiniteness of my early stuff.) & sec-

42. HPL to Lillian D. Clark, 16 July 1931; *Letters to Family and Family Friends* 942.

> ondly, that all the tales are uniformly macabre in mood to stand collected publication. This second reason is sheer bull—for as a matter of fact unity of mood is a positive asset in a fictional collection. But I suppose the herd must have their comic relief![43]

I think Lovecraft is on target in this evaluation. He may have overstated the degree to which his stories were over-explanatory; as he evolved as a writer, he largely abandoned the nebulously macabre manner of "The Music of Erich Zann" for the pseudo-scientific manner of "The Call of Cthulhu" and *At the Mountains of Madness,* and that necessitated a certain precision in the nature of the horrors in those tales. In effect, the stories were so dense in their language and intense in their atmosphere that an editor like Shiras, who was probably unfamiliar with the weird, found them difficult to take without the "comic relief" that Lovecraft rightly despised.

A third rejection came at the hands of Harry Bates, editor of the short-lived pulp magazine *Strange Tales of Mystery and Terror* (1931–33). Lovecraft had submitted five stories to Bates, but all were rejected. These were, however, among his poorest ("Beyond the Wall of Sleep," "The Nameless City," "The Doom that Came to Sarnath," etc.), and had all been previously rejected by Wright.

One of these stories was "In the Vault." Wright himself rejected it when it was submitted to him in late 1925. Wright's rationale—that "its extreme gruesomeness would not pass the Indiana censorship"[44]—refers to the fact that, when C. M. Eddy, Jr.'s "The Loved Dead" (extensively revised by Lovecraft) appeared in the May–June–July 1924 issue, the state of Indiana evidently banned the issue for obscenity. Ever since then, Wright became hesitant to take stories that featured the kind of grisliness

---

43. HPL to J. Vernon Shea, 7 August 1931; *Letters to J. Vernon Shea . . .* 30.

44. HPL to Lillian D. Clark, 2 December 1925; *Letters to Family and Family Friends* 498.

that "The Loved Dead" had (although of course that story did indeed approach the borderline of good taste by actually hinting that the protagonist had sex with corpses—and there was no corresponding sexual element in "In the Vault"). Wright had previously rejected "Cool Air" in early 1926 for the same reasons, and it had to appear in the poorly paying *Tales of Magic and Mystery* (March 1928). In early 1932 August Derleth, in his conventional way, was taken with "In the Vault" and retyped Lovecraft's fraying typescript, then badgered his friend to re-submit the story; this time it was accepted.

One more book project emerged in 1932, only to fizzle quickly. In March, Vanguard asked about a possible volume of some kind. Vanguard was a second- or third-tier publisher at best, and it would have been no especial feather in Lovecraft's cap to have had a book published with it; but it would have been something. His friend Arthur Leeds—a columnist for *Writer's Digest*—had spoken to a Vanguard editor, one Percy Elias, on Lovecraft's behalf. Lovecraft sent four stories—"The Call of Cthulhu," "The Rats in the Walls," "Pickman's Model," and "The Dunwich Horror"[45]—even though he notes that the editor wasn't "so keen"[46] on short stories, preferring a novel. I cannot find a contemporaneous discussion of the upshot of this submission; but the fact that, about a year and a half later, Lovecraft is speaking of "the Putnam & Vanguard fiascos"[47] suggests an eventual rejection.

Given these twin débâcles, it is not likely that Lovecraft received more than transient pleasure in the esteem accorded to him by one J. Randle Luten in an article, "What Makes a Story

45. HPL to August Derleth, 25 March 1932; *Essential Solitude* 466.

46. HPL to Wilfred B. Talman, 22 March [1932]; *Letters to Wilfred B. Talman and Helen V. and Genevieve Sully* 208.

47. HPL to Clark Ashton Smith, [3 October 1933]; *Dawnward Spire* 447.

Click?" in the *American Author* (July 1932). This periodical (1929–41) was one of the poorest of the "writers' magazines" then published—the *Writer, Writer's Digest, Writer's Monthly,* among others—because it catered relentlessly to authors seeking to land material in pulp or popular magazines of low grade. And, to be blunt, J. Randle Luten is an idiot. The article chooses, apparently at random, three stories from the April 1932 *Weird Tales*—Clark Ashton Smith's "The Gorgon" (which Luten repeatedly misspells as "Gorgan"), Edmond Hamilton's "The Earth-Brain," and Lovecraft's "In the Vault"—to single out for praise in narration, creation of suspense, and ill-defined "glamor." His view of what constitutes suspense is crude and simplistic: "Suspense is the withholding of data—important data—from your readers. If it is a love story, do not let the reader know whether the heroine is going to love the hero or not, or vice versa" (*WW* 58). As for "glamor," this is "the thing in the story that is remembered by the reader, even after the story is finished and the magazine laid aside." Not very helpful; but we learn that Poe "is a master of *glamor*" (*WW* 60). The mere fact that he singles out "In the Vault"—which nearly everyone aside from August Derleth regards as one of Lovecraft's poorest stories—says it all.

Lovecraft could still find solace in the continued appeal of his work to readers of *Weird Tales.* It was perhaps to be predicted that readers would enthuse about "The Lurking Fear" (June 1928) and "The Dunwich Horror" (April 1929), as these are just the sort of 'rousing good yarns' that devotees of the pulps slavered over. And even though the latter is a significant elaboration upon the Cthulhu Mythos, introducing Yog-Sothoth (for the first and, essentially, the last time) as a significant presence, its naïve good-vs.-evil scenario, where the valiant librarian Henry Armitage and his colleagues do battle against the 'evil' Old Ones and manage to banish them, also suited the tastes of conventional readers.

Paul Hendrickson thought "The Lurking Fear"—which Lovecraft only grudgingly submitted to Wright, thinking it at least marginally better than "Herbert West," which he refused to send in—was "his best so far" (*WW* 68), an opinion that would have made Lovecraft cringe. A. V. Pershing, in commenting on "The Dunwich Horror," follows the lead of several previous letter-writers by actually trying, grotesquely, to imitate Lovecraft's richly textured prose, producing ludicrous bombast:

> The bare remembrance of such matter-of-fact acquaintances with the gibberish 'terrors' of his pen freezes my brain, the while my thoughts scatter and flee panic-stricken to the crumbling recesses of ancient hyper-space where laughing, screeching demons of all the crystallized filth and anguish of a universe obscenely chant the orgies of the insane existence we term, 'reality.' (*WW* 69)

Well, he would not be the last to engage in such empty theatrics. And his critical judgment might be questioned when he states that "Again I say that surely Lovecraft is as great a writer as ever lived" (*WW* 69).

Lovecraft's friend Bernard Austin Dwyer chimed in with a slightly less flamboyant encomium: "I regard him as the greatest weird writer living today." Later in the letter he states: "Lovecraft, I am sure, will in after days be noticed as one of the very greatest writers of the weird and the grotesque that ever lived. Indeed I consider him as equal to Bierce and Blackwood, and at times equal to Poe—'The Outsider', for instance" (*WW* 69–70). Even if such an opinion is now quite plausible, it seemed to Lovecraft absurdly extravagant, leading him to declare to J. Vernon Shea: "You don't call us clumsy W.T. jacks 'real authors' do you? [. . .] The difference between the veriest novice & this grade of scribbler is infinitely less than that between such scribblers & the Blackwood-Dunsany-Machen-James type."[48]

It is of some interest see, as early as 1929, readers asking whether the *Necronomicon* is real (see E. L. Mengshoel in the August 1929 issue and N. J. O'Neail in the March 1930 issue [*WW* 70, 71]); but this point relates to the expansion of the Cthulhu Mythos, which I have discussed elsewhere.[49] Charles Rush, Jr. gave Lovecraft added impetus to be doubtful of *Weird Tales* readers' critical acumen when he noted, in response to the reprint of "The Rats in the Walls" (June 1930), that Lovecraft "has held a standard unsurpassed by any of your other authors"—with the "possible exception," of course, of Seabury Quinn, Edmond Hamilton, and Robert E. Howard (*WW* 73)! "The Whisperer in Darkness" (August 1931), a 25,000-word novella, understandably came in for its share of praise. Duke Williamson, speaking more generally, waxed poetic about Lovecraft:

> Before you read a page of a Lovecraft story you are engulfed in a whirlpool, as it were, of deep mists, eery whispers and deadly foreboding which continues and rises until the very last page, when the climax shatters all and leaves the reader breathless. [. . .] By no means secondary are the vivid and brilliant descriptions with which Mr. Lovecraft paints his backgrounds; one could actually hear those swirling, trickling brooks, those buzzing voices, and the wind in the trees, through the magic of the author's words. (December 1931; *WW* 75)

What Williamson is awkwardly trying to say is that Lovecraft is effective in creating weird atmosphere; that his story construction is impeccable in creating a sense of cumulative horror; and that his portrayal of topography is vital to the power of his tales. All these points are quite sound and would be elaborated upon by genuine critics decades later.

48. HPL to J. Vernon Shea, 28 September 1931; *Letters to J. Vernon Shea* . . . 57.

49. See *The Rise, Fall, and Rise of the Cthulhu Mythos* (2015).

But *Weird Tales*—not its readers, but its editor—played a critical role in another catastrophic event in Lovecraft's life: the decline of a story collection by Alfred A. Knopf. Knopf was a relatively new publisher (it began issuing books only in 1915), but it quickly attained high regard, in part because of the early involvement of H. L. Mencken as an informal editorial director. (Mencken, however, strongly disapproved of Knopf's many reprints of Arthur Machen's work, writing a scathing review of them in 1923.)[50] In August 1933, on the suggestion of Samuel Loveman, an editor at Knopf, Allan G. Ullman, wrote to Lovecraft asking to see some manuscripts for possible book publication. In two separate packages Lovecraft sent a total of twenty-five stories. I have previously criticised the self-deprecatory comments that Lovecraft made in the cover letters accompanying these stories—comments that he probably thought to indicate gentlemanly humility but which Ullman may have interpreted as the author's lack of confidence in his own work.

What have now come to light, however, are the readers' reports on these stories; and they are highly illuminating. The two readers were Cary Abbott and Louis Kronenberger. Abbott had previously been the managing editor of the *Yale Literary Magazine* but otherwise had few literary credits to his name. Kronenberger (1904–1980) was a different story. Although at this time in the early stages of his career as a journalist, editor, and author (he had begun working for the *New York Times* in 1924 and had previously served in the editorial office of Boni & Liveright before joining Knopf in 1933), he published a well-regarded novel, *The Grand Manner,* in 1929.

Abbott's reader's report notes that the material in question

50. "Biography and Other Fiction," *Smart Set* 71, No. 4 (August 1923): 138–44; rpt. in *Writings in the* Smart Set, *Volume 8:1922–1923,* ed. S. T. Joshi (Seattle: Sarnath Press, 2019), 331–35.

was "a collection of horror stories by a well-known writer in this type of tale. As a rule he gives a very good performance in this slow, dignified, rather old-fashioned style which accelerates to a wild tempo toward the climaxes." Kronenberger wrote: "Quite good in an old-fashioned way, though perhaps too much alike, and too much given to atmosphere and not enough to action. In their own way, however, they are effective."[51] The upshot of these reports, apparently, was tolerably favourable, but the question (pointed at by Kronenberger when he remarked: "Lots of people undoubtedly like this kind of thing: the whole question is, are they book-buyers or pulp readers?") was whether such a book would sell. Ullman approached Farnsworth Wright, asking whether 1000 copies of a book of Lovecraft's stories could be sold through *Weird Tales.* Wright said he couldn't be sure, so Ullman turned the book down.

Was Wright being too cautious? He no doubt recalled the spectacular failure of *The Moon Terror* six years earlier, which led to the demise of a Lovecraft volume in 1927–28; and that was before the worst phases of the Depression went into effect. With FDR's New Deal only a few months old, and unemployment still rampant, Wright felt he had to be extremely judicious in making such promises as Ullman had requested. But the end result was another painful disappointment—perhaps the worst that Lovecraft ever suffered. It was the *At the Mountains of Madness* scenario all over again: Wright thought highly of the work but did not think it was commercially viable as a serial;[52] and

51. David E. Schultz, "'Whaddya Make Them Eyes at Me For?': Lovecraft and Book Publishers," *Lovecraft Annual* No. 12 (2018): 59, 60.

52. It can be noted here that Wright twice declined the novella "The Shadow over Innsmouth" when it was surreptitiously submitted to him by August Derleth. See *The Shadow over Innsmouth,* ed. S. T. Joshi and David E. Schultz (West Warwick, RI: Necronomicon Press, rev. ed. 1997), 10–11.

Knopf's Ullman came to a similar conclusion in regard to the book venture.

It need hardly be said that a book of Lovecraft's stories would have been a towering achievement in his personal and professional career—and may have been a turning point in the entire history of weird fiction. But it was not to be, and so Lovecraft had to plug along as best he could. But the remaining three and a half years of his life continued to be dogged by rejection and disappointment.

The year 1933 is a landmark in a very different way, in that it was the year when the *Fantasy Fan*—acknowledged to be the first "fan" magazine in the field of weird fiction—appeared. And yet, although Lovecraft appeared extensively in its pages—ranging from stories that had been rejected by professional publishers to the uncompleted serialisation of the revised version of "Supernatural Horror in Literature"—not a single article explicitly or entirely about Lovecraft appeared in its pages, not even in the October 1934 issue, dedicated to him. Perhaps this is not so unusual. A biographical article by F. Lee Baldwin, clearly based on his correspondence with Lovecraft, did appear as "H. P. Lovecraft: A Biographical Sketch" in *Fantasy Magazine* (April 1935), but even this is a singular item in the fan press prior to Lovecraft's death.

The ever-faithful *Weird Tales* readership continued to laud Lovecraft's work; but, with the increasing appearance of his revised or ghostwritten tales in the magazine, readers understandably had trouble distinguishing his work from these commissioned tales. The most piquant remark came from Bernard J. Kenton, who wrote in the May 1934 issue: "Of the recent writers, Hazel Heald strikes my fancy most, for whenever did anything to strikingly horrible as 'The Horror in the Museum' appear in print? Even Lovecraft—as powerful and artistic as he is with macabre suggestiveness—could hardly, I suspect, have surpassed the grotesque scene in which the other-dimensional shambler leaps out upon the hero" (*WW* 77). Kenton is the pseudonym of Jerome Siegel, the co-creator of Superman; he was twenty years old when this letter was written. John Malone spoke more truly than he knew when he stated, in reference to "Out of the Aeons," that the story "was like a masterpiece by H. P. Lovecraft" (June 1935; *WW* 78); and B. M. Reynolds analogously referred to Heald as "veritably a female Lovecraft" (June 1935; *WW* 79).

Readers did clamour for new stories by Lovecraft, but had to be satisfied with reprints, since after the rejection of *At the Mountains of Madness* he himself submitted only a single story ("In the Vault") prior to late 1936. Robert Nelson—a brief correspondent of Lovecraft prior to his early death in 1935—wrote in to praise "The Music of Erich Zann" (March 1935), while Charles H. Bert maintained that "The Outsider" was founded on the life of Kaspar Hauser (1812?–1833), a German boy who claimed that he had spent nearly his entire life in a dungeon, tended to by some mysterious man who hid his face from him. But there is no evidence that Lovecraft knew of Hauser before writing the story.

One interesting letter came from Jacques Bergier, who wrote in the March 1936 issue that Lovecraft "is the only writer of today who is really *haunted*" (Bergier's emphasis). He goes on to rank Lovecraft with the titans: "Some of his stories, such as 'Pickman's Model' and 'The Rats in the Walls', surpass even Poe, Blackwood, and Machen" (*WW* 80). We will hear more of Bergier in the decades to come.

By this time, however, Lovecraft had, by a serious of accidents, landed two long stories—*At the Mountains of Madness* and "The Shadow out of Time"—in *Astounding Stories*. *Astounding*, founded in 1930 by Clayton Magazines (publisher of some of the cruder pulp magazines of the era, including *Ghost Stories*) and edited by Harry Bates, folded in early 1933. It was then revived by Street & Smith, who installed F. Orlin Tremaine as editor. Nothing in Tremaine's background suggested that he would be an especially adept editor of a flagship science fiction magazine; his prior stints included work on a line of romance and detective magazines published by the Macfadden group, an even more plebeian publisher than Clayton. It may seem superficially impressive that he edited the *Smart Set* for three years (1924–26); but this was exactly the time when the publisher of that magazine ousted H. L. Mencken and George Jean Nathan in order to turn the magazine into a venue for crude popular fiction and celebrity profiles.

Tremaine was first approached in late 1935 by the young Julius Schwartz, who was attempting to establish himself as an agent. Schwartz had persuaded Lovecraft to let him handle *At the Mountains of Madness,* which had been sitting idle since its rejection by Farnsworth Wright four years earlier. Tremaine reportedly accepted the story without reading it, merely on the strength of Lovecraft's name. He did the same when Donald Wandrei followed suit and brought over "The Shadow out of Time" for Tremaine's examination. If nothing else, these quick acceptances indicate Lovecraft's celebrity in a field outside his chosen realm of weird fiction.

But Lovecraft saw red when he noted the butchery that his Antarctic novel suffered (*Astounding Stories,* February, March, and April 1936), especially in the third instalment. The omission of vital text, the chopping up of Lovecraft's long, leisurely paragraphs into shorter ones, and the overhauling of his punctuation infuriated Lovecraft, who referred to Tremaine as a "god-damn'd dung of a hyaena."[53] Needless to say, it is unlikely that Tremaine

---

53. HPL to R. H. Barlow, 4 June 1936; *O Fortunate Floridian* 335.

himself made these textual revisions; no doubt some underling did so, and Tremaine either sanctioned them or didn't care one way or the other. Lovecraft repeatedly declared to correspondents that "The Shadow out of Time" (June 1936) didn't suffer the same fate; but in fact, it was also extensively re-paragraphed, among other alterations.

As for the response to the two stories among the readers' column ("Brass Tacks") of the magazine—the degree to which it was hostile to Lovecraft has been consistently overstated by critics.[54] In fact, a slight majority of the letters were favourable to Lovecraft, even if a number of these were written by Lovecraft's own colleagues. Still, some of the negative letters do contain some pungent zingers, as in Robert Thompson's comment: "I am glad to see the conclusion to *At the Mountains of Madness* for reasons that would not be pleasant to Mr. Lovecraft" (*WW* 113). Cleveland C. Soper, Jr. wrote at length about his disdain for the story:

> First, why in the name of science-fiction did you ever print such a story as *At the Mountains of Madness* by Lovecraft? Are you in such dire straits that you must print this kind of drivel? In the first place, this story does not belong in Astounding Stories, for there is no science in it at all. You even recommend it with the expression that it was a fine word picture, and for that I will never forgive you.
>
> If such stories as this—of two people scaring themselves half to death by looking at the carvings in some ancient ruins, and being chased by something that even the author can't describe, and full of mutterings about nameless horrors, such as the windowless solids with five dimensions, Yog-Sothoth, etc.—are what is to constitute the future yarns of Astounding Stories, then heaven help the cause of science-fiction. (*WW* 114)

There are several curious things about this letter. How Soper

---

54. See Robert E. Weinberg, "Lovecraft in Astounding Stories," *Nyctalops* 2, No. 3 (January–February 1975): 3–5, 43.

could say "there is no science in it at all" is hard to understand; Lovecraft drew extensively on his own knowledge of geology, palaeontology, astronomy, and other sciences to create verisimilitude, especially in the first half of the text. Possibly Soper was displeased that the story was largely set in the remote past rather than a future full of space ships and other technological advances, even though such works as John Taine's *Before the Dawn* (1934) are of the same sort. (Some have speculated that Lovecraft was in part influenced by Taine's *The Greatest Adventure* [1929], another story about Antarctic exploration.) And as for Lovecraft's failure to describe the shoggoth at the end: as in other tales, he may refer to it as "indescribable" or "nameless" or such, but in fact he provides a compelling portrayal of its nature and properties in what might be the most chilling tableau in the entire history of weird fiction.

But Soper's overall comment clearly betrays a scorn for any admixture of weirdness in the genre of science fiction—the same intolerance that led Forrest J Ackerman to condemn Smith's "The Dweller in the Gulf" (published under an altered title) as an inappropriate contribution to *Wonder Stories:* "it seems to me that Wonder Stories is going far afield when it takes such a horror story as Mr. Smith's 'Dweller in Martian Depths' and, because it is laid on the Red Planet, prints it in a magazine of scientific fiction."[55] The 1930s also saw a lively discussion in *Weird Tales* as to whether that magazine should remain purely "weird" or include some science fiction/weird hybrids.

It is this line of thinking that led Harold Z. Taylor, in what is presumably (but not definitely) a parodic or sarcastic letter, to say that the story "was rather dry, although a pretty girl and the appearance of the Elders [?] would have made it an excellent sto-

---

55. "The Boiling Point," *Fantasy Fan* (September 1933); in *Dawnward Spire* 689.

ry for a weird magazine" (*WW* 114). Andy Aprea, Jr., soberly agreeing with Cleveland C. Soper that *At the Mountains of Madness* was "drivel," states flatly that "Lovecraft is out of place in Astounding" (*WW* 115–16).

Other hostile comments on *At the Mountains of Madness* focused predictably on Lovecraft's narrative style, as when Cameron Lewis stated that the story "dragged horribly and the absence of conversation spoiled it" (*WW* 114). Gene Noguere, incredibly, thought the "ending was altogether boring and not up to average" (*WW* 113), whatever the "average" may be. Just as remarkably, L. M. Jensen, speaking only of the first instalment, believes it "a fine story" but criticises it for "a lack of attention to detail and too much repetition; too many specific references to the Necronomicon" (*WW* 110). Peter Ruzella, Jr. goes so far as to say the story was "trash" (*WW* 115).

But in contrast to these brickbats, we have Lyle Dahlbrun coming forth with the critical gem that *At the Mountains of Madness* is "one keen yarn" (*WW* 111). Gene Pigg, in contrast to Jensen, states "I believe it is one of the most fascinating stories that I have read, because of the realistic style of writing" (*WW* 111). James L. Russell raves: "His masterful description and his repetition of certain themes casts an almost hypnotic trance upon the reader which persists long after the story is finished" (*WW* 112). A host of Lovecraft's friends wrote in support of the tale, from Lloyd Arthur Eshbach to August Derleth to Corwin F. Stickney.

"The Shadow out of Time" inspired fewer negative letters. Cameron D. Lewis, who didn't care for *At the Mountains of Madness,* found "Shadow" to his liking: "Part of it actually sent chills up my spine, which a story seldom does" (*WW* 114). But W. B. Hoskins presents an admirable defence of Lovecraft as both an intrinsically meritorious writer and one who belongs in *Astounding:*

> Lovecraft refuses to add the usual space ships and disintegrators to his tales; therefore, he does not write science-fiction. All right, he doesn't! But his stuff is worth admitting to the magazine on literary merit alone.
>
> You have only three or four authors who could qualify as authors *only,* not merely as authors of science fiction, and Lovecraft is one of them. His stories stand rereading better than almost any others you have printed.
>
> Lovecraft does much the same thing in his stories that Tschaikowsky does in his music—his climaxes are obvious, yet you always get a kick out of them. In my own case, at least, his description is so convincing that I wonder: Is this man chiseling his stories out of fresh, uncut granite, or is he merely knocking away the detritus of some age-old carving? His lore has all the sombre ring of truth. You get the general idea. I like Lovecraft. (*WW* 118)[56]

But Lovecraft would not have an opportunity to rile up the readers of *Astounding* with any more contributions: he would be dead less than a year after "The Shadow out of Time" appeared.

In 1935–36 two more book proposals occurred, only to come to naught. Early in 1935, Loring & Mussey asked to look at some of Lovecraft's stories for a possible collection. The firm, established by Percy Loring and Barrows Mussey, was distinctly a second-tier publisher, far inferior to Putnam's and Knopf. The solicitation came at the urging of August Derleth, whose "Judge

---

56. Another reader who enjoyed HPL's stories but, like Fritz Leiber, neglected to send in a letter of comment was the young Arthur C. Clarke. Decades later, in his autobiography, he speaks of how both stories thrilled him. In *At the Mountains of Madness,* "the author's remarkable erudition—he had more than a nodding acquaintance with all the sciences—makes his account of an ill-fated expedition to the Antarctic very convincing, through his use of geographical, historical, and geological details." *Astounding Days: A Science Fictional Autobiography* (New York; Bantam, 1990), 129.

Peck" detective novels (and also his first mainstream work, *Place of Hawks* [1935]) had appeared under its imprint beginning in 1934. The publishers took their time making a decision. Things didn't look good by the end of May: "Mussey is indecisive; his wife (who is in the business) doesn't like the stories & wants to turn them down; & Loring hasn't read them."[57] A definite rejection came in the middle of July. Perhaps this was just as well: the firm suffered financial troubles and essentially went out of business in 1936–37. Derleth himself, as we shall see, deftly moved to Scribner's, a far more prestigious publisher.

At the very end of Lovecraft's life, October 1936 and extending on into early 1937, his friend Wilfred Blanch Talman approached William Morrow & Co. with some kind of proposal for a Lovecraft volume. The firm had been founded in 1926, hence was a relative newcomer to New York publishing, but it was rapidly rising in stature. Talman initially suggested a short story collection, but Morrow was cool to the idea. What happened next is not entirely clear, but it appears that Talman, on his own initiative, made a quasi-firm promise on his friend's behalf that Lovecraft would produce a novel in the near future. Lovecraft, of course, was not in any sense prepared to undertake such a task, all apart from his overriding health issues (which he kept secret from Talman as he did from almost all his other colleagues). Lovecraft was simply not one who could write anything to order—not anything, at any rate, that he regarded as genuine literature as opposed to hackwork like "Herbert West—Reanimator." The result was a long and apologetic letter to Talman, expressing his regrets for being unclear on his stance. He certainly didn't wish Morrow (or anyone) to dictate the substance of such a novel as he might produce in the future, and the best he could produce in the near term was a synopsis:

57. HPL to R. H. Barlow, [24 May 1935]; *O Fortunate Floridian* 273.

> Let me repeat for clearness' sake: the course you advise—to give a reasonably strong promise of a synopsis sooner or later, & much less definite suggestions regarding a complete or fractional novel-manuscript in the remote future—will be acceptable to me if you prefer it. But I also give you leave to terminate all discussion if you ever find it advisable for your own sake or the firm's.[58]

It is abundantly clear that Lovecraft was not wishing to commit himself at all to any such project, and the discussion quickly petered out.

What did appear around this time was Lovecraft's "first book"—if it could be called that. But this book—*The Shadow over Innsmouth,* issued by William L. Crawford's Visionary Publishing Co. (Everett, Pennsylvania)—was a fiasco from beginning to end. Crawford, the editor of the semi-professional magazines *Marvel Tales* and *Unusual Stories,* had come into contact with Lovecraft in the fall of 1933. In the spring of 1935 he proposed a variety of book projects—either *At the Mountains of Madness* or "The Shadow over Innsmouth" or both in one volume. He finally resolved on "Innsmouth," and the tedious work of typesetting—and the even more tedious work (for Lovecraft) of reading the proofs—began. The project dragged on and on. The title page of the book states that it was published in April 1936, but Lovecraft did not get copies until November. And in spite of his repeated proofreading, he found the published book so full of errors that he demanded that Crawford issue an errata sheet. The initial version of the errata sheet was itself so misprinted as to be virtually useless. And the final version listed only a small number of the errors in the book.

Crawford claimed that 400 copies were printed, but only 200 of these were bound. The other 200 were later destroyed.

---

58. HPL to Wilfred B. Talman, 10 November [1936]; *Letters to Wilfred B. Talman and Helen V. and Genevieve Sully* 275.

The book sold for $1. As can be imagined, it generated virtually no discussion in even the publications devoted to fantasy, horror, and science fiction. Exactly two reviews are known to have appeared: one in *Amazing Stories* (August 1937) and the other in Ray H. Zorn's fanzine, the *Nix Nem Quarterly Review* (December 1937). I have not had access to the former. The latter speaks highly of the work ("The story itself is a good example of Lovecraft's gift of portraying mounting horror"[59]), but is otherwise unremarkable.

But Lovecraft was past the point of caring about such notices. He would die painfully on March 15, 1937. He could not possibly know that the celebrity and critical acclaim he had never sought in life would come to him only in the decades that followed.

59. *Nix Nem Quarterly Review* 7, No. 3 (December 1937): 8.

III. Arkham House: The Early Years (1937–1945)

Since Lovecraft died at 7:15 A.M. on the 15th (according to his death certificate), an obituary managed to appear that evening in the *Providence Evening Bulletin*. It is substantially similar to a four-paragraph obituary that appeared in the *Providence Journal* (a morning paper) on March 16. Although full of errors (it states that Lovecraft actually graduated from Hope Street High School and that he "secured the equivalent of a college education from private tutors"—in fact, his private tutoring had occurred much earlier, in the years prior to his entry into high school), it made a provocative comment about his final days in Jane Brown Memorial Hospital: "As he neared the end of his life, he turned his scholarly interest to a study of his own physical condition and daily wrote minutely of his case for his physician's assistance. His clinical notes ended only when he could no longer hold a pencil."[1] This too appears to be somewhat of an exaggeration. But it caused the Associated Press to write a one-paragraph notice that was picked up by the *New York Times* on the morning of March 16 (and, presumably, other newspapers):

Writer Charts Fatal Malady

PROVIDENCE, R. I., March 15 (AP).—Howard Phillips

---

1. "H. P. Lovecraft Dead in Hospital," *Providence Evening Bulletin* (15 March 1937): 26. "H. P. Lovecraft, Author, Is Dead," *Providence Journal* (16 March 1937); 18; rpt. in facsimile in Everts, *The Death of a Gentleman* 14.

> Lovecraft, 46 years old, a writer of horror tales, died early today of an illness from which he had suffered from childhood. During the past month, when his condition became serious, he devoted his writing to a minute clinical study of his disease as an aid to science, continuing the daily chart until he could no longer hold his pencil. His sole survivor is an aunt, Mrs. Phillips Gamwell of this city.[2]

The date of the notice, and the fact that it appeared in morning papers throughout the country (as did the *Providence Journal* obituary), clearly mean that its information was derived from the *Evening Bulletin*. Frank Belknap Long—ignorant, as the great majority of Lovecraft's other friends and correspondents were, of the severity of Lovecraft's illness—learned of his friend's passing while reading the paper in New York that day.

Expressions of sorrow and grief, as well as brief attempts at critical analysis, appeared widely in the pulp magazines, amateur journals, and magazines devoted to fantasy fandom. Given that *Weird Tales,* as was common among both pulp and "slick" magazines of that time, appeared a month or two before its cover date, "The Eyrie" did not carry any letters of comment until the June 1937 issue. These letters—which fill three entire pages—were prefaced by a substantial paragraph by Wright (unsigned) lamenting Lovecraft's death: "He was a titan of weird and fantastic literature, whose literary achievements and impeccable craftsmanship were acclaimed throughout the English-speaking world" (*WW* 81). How's that for exaggeration? Wright seems to have anticipated Lovecraft's worldwide acclaim by at least six decades. Wright concluded poignantly: "His death is a serious loss to weird and fantastic fiction; but to the editors of *Weird Tales* the personal loss takes precedence. We admired him for his great literary achievements, but we loved him for himself; for he was a courtly and noble gentleman, and a dear friend. Peace be

2. *New York Times* (16 March 1937): 5.

to his shade!" (*WW* 82). Lovecraft might have wondered why Wright did not show greater admiration for his "literary achievements," instead of rejecting *At the Mountains of Madness,* "The Shadow over Innsmouth," and other now classic tales.

What is remarkable is that persons who knew Lovecraft only through the pages of *Weird Tales* echoed Wright's sense of personal loss. Robert Leonard Russell wrote: "I feel, as will many other readers of *Weird Tales,* that I have lost a real friend" (*WW* 83). Others made routine assessments of his place in literary history (Lorne W. Power: "He was nothing less than a genius, and the greatest writer of weird fiction since Poe" [*WW* 82]). N. J. O'Neail, in the August 1937 issue, wrote at significant length, stressing Lovecraft's artistic restraint: "While some writers exhaust the dictionary in their efforts to picture the horror with which they are dealing, Lovecraft's technique was far superior, for he gave the impression always of striving to conceal or to minimize horror, instead of painting it in rainbow colors and in circus poster type" (*WW* 88). This stands (correctly, in my judgment) in stark contrast to many assessments over the next several decades that mechanically censured Lovecraft for being verbose, flamboyant, and over-the-top.

But the most sensitive comments came from a bevy of Lovecraft's colleagues, early and late. Robert Bloch (who, let us recall, never met Lovecraft but only corresponded with him for four years) wrote: "He was a great writer, but an even greater friend; a real New England gentleman of the old school. I think we ought to count ourselves proud to have known him" (*WW* 84). Henry Kuttner, who corresponded with Lovecraft for only a year, stated: "I've been feeling extremely depressed about Lovecraft's death. Even now I can't realize it" (*WW* 86).

Kenneth Sterling, who had known Lovecraft only since 1935, stressed that "Lovecraft was a confirmed materialist and iconoclast . . . His conversation was transcendently brilliant, outshining even his excellent writings. . . . I think it would be most fitting if Lovecraft were remembered as a scholar and thinker as well as an author" (*WW* 85). These remarks are also far ahead of their time. No less so was Robert A. W. Lowndes's comment, after receiving only two letters from Lovecraft: "Can we readers hope that eventually someone will collect all of his works and publish them in a single volume? What a treasure for the lovers of the weird and the fantastic that would be! An even greater treasure would be a compilation of his masterly though enormous correspondence; yet what splendid reading his letters would make, even though they ran to a number of volumes!" (*WW* 90). Francis Flagg (the pseudonym of Henry George Weiss, a communist with whom Lovecraft had been sporadically corresponding since 1930) echoed Kenneth Sterling's remark by noting: "Lovecraft was never more the materialist than when he was the weird artist. There is a psychological realism in many of his tales that could only have been set down by a materialist thinker" (*WW* 91).

Clark Ashton Smith, who had been a correspondent since 1922 although they had never met, expressed his sorrow: "I am profoundly saddened by the news of H. P. Lovecraft's death after a month of painful illness. The loss seems an intolerable one, and I am sure that it will be felt deeply and permanently by the whole weird fiction public" (WW 85). Harold S. Farnese, the composer who had been corresponding sporadically with Lovecraft since 1932, wrote extravagantly: "But has it ever occurred to you that in Lovecraft you had the greatest genius that ever lived in the realm of weird fiction?" (WW 87). Then there was Jacques Bergier, the Frenchman who never met or corresponded with Lovecraft (although in later years he claimed he did), who intoned: "I believe that Lovecraft was one of America's greatest writers, an equal to Poe. I believe that recognition of this fact will come after a lapse of years, as with Poe. . . . The passing of Lovecraft seems to me to mark an end of an epoch in the history of American imaginative fiction" (*WW* 91).

In the realm of amateur journalism, we can take note of one significant publication: the Summer 1937 issue of the *Californian,* edited by Hyman Bradofsky, who had been corresponding with Lovecraft since 1934. Bradofsky was clearly grateful that Lovecraft had defended him in various amateur controversies in 1935–36 (in the course of which Lovecraft wrote the eloquent plea for a cessation of vitriol in the amateur community, "Some Current Motives and Practices" [1936]). The Summer 1937 issue contained Rheinhart Kleiner's memoir "Howard Phillips Lovecraft"; a poem by Frank Earle Schermerhorn, "Yet Still We Mourn"; "By Post from Providence," extracts of Lovecraft's letters to Kleiner discussing amateur journalism; and a "Group of Poems" (six poems—two of which are not by Lovecraft).[3] Bradofsky's own editorial in the issue, "Amateur Affairs," has an eloquence all its own:

> The news that Howard Lovecraft was gone seemed incredible. It was like an unicorn dying, or an amoretto, or one of those sinewy and eternal children of Pan. It came like a shock, as if a calamity had happened. There was an eternal quality in him, and his passing disturbed our feeling of the essential durableness of things. [. . .]
>
> Great as was Howard Lovecraft in heart and mind, we of today are unable to evaluate him at his true worth. Time and the march of events will bring increased understanding of him and of his tangible legacies. (*WW* 22–23)

Some of Lovecraft's letters now began to be published in the fantasy fandom community. Six letters—three to Jim Blish and

3. See my essay "Two Spurious Lovecraft Poems," in *Lovecraft and a World in Transition* 437–39.

William Miller, Jr., and three to Nils H. Frome—appeared in *Phantastique/The Science Fiction Critic* (March 1938). This fanzine had begun life in 1935 as the *Science Fiction Review,* edited by the teenage Claire Beck (of whom more below); later that year it changed its title to the *Science Fiction Critic.* Its last issue appeared in July 1938. The letters are of significance chiefly because Blish, a very late correspondent of Lovecraft, went on to become one of the most distinguished writers of science fiction in subsequent generations.

At this point I wish to take notice of only a single article from the fan press—a very curious piece by one R. W. Sherman (about whom almost nothing is known) entitled "Disbelievers Ever." This was published in the September–October 1937 issue of *Amateur Correspondent,* Corwin F. Stickney's successor to Willis Conover's short-lived *Science-Fantasy Correspondent.* He writes: "throughout the course of his entire literary career he found himself wedged between two factions—a group of enthusiastic followers who worshipped his very name, and a clique of vehement scoffers who seemed to achieve delight in the berating of this master. Which one was the more irritating remains a moot question" (*WW* 127). It is not at all clear what Sherman could be referring to; his comment would have applied far more accurately to controversies several decades hence. Sherman concludes that Lovecraft's death largely silenced his critics, and that "the seed of the genius of the man takes root in their minds" (*WW* 127). Would that it were so!

One name obtrusively absent from the *Weird Tales* letter column in the months—indeed, the first four years—following Lovecraft's death was August Derleth. He has testified eloquently to his emotional reaction when hearing of his friend's passing:

> When Howard Wandrei, then in New York, wrote to tell me that Lovecraft had died, I read his letter on my way into the marshes below Sauk City, where I frequently went to sit in the sun and read, and where that day I had along a volume of Thoreau's *Journal.* Instead of reading, however, I sat at a railroad trestle beside a brook and thought of how Lovecraft's best stories could be published in book form.[4]

But before Derleth fully realised his goal of publishing Lovecraft in book form, he had other concerns. His first concern was simply what authority he had to market Lovecraft's work in any fashion. Derleth must have known that he himself was not Lovecraft's chosen literary executor; instead, Lovecraft had—in the document titled "Instructions in Case of Decease," probably written in December 1936 or January 1937, when Lovecraft knew he was going to die—chosen R. H. Barlow for the role. "Instructions" was not a legal document, but Lovecraft's surviving aunt Annie E. P. Gamwell made the executorship legal by a document filed in the Rhode Island Probate Court on 26 March 1937. (Whether even that document was legal is an open question, since Barlow was still underage at the time—not quite nineteen years old. Adult status at that period was conferred only at the age of twenty-one.)

Derleth himself may have relied on a passing remark that Lovecraft made in a 1932 letter to him: "Yes—come to think of it—I fear there might be some turbulent doings among an indiscriminately named board of literary heirs handling my posthumous junk! Maybe I'll dump all the work on you by naming you sole heir."[5] Whether Derleth actually relied on this passage as authority for his actions in assembling Lovecraft's work is unclear;

---

4. "Arkham House: 1939–1969" (from *Thirty Years of Arkham House*), in Joshi, *Sixty Years of Arkham House* 3.

5. HPL to August Derleth, 14 April [1932]; *Essential Solitude* 472.

if he did, he clearly overlooked its whimsical and self-parodic tone.

In any event, Derleth simply assumed informal control of Lovecraft's literary properties, and his first order of business was to keep his friend's name alive by having additional stories published in *Weird Tales*. To his credit, Derleth gave the proceeds of these sales to Annie Gamwell. The number of tales published in *Weird Tales* from 1937 to 1943 is impressive:

"The Shunned House" (October 1937)
"Polaris" (December 1937)
"From Beyond" (February 1938)
"Beyond the Wall of Sleep" (March 1938)
"The Doom That Came to Sarnath" (June 1938)
"The Tree" (August 1938)
"The Other Gods" (October 1938)
"The Quest of Iranon" (March 1939)
"The Wicked [*sic*] Clergyman" (April 1939)
"Celephaïs" (June/July 1939)
"Cool Air" (September 1939)
The Case of Charles Dexter Ward (May & July 1941; abridged)
"The Shadow over Innsmouth" (January 1942)
"Herbert West—Reanimator" (March, July, September, November 1942; September & November 1943)

This includes many stories previously rejected by Farnsworth Wright, notably "The Shunned House" and "The Shadow over Innsmouth," along with many of Lovecraft's "Dunsanian" tales (several of which had also been rejected in Lovecraft's lifetime). The list does not include three stories that were reprinted between 1937 and 1952; four revisions or collaborations ("The Diary of Alonzo Typer" [accepted in Lovecraft's lifetime], "In the Walls of Eryx," "Medusa's Coil," and "The Mound"—the latter two published in truncated form); and twenty poems, including numerous sonnets from *Fungi from Yuggoth.* Clearly, as we shall see presently, Lovecraft remained a dominant presence in *Weird Tales.*

Derleth also wrote a few pieces on Lovecraft in the wake of the latter's death. One was "A Master of the Macabre" (*Reading and Collecting,* August 1937), which was apparently begun during Lovecraft's lifetime as a review of *The Shadow over Innsmouth* but awkwardly morphed into a brief survey of his life and work. Another piece written at this time, "H. P. Lovecraft, Outsider" (*River,* June 1937), is notorious for introducing a spurious quotation (purportedly from a Lovecraft letter, but in fact supplied to Derleth by Harold S. Farnese) that justified Derleth's distorted view of the Cthulhu Mythos.

I shall not be discussing the dissemination of the Mythos in this book except insofar as it has some bearing on the ascent (or descent) of Lovecraft's reputation and on the developing critical analysis of his work;[6] but it is worth noting how Derleth, here as elsewhere, seems to go out of his way to disparage Lovecraft. Perhaps this was not his explicit intent, but that is the effect. "Lovecraft himself had no very high opinion of his work," Derleth writes (*WW* 123), going on to quote several derogatory comments on his own tales. He concludes:

> Neither his prose nor his poetry will ever attain the status of world recognition, but his genius will be recognized, his work will be appreciated by that comparatively small but widespread public who read Machen, de la Mare, Dunsany, Blackwood, and Montague Rhodes James . . .
>
> I salute not only his curious genius, but his magnificent spirit. As a writer, he stands among the best in his field, however limited that may be . . . (*WW* 124)

6. On this topic see my *The Rise, Fall, and Rise of the Cthulhu Mythos.*

At the end of "A Master of the Macabre" Derleth announces that "There is now in preparation a comprehensive collection of the writings of H. P. Lovecraft, and a first volume, *The Outsider*, . . . may appear before the year is out" (*WW* 126). Derleth's estimate was off by a full two years, but numerous remarks in various documents make clear that he began to undertake the task almost immediately upon Lovecraft's death. He made a trip to Providence (as did Barlow) to look over the Lovecraft material, which Barlow was in the process of turning over to the John Hay Library of Brown University. In one of his earliest statements regarding the early history of Arkham House, Derleth writes:

> Immediately on receiving word of Lovecraft's death, I wrote Donald Wandrei that something should be done to keep Lovecraft's work alive; in this opinion he heartily concurred. It should be pointed out that my initial plan was to recover only the work which appeared in the first Arkham House omnibus; it was Donald Wandrei who envisioned collecting all the work, including a substantial editing of the forthcoming work, the *Selected Letters*. In this, I in turn concurred, and we set about the preparation of the initial manuscript, submitting it to Simon & Schuster and to Charles Scribner's Sons.[7]

The account in *Thirty Years of Arkham House* takes up the story from there:

> Since Charles Scribner's Sons were then my publishers, I sent the manuscript to them. They were sympathetic to the project and recognized the literary value of Lovecraft's fiction; but in the end they were forced to reject the manuscript because the cost of producing so bulky a book, combined with the public's then sturdy resistance to buying short story collections and the comparative obscurity of H. P. Lovecraft as a writer, made the project financially prohibitive. Simon & Schuster, to whom

7. "Arkham House: A Thumbnail Story" (1950), in Joshi, *Eighty Years of Arkham House* 201.

the manuscript was next submitted, rejected for similar reasons.[8]

I have quoted these passages at such length because they are so crucial to what Derleth then did—and how Lovecraft's popular and critical acclaim may have been delayed or derailed because of these fateful decisions. It is evident from Derleth's own telling that Scribner's might well have accepted a smaller volume than the 500,000-word *Outsider and Others,* which even Derleth, when he published it with Arkham House, had to charge the unprecedented price of $5.00 (the average price of a hardcover book of fiction at the time was $2.00 or $2.50). The prejudice—by publishers and perhaps by readers—against weird short story collections may still have applied, but we will see that such a prejudice did not deter readers from buying just such a volume of Lovecraft's "best" stories published only a few years later.

Derleth seemed so fixated with bringing out *The Outsider and Others* in exactly the form he had initially compiled it that he could brook no alternative. Indeed, in a moment of unwitting candour Derleth noted: "By this time, however, the effort of trying to find a publisher for the omnibus was proving too irritating for me."[9] In other words, his own busy writing schedule militated against any further solicitations on behalf of the friend whose work he claimed to want preserved in the most distinguished possible manner.[10] Had Derleth been a bit more persistent, or a bit less pig-headed in what kind of offer he was prepared to accept from a major publisher, the entire history of Lovecraft's posthumous reputation might have been very differ-

8. "Arkham House: 1939–1969" 4.

9. "Arkham House: A Thumbnail Story" 202.

10. It was the press of Derleth's own writing—as well as his own lack of expertise in textual studies—that impelled him to assemble HPL's texts, from 1937 all the way to his death, in a way that was criminally careless as far as textual accuracy was concerned.

ent. There is, in addition, a distinct possibility that Derleth did not wish the Lovecraft material to slip too far out of his own direct control, as might have happened if a standard book publisher had issued it at this time. Derleth's own claim to act on behalf of Lovecraft's literary estate was quite dubious, as he probably knew; and by publishing the book himself he could assert ownership in a manner that, at least in the weird fiction community, was not likely to be challenged.

So Derleth and Wandrei set about publishing *The Outsider and Others*. It is hardly profitable to go into how they came up with the name of their press (at one point someone suggested Derwan House, using the initial syllables of the last names of the two colleagues), nor the financial difficulties that these two "impecunious writers"[11] faced in bringing out the book. It did in fact appear in December 1939, in a print run of 1268 copies. Issued in an oversize (6.5″ × 9.5″) format that Arkham House used for several other large volumes published in its early years, it contained thirty-six stories (arranged in no particular order) plus the essay "Supernatural Horror in Literature." It filled 553 pages and contained an evocative dust jacket by Virgil Finlay.

While the list price was $5.00, Derleth had offered a prepublication price of $3.50, but received only 150 advance orders.[12] Indeed, Willis Conover wrote an indignant letter to *Weird Tales* just at the time *The Outsider* was about to be released, berating Lovecraft fans for failing to support the venture:

> August Derleth and Donald Wandrei have worked on this volume for two years, confident that HPL's followers would back them up when the time came. Well, the time has come, and what's happened? About *one-tenth* of the money necessary to pay for publication has been received! If all the Lovecraft fans came through, there would be no diffi-

11. "Arkham House: 1939–1969" 4.
12. "Arkham House: A Thumbnail Story" 202.

> culty in putting out this book, plus succeeding volumes of selected letters, etc. (*WW* 98)

But Derleth and Wandrei weren't the only impecunious ones; weird fiction fans, then and now, are themselves notoriously short of funds, and an outlay of $5.00 was not an insignificant one at a time when the Depression was still raging. Derleth reports that it took four years for the book to go out of print.[13]

But the book was on the whole well received by the wider literary community. I have located seven reviews in both the mainstream press and in fantasy/weird fiction periodicals. The latter amount to very little, but Will Cuppy's review in his "Mystery and Adventure" column in *New York Herald Tribune Books* (17 December 1939) is, in his customarily informal manner, enthusiastic:

> Mystery fans might do worse than dig into the devil-haunted depths of this book for strange thrills and a general review of dreams, drugs, demons, magic, nameless crimes, the unspeakable Shub-Niggurath, the Hooded Thing that bleats, and why it is that in Ulthar, which lies beyond the river Skai, no man may kill a cat. You'll never be the same again, we promise you, if you attempt to swallow all these heady compositions at one sitting. (*WW* 179)

That final sentence is one more indication that Derleth would have been better off assembling a smaller volume. More impressively, T. O. Mabbott—the leading Poe scholar of his generation—wrote a brief review in the academic journal *American Literature* (March 1940) unstintedly praising Lovecraft, both for his fiction ("Time will tell if his place be very high in our literary history; that he has a place seems certain") and for "Supernatural Horror in Literature" ("it contains discussions of Poe, Hawthorne, and Bierce, so penetrating, sympathetic, and imaginatively

---

13. "Arkham House: A Thumbnail Story" 202.

keen that scholars will not want to miss them" [*WW* 183]).[14]

But the most remarkable notice was an anonymous review-article in *Publishers' Weekly* (24 February 1940) that took up two full pages. Titled "Horror Story Author Published by Fellow Authors," it acknowledges that the book is largely a testament to the devotion of Lovecraft's friends: the writer actually interviewed Derleth and Wandrei (in the course of which Derleth stated that the manuscript of the book was sent to "three different publishers" [*WW* 181], although this is probably an error) and records the expense and labour involved in actually bringing the book out. Not a single word is devoted to an assessment of the stories themselves, although the article begins by stating that Lovecraft "had won a considerable following, almost a cult of worshippers, for his horror tales" (*WW* 180).

An entire lengthy paragraph is devoted to Derleth's travails in accumulating and transcribing Lovecraft's letters, which leads to a striking statement toward the end: "Arkham House will publish two more books to complete the job. The second volume will consist of Lovecraft's two long, unpublished novelettes, a few stories that he wrote in collaboration, his complete poems and a selection of letters. The third volume will contain letters alone" (*WW* 182). Things did not transpire according to this plan, but it is of interest to see that Derleth was already planning to publish *The Dream-Quest of Unknown Kadath* and *The Case of Charles Dexter Ward* (the manuscripts of which he had presumably seen on his trip to Providence, and which he subsequently borrowed for transcription), and that he was already deeply involved in securing Lovecraft's letters.

---

14. Some months earlier, in the August 1939 issue of *Weird Tales,* Mabbott had written a brief letter to "The Eyrie" lamenting the passing of HPL and Robert E. Howard and wondering: "is there no chance of a collected edition of Lovecraft? He deserves one" (*WW* 97).

It is possible that the appearance of *The Outsider and Others*—or word of its imminent publication—spurred a renewed discussion of Lovecraft in the fantasy and science fiction fan press. Lovecraft-related activity had in fact never ceased, and his death impelled the publication of his lesser or obscure work, much of it for the first time. Corwin F. Stickney, Willis Conover's colleague in the *Science-Fantasy Correspondent,* issued a booklet of 23 pages simply titled *HPL* (1937), and containing eight poems by Lovecraft. It was printed in an edition of only 25 copies and given free to whoever paid a year's subscription (which cost 25¢) to Stickney's *Amateur Correspondent.* In that fanzine he published Lovecraft's "Notes on Writing Weird Fiction" in the May–June 1937 issue, which featured a stunning cover illustration by Virgil Finley depicting Lovecraft as an eighteenth-century gentleman.

In late 1937 Wilson Shepherd, a late correspondent, issued a four-page pamphlet, *A History of the Necronomicon,* as a "Limited Memorial" edition in 80 copies. More significantly, R. H. Barlow prepared an edition of Lovecraft's *Notes and Commonplace Book* and had it published by his friends Claire and Groo Beck (Lakeport, California) in May and June 1938, in an edition of 75 numbered copies. Half of these were bound in hardcover, the others remaining as unbound sheets.

Around the time of *The Outsider,* a peculiar debate flared up in the fan press. John B. Michel, a young devotee of science fiction, wrote an article, "The Last of H. P. Lovecraft" (*Science Fiction Fan,* November 1939), telling of how he and Donald Wollheim went to Lovecraft's house in Providence, met Annie Gamwell, and found themselves in Lovecraft's living quarters at 66 College Street. But the article is no paean to a fallen titan; it concludes:

> Lovecraft, for all his giant knowledge and piercing, calculating

> intellect, was the deadly enemy of all that to me is everything, an inflexible Jehovah-man, a gaunt, prophet-like high priest of dark rites and darker times, clad in funereal robes and funereal visage, gazing with suppressed hate upon a great new world which placed more value upon the sanitary condition of a bathroom fixture than all the greasy gold and jewels. The bones and dirt-crushed half knowledge of a thousand and a thousand-thousand kingdoms of the hoary past, whose faithful chronicler he was and in which he lived. (*WW* 131)

This not entirely comprehensible diatribe signals Michel's own leftist politics, which would manifest itself later in his joining the Young Communist League. It is not at all clear how representative Michel's views were at the time; and, of course, Michel was ignorant of Lovecraft's own late conversion to moderate (non-Marxist) socialism, although he remained an aesthetic conservative to the end of his days.

The article inspired a furious rebuttal by someone masquerading under the pseudonym "Autolycus," who wrote an article, "What of H. P. Lovecraft? or, A Commentary upon J. B. Michel" (*Science Fiction Fan,* January 1940), where he states: "if all writing were to become class conscious we would lose a universe of beauty, of grandeur, of exquisite aesthetic satisfaction" (*WW* 133). As for Lovecraft himself, he "was a man of genius . . . His mind traversed immeasurable distances in time and space, he saw vistas of magnificence as well as of horror which are forever beyond the visions of most of us." In conclusion, Autolycus defends Lovecraft's deliberate choice not to write about the mundanities of present-day life:

> He lived in a world of his own, a world of past and future, a world of other dimensions, an alien, unreal world where unhuman entities prowled. He was set aside from the hustle of today, from our social and economic problems. He took no part in present struggles. Why not? Surely in this world of ours there are enough warriors to fight in the cause of justice and righteousness to permit an occasional faery mind to roam as it will in space and time. (*WW* 134)

The remark was sound then—and is perhaps more sound today.[15]

From a very different perspective, J. Chapman Miske, a leading science fiction and fantasy fan of the 1940s, wrote an admirably sane and accurate biographical sketch, "H. P. Lovecraft: Strange Weaver," in *Scienti-Snaps* (Summer 1940). The fanzine had been founded in 1938 by Walter E. Marconette; Miske served as associate editor for several years. At nearly 2000 words, the piece provides a clear overview of Lovecraft's literary career and a balanced account of his character ("Not freakish, simply different, by temperament, tastes, and, to certain degrees, actions" [*WW* 135]). Less to Miske's credit, he published a portion of a Lovecraft letter to Donald Wandrei in *Bizarre* (January 1941), the successor to *Scienti-Snaps,* under the title "The Thing in the Moonlight," adding his own introductory and concluding paragraphs without notifying readers that he was the author of them.

The world of amateur journalism was also busy in paying tribute to Lovecraft. One of Lovecraft's oldest colleagues, Edward H. Cole, who had established contact with the Providence writer as early as 1914, resurrected his journal, the *Olympian,* after a twenty-three-year hiatus by publishing an issue (Autumn 1940) devoted entirely to Lovecraft and containing memoirs by Ernest A. Edkins, James F. Morton (the only memoir that Morton—who had known Lovecraft since 1922—ever wrote), and W. Paul Cook, as well as one (the lengthiest of the lot) by himself. Somewhat earlier, the amateur journal *O-Wash-Ta-Nong,* edited by George W. Macauley (whose correspondence with Lovecraft dated back to 1915), published several short memoirs by Ira A. Cole, Maurice W. Moe and his son Donald J. Moe, and some anonymous pieces in a 1937 issue.

---

15. Michel responded to this article in "Some Further Notes on Lovecraft," *Science Fiction Fan* 5, No. 2 (September 1940): 2–8.

The piece by Cook in the *Olympian* was an extract of a substantial memoir that he was writing at this time, and which appeared as *In Memoriam: Howard Phillips Lovecraft—Recollections, Appreciations, Estimates* (Driftwind Press, 1941), in a print run of 94 copies. It is difficult to overstate the brilliance of this 20,000-word memoir. All apart from the engaging anecdotes it relates—the boy Lovecraft setting a fire exactly one foot by one foot, as a testament to his scientific precision; Lovecraft staying up all night because he did not wish to disturb the kitten that had fallen asleep on his lap—it paints what appears to be a fundamentally true portrait of Lovecraft as reserved but cordial and devoted to his friends, and relentless in his antiquarian travels. He observes that Lovecraft's two years in New York had been supremely painful but that he had emerged from them a changed, and a better, man: "He had been tried in the fire and came out pure gold" (*AV* 43).

But it was in the fan world where much of the more interesting, and perhaps even the more pioneering, work on Lovecraft was being conducted. Late in 1943 Francis T. Laney and William H. Evans published *Howard Phillips Lovecraft (1890–1937): A Tentative Bibliography*. This 12-page publication made a stab at charting the seemingly innumerable publications of Lovecraft's stories, essays, and poems in the amateur press, the pulp magazines, and elsewhere. Of Laney we shall speak at greater length later; of William H. Evans I know nothing, aside from the fact that he issued a pamphlet, *Fungi from Yuggoth* (containing only the first thirty-three sonnets of the cycle), earlier in 1943 and distributed it through the Fantasy Amateur Press Association, as the bibliography itself was distributed. In a foreword, Laney acknowledges the assistance of numerous individuals, including Derleth, Barlow, and C. W. Smith (editor of the *Tryout*). Needless to say, the work—more a checklist than a bibliography—is massively incomplete; at times (especially in the poetry section), it merely provides a title with the note: "(Where published?)" More dubiously, Laney spends two pages listing "Stories of the Cthulhu Mythology" by eighteen different writers—not only Lovecraft's predecessors (Poe, Machen, Bierce, etc.) but authors whose works that are not derived from Lovecraft at all (such as George Allan England's "The Thing from—Outside" [1926]). But for all its deficiencies, it is an able start at what would become the immensely complicated task of recording the full array of publications by and about Lovecraft.

Derleth, after publishing a collection of his own, *Someone in the Dark* (1941) and one by Clark Ashton Smith, *Out of Space and Time* (1942), brought out the second Lovecraft omnibus, *Beyond the Wall of Sleep,* in late 1943. At 458 pages in an oversize format, it is shorter than *The Outsider and Others* but certainly big enough. Far and away its most significant components are the two novels, *The Dream-Quest of Unknown Kadath* and *The Case of Charles Dexter Ward.* For the former, Derleth made use of a typescript of about half the text that Barlow had prepared during Lovecraft's lifetime; the balance of the text was presumably transcribed from the autograph manuscript by Derleth's secretary at Arkham House, Alice Conger. For the latter, Derleth unwisely ignored a partial typescript (comprising only about a fifth of the text) that Barlow had prepared, as Conger's transcript fails to take note of some revisions that Lovecraft had made in Barlow's typescript and makes numerous other errors.

Derleth allowed an abridged version of *The Case of Charles Dexter Ward* to appear in *Weird Tales* (May and July 1941). Accompanying the first instalment was a letter in "The Eyrie," signed by both Derleth and Donald Wandrei,[16] chronicling their

16. In a phone conversation with me, c. 1980, Wandrei denied writing any

arduous attempts to prepare the text. The letter seems to contain numerous inaccuracies and exaggerations, such as the notion that the full text of *Ward* was temporarily "lost beyond any hope of recovery" (*WW* 100) when in fact it had been resting comfortably in the John Hay Library (albeit probably uncatalogued) ever since Barlow had deposited the manuscript there. Derleth also asserts that "*Ward* is one of the earliest stories in which he used the 'Cthulhu' mythology" (*WW* 100)—an assertion based on fleeting and unexplained mentions of Yog-Sothoth toward the end of the text.

In any case, the two short novels, however badly mistranscribed, had finally achieved print, a decade and a half after their writing. *Beyond the Wall of Sleep* contained nine stories (out of a total of thirty-four that have now been identified) that Lovecraft wrote in collaboration or as "revisions" of various clients' work. And of course it did not include anything approaching Lovecraft's "complete poems" (as the *Publishers' Weekly* review of *The Outsider* had noted), but only twenty-nine poems—a mix of occasional verse and weird poetry—plus all thirty-six sonnets of *Fungi from Yuggoth*. Evidently these were simply the poems that Derleth could secure without too much effort. Derleth deserves praise for including an abridged version of W. Paul Cook's memoir, but quite otherwise for publishing Francis T. Laney's error-filled "The Cthulhu Mythology: A Glossary."

Reviews were on the whole cordial. I have located eight of them, scattered among leading newspapers and the fan press. *Publishers' Weekly* did not take note of the book, but the *New York Times Book Review* (16 January 1944) did. One William Poster makes numerous errors in his brief account of Lovecraft, apart from referring to Wandrei as "Clark Wandrei." He does

part of the letter; but probably he did contribute to it and had forgotten.

appreciate the newly published *The Case of Charles Dexter Ward* (it "is a good story in the New England witchcraft tradition, well seasoned with alchemy, vampirism, ancient documents and mummy-stealing") and concludes: "Though nothing in it equals the best in the first volume, this second installment does contain a sufficient quantity of first-rate 'weird writing' in its 450-odd pages of microscopic print to keep a responsive reader's hair standing on end for days" (*WW* 196).

Considerably less charitable was Peter De Vries in his review in the *Chicago Sun Book Week* (26 December 1943). De Vries would become a prolific mainstream novelist, but at this time he was only thirty-three and had published only two novels. He admits that "H. P. Lovecraft . . . is not quite on my wavelength," apparently disliking Lovecraft's archaic prose and fantastic imagery. It is abundantly clear that De Vries has little sympathy or sensitivity toward the weird. Quoting a particularly lurid paragraph from "The Hound," De Vries concludes: "At least, to say that it is difficult to read [such a passage] without a smile is putting it mildly" (*WW* 195). Perhaps De Vries is to be excused for not detecting that the story is a self-parody.

Will Cuppy, however (*New York Herald Tribune Weekly Book Review,* 2 January 1944), was enthusiastic. "We herewith recommend to fandom this outsized volume, stuffed and crammed with some of the weirdest material on record," he writes. "We confess that we are knocked silly by the mass of mania, nightmare and such in these Lovecraft collections, both of which should be possessed, or at least perused, by any citizen who goes for hideous dream states, demons from the vast abyss, humans doomed and damned, things unnamable and so forth in truly astonishing variety" (*WW* 194).

Perhaps the most interesting review, from both a biographical and historical perspective, is that by Vincent Starrett in his long-running "Books Alive" column in the *Chicago Sunday Tribune* (2 January 1944). Starrett had corresponded for about a year with Lovecraft (1927–28), having found some interest in "Supernatural Horror in Literature." His review was the first of several he wrote of Lovecraft's posthumous publications, extracts of which he gathered in his volume *Books and Bipeds* (1947). The current review makes some celebrated claims:

> But to me Lovecraft himself is even more interesting than his stories; he was his own most fantastic creation—a Roderick Usher or C. Auguste Dupin born a century too late. . . .
>
> But if Lovecraft was a self-conscious *poseur,* a macabre *precieuse,* he was genuine too: his poses never had any relation to commercial success, which he didn't achieve, and there is no question about the sincerity of his artistry. In his field he was important. . . .
>
> He was a born eccentric, a dilettante, and a *poseur par excellence;* but he was also a born writer, equipped with a delicate feeling for the beauty and mystery of words. The best of his stories are among the best of their time, in the field he chose to make his own. (*WW* 197–98)

While Starrett's apparent vaunting of Lovecraft the man and the "eccentric" over Lovecraft the writer may be unfortunate, he still delivers enough sound praise to make his review significant.

Derleth followed up *Beyond the Wall of Sleep* with *Marginalia* in late 1944. By this time it had become obvious that the proposed volume of letters that was to be the third volume of the series would have to be indefinitely postponed, given the staggering number of letters Derleth received from correspondents and also given that Donald Wandrei's involvement with the firm would, because of his entry into the U.S. Army, have to be radically curtailed. And yet, *Marginalia* is perhaps the most substantial of the four "miscellany" volumes that Derleth published over the next twenty-two years. It set the pattern by containing a mix of previously unpublished or uncollected Lovecraft texts, memoirs or critical assessments of Lovecraft, and various other matter. Here we find four more "revisions" or ghostwritten tales (including the tale he wrote for Houdini); eight essays, including two of his splendid travel pieces; two juvenile stories; five story fragments (including, unfortunately, "The Thing in the Moonlight);[17] and, most vitally, seven essays on Lovecraft and eight poems, including Clark Ashton Smith's exquisite elegy "To Howard Phillips Lovecraft" (first published in *Weird Tales,* July 1937).

Of the essays (all previously unpublished), Winfield Townley Scott's "His Own Most Fantastic Creation" remained the most significant biographical essay on Lovecraft until the work of Kenneth W. Faig, Jr. in the 1970s. Memoirs by Frank Belknap Long, R. H. Barlow, Kenneth Sterling, and Donald Wandrei are highly notable; Derleth's own memoir, "Lovecraft as a Formative Influence," is largely a string of lengthy extracts from his correspondence with Lovecraft, since of course he never met Lovecraft and had no personal encounters to discuss.

The final piece is a brief critical essay, "H. P. Lovecraft: An Appreciation," by T. O. Mabbott, who opens with the remarkable statement: "Lovecraft is one of the few authors of whom I can honestly say that I have enjoyed every word of his stories." He goes on to make the significant statement that Lovecraft was "a scientist at heart" but that "he was also a dreamer," and that the fusion of these two qualities is the secret to the success of his work. And he adds: "There must be a narrative power for the writer of stories to excel, and that narrative power was the great-

---

17. J. Chapman Miske, upon seeing the volume, wrote to Derleth to notify him of the half-spurious nature of the "fragment." But Derleth evidently forgot about this and went on to reprint "The Thing in the Moonlight" in *Dagon and Other Macabre Tales* (1965). See David E. Schultz, "'The Thing in the Moonlight': A Hoax Revealed," *Crypt of Cthulhu* No. 53 (Candlemas 1988): 12–13.

est of Lovecraft's gifts." This is a point that even contemporary criticism has not sufficiently emphasised or analysed. And he concludes poignantly: ". . . while I think it too soon to say what place Lovecraft will have in American Literature, I have no doubt that it is an honorable place that should be accorded this truest amateur of letters."[18] What a contrast from those reviews, however enthusiastic they may be, who merely admire Lovecraft as a shudder-coiner!

Reviews of *Marginalia* were somewhat mixed. Will Cuppy chimed in again with another enthusiastic review (*New York Herald Tribune Weekly Book Review,* 11 February 1945), although it was only a paragraph long. Vincent Starrett wrote a few paragraphs on the book in the *Chicago Sunday Tribune* (4 March 1945), maintaining that the various essays and memoirs of Lovecraft "seem to me to confirm my own notion that Lovecraft the man is more interesting than his work" (*WW* 204).

More surprisingly, William Rose Benét, in his "The Phoenix Nest" column in the *Saturday Review of Literature* (17 March 1944), wrote that "his tales have a singularly weird quality. In a sense he remained a gifted amateur, but he did the sort of thing for which I myself have a great fancy" (*WW* 206). In an article written several years earlier,[19] Benét made the startling claim that his brother, the noted poet Stephen Vincent Benét (also the author of such weird tales as "The Devil and Daniel Webster"), "was entirely familiar with the work of H. P. Lovecraft long before that little-known master of horror was brought to the attention of the critics" (*WW* 231).

But in an indication that mainstream critical opinion may have been turning away from Lovecraft, Marjorie Farber, in a

---

18. *Marginalia* 338–40.

19. "My Brother Steve," *Saturday Review of Literature* 24, No. 30 (15 November 1941): 25.

review derisively entitled "Poesque Doodles" (*New York Times Book Review,* 25 February 1945), gave an emphatic thumbs-down on the book. Noting Lovecraft's apparent reclusiveness and the coddling he received from his mother and aunts, she wrote:

> Thus closeted, cosseted and protected, Lovecraft achieved a kind of "famous obscurity" as an amateur and later as a pulp writer. Since he never put his genius to any stringent professional test, he was able to use the horror story as a presumable means of gaining personal mastery over nightmares and delicate health. . . . A professed naturalist, scholar, and littérateur, his whole career seems an effective protest against "natural laws," against genuine scholarship and against literary craftsmanship. Only as an *undiscovered* genius can a writer really protect himself from failure. (*WW* 203–4)

This passage is about as good an example as one would want of the dangers of assessing a writer's merits on the basis of his biography, to say nothing of the dangers of armchair psychoanalysis.[20]

Another notable volume in 1944—not so much intrinsically but as a harbinger of the future—was the first Lovecraft paperback volume: *The Weird Shadow over Innsmouth* (Bartholomew House, 1944). The editor of this volume was none other than F. Orlin Tremaine, the erstwhile editor of *Astounding Stories* who had allowed the butchery of *At the Mountains of Madness* and "The Shadow out of Time" in 1936. Containing only five stories (two novellas and three short stories), it filled only 190 pages; and Tremaine continued his humiliation of Lovecraft by altering the title of the title story and by slapping on a lurid cover that relegated the book to the level of hackwork. Tremaine requested an initial print run of 100,000, and, incredibly, it must have sold

---

20. Farber made a further, and still more amateurish, attempt to psychoanalyse HPL in the article "Subjectivity in Modern Fiction" (*Kenyon Review,* Autumn 1945).

well, for by November 1944 he was proposing a second volume. Interestingly enough, one of his ideas was to issue the two stories he had bought for *Astounding* together in one volume. This plan did not materialise, but what did emerge in 1945 was *The Dunwich Horror,* containing only three long stories.[21]

The year 1944 would, however, have been noteworthy for Lovecraft had *Marginalia* and *The Weird Shadow over Innsmouth* never appeared; for it saw the publication of the immense *Great Tales of Terror and the Supernatural,* edited by Herbert A. Wise and Phyllis Fraser, and issued by the Modern Library. This 1080-page volume, whose contents are divided into two parts ("Tales of Terror" and "Tales of the Supernatural"), each arranged chronologically based on the birth date of the author, concludes with "The Rats in the Walls" and "The Dunwich Horror." This volume may still be the greatest anthology of weird tales ever issued, and the inclusion of not one but two Lovecraft stories—only Poe, Maupassant, M. R. James, Rudyard Kipling, E. F. Benson, and Algernon Blackwood are granted a similar privilege—is highly notable. In effect, it canonised Lovecraft within the field of weird fiction as no other volume or critical judgment had done up to this point. The editors make no reference to Lovecraft in their brief introduction, but their lengthy headnote to "The Rats in the Walls" (which serves as a general headnote to Lovecraft, since there is no separate headnote to "The Dunwich Horror") they observe: "Although his stories were widely circulated among the readers of the pulp mystery and horror magazines during his lifetime, they were neglected in other circles that should also have welcomed them for their originality and

21. See David E. Schultz, "The Bart House Paperbacks," *Crypt of Cthulhu* No. 65 (St John's Eve 1989): 27–28.

their gruesome terror."[22] The editors are referring to the several book publishers who turned down proposed volumes of Lovecraft in his lifetime. The volume was kept in print for many years.

Another noteworthy anthology appearance occurred the following year, when Donald A. Wollheim chose "The Shadow out of Time" for *The Portable Novels of Science* (Viking Press, 1945), along with novels by H. G. Wells, John Taine, and Olaf Stapledon. Lovecraft's presence as a pioneer of science fiction was well under way.

Meanwhile, Derleth forged ahead with other Lovecraft-related projects beyond Arkham House. He lent his authority to a Lovecraft volume published by the Editions for the Armed Services, an organisation designed to provide reading matter for soldiers stationed overseas during and after World War II. The date of publication of the volume (*The Dunwich Horror and Other Weird Tales*) is unclear, but probably it occurred in 1945. It contained twelve stories, a mix of longer and shorter tales, although with a few unfortunate choices ("In the Vault," "The Moon-Bog"), preceded by a brief introduction by Derleth. It was published in the distinctive 6½″ × 4″ paperback format—i.e., longer than it was tall, and printed in two columns on a page. There are reports that it was read widely by servicemen who remained overseas after the end of the conflict.

Derleth also prepared an edition of *Supernatural Horror in Literature* for Ben Abramson, a Chicago publisher and bookseller who had actually corresponded briefly with Lovecraft at the end of the latter's life. This was published in 1945; the first hardcover edition was full of typographical errors, which were corrected in a new printing later that year.

Even more important was *The Best Supernatural Stories of*

---

22. *Great Tales of Terror and the Supernatural* (New York: Modern Library, 1944), 1010.

H. P. Lovecraft, a 307-page "best of" collection published in hardcover by the World Publishing Company in April 1945. It went through three printings (September 1945, June 1946, and September 1950). Containing fourteen stories, it could well be said to contain many of Lovecraft's best tales, with the exception of his three short novels. Once again, however, Derleth chose the mediocre and conventional "In the Vault"—which, in fact, led off the volume.

The significance of this volume is that, even though it was issued by a second-tier publisher operating out of Cleveland rather than New York, it was exactly the sort of substantial but modest-sized book that Derleth should have published at the outset instead of *The Outsider and Others.* By the end of 1946 the volume had sold 67,254 copies in hardcover; by mid-1949 sales had reached 73,716.[23]

These 1945 volumes received almost no reviews. *The Best Supernatural Stories* and *The Weird Shadow over Innsmouth* were, so far as is known, reviewed only by Winfield Townley Scott in the *Providence Sunday Journal.* But a surprising review of *Supernatural Horror in Literature* appeared in the prestigious academic journal *American Literature* (May 1946). It was written by Fred Lewis Pattee, who spent much of his career at Pennsylvania State College (later Penn State University) and who, strangely enough, wrote a semi-weird novel, *The House of the Black Ring* (1916), that Lovecraft owned. Pattee expressed wholesale admiration for the book: "It is a brilliant piece of criticism" (*WW* 207). Otherwise, the review is largely a summary of the book, but its mere appearance in such a distinguished venue is notable.

The fan world was doing its bit to promote Lovecraft and to

23. See David E. Schultz, "Lovecraft's *Best Supernatural Stories,*" *Crypt of Cthulhu* No. 66 (Lammas 1989): 15–17.

dissect his life and work. Most notably, Francis T. Laney and others initiated the first Lovecraft-related fanzine, the *Acolyte,* whose first issue appeared in Fall 1942 and which continued until its final issue in Spring 1946. Laney enlisted the assistance of such former Lovecraft correspondents as Duane W. Rimel and F. Lee Baldwin, who appeared on the masthead as "Contributing Editors." R. H. Barlow—who, in the years immediately following Lovecraft's death, had largely been shoved aside by Derleth and Wandrei as Lovecraft's literary executor, chiefly because of Wandrei's implacable hatred for him—reappeared on the scene to contribute random bits.

The first two issues were run off on ditto, a crude reproductive method that has now rendered these issues virtually illegible; the rest are reproduced by mimeograph. The focus is not entirely on Lovecraft, as other writers of weird fiction come in for occasional discussion, and there is an abundance of fiction, not all—or even much—of it "Lovecraftian" in any meaningful sense. But the emphasis, even if sporadic, was clearly to shed additional light on lesser-known aspects of Lovecraft's life and work. Rimel prepared a brief series of extracts from Lovecraft's letters to him, publishing them as "Excerpts from the Letters of H. P. Lovecraft" (Fall 1942); Baldwin published a 1934 letter to him as "Lovecraft as an Illustrator" (Summer 1943), which even included a reproduction of a drawing by Lovecraft. Barlow probably provided the text of a Lovecraft letter to Elizabeth Toldridge, published as "Poetry and the Artistic Ideal" (Spring 1943), and he wrote a brief article on "Pseudonyms of Lovecraft" (Summer 1943).

Several rare or obscure Lovecraft items appeared for the first time in the pages of the *Acolyte,* including a discarded draft of "The Shadow over Innsmouth" (Spring 1944); the poem (actually a translation of a Latin translation of a Runic ballad) "Regner Lodbrog's Epicedium" (Summer 1944); and the Lovecraft/Barlow spoof "The Battle That Ended the Century" (Fall 1944—although of course the whimsy had been "published" as a mimeographed pair of sheets and sent out to mutual colleagues in 1934). Memoirs by E. Hoffmann Price and Stuart M. Boland, and several illuminating critical articles by Fritz Leiber, also appeared. The Lovecraftian content actually dwindled as the magazine proceeded, and almost no Lovecraft material appeared in the two issues for 1946.

But among the most valuable parts of the *Acolyte* were the numerous letters that appeared in nearly every issue. These did not necessarily comment on specific items in the magazine, but were often reflections on Lovecraft and the state of the field. T. O. Mabbott contributed several interesting letters; in one he expressed regret that he never looked up Lovecraft when he was teaching at Brown University in 1928–29 (Summer 1944; *WW* 145); in another he ruminates on the Lovecraft "Mythology," as a response both to an article by Fritz Leiber that touched on the subject and also, perhaps more indirectly, on August Derleth's now relentless flogging of the Cthulhu Mythos in articles, pastiches, and "posthumous collaborations." This leads to a thoughtful discussion of Lovecraft as a philosopher, and Mabbott concludes: "I think Lovecraft's 'mythological' characters represent extraordinary powers *within* natural law" (Spring 1945; *WW* 147).

Robert Bloch, Matthew H. Onderdonk, E. Hoffmann Price, and numerous others also contributed letters that broached a number of issues relating to Lovecraft's life and work. These ongoing discussions provided a forum for Lovecraft devotees to debate topics of importance in a tolerably respectful manner, setting the stage for further critical work by these and other critics.

The publication *Rhode Island on Lovecraft* (1945) cannot precisely be said to have emerged out of the fan world. It is largely an amateur undertaking—but no less notable for all that. At only 26 pages, it seems a slim and insubstantial item, but it has a number of worthy pieces. Edited by Donald M. Grant (subsequently to become a highly regarded publisher in the weird fiction field) and Thomas P. Hadley and published by the editors, it features perhaps the most reliable memoir by Muriel E. Eddy (wife of Lovecraft's sometime collaborator C. M. Eddy, Jr.), who in subsequent years appears to have systematically exaggerated the extent of her relations with the Providence writer; brief memoirs by Marian F. Bonner (a friend of Annie Gamwell's with whom Lovecraft carried on a delightfully playful correspondence in 1936) and Mary V. Dana (the wife of the bookseller H. Douglass Dana); and two critical articles, one by Winfield Townley Scott ("Lovecraft as a Poet") and the other by Dorothy C. Walter ("Lovecraft and Benefit Street"), the latter of which had previously appeared as a pamphlet (1943) published by W. Paul Cook. If nothing else, the booklet denotes the beginning of a long struggle to get Lovecraft better-known in his native state.

The year 1945 could be regarded as a kind of *annus mirabilis* for Lovecraft. All apart from the slim *Rhode Island on Lovecraft,* we have *The Best Supernatural Stories, Supernatural Horror in Literature,* the paperback *Dunwich Horror,* and the Armed Services Edition. Derleth also published the first and longest of his "posthumous collaborations" with Lovecraft, *The Lurker at the Threshold* (Arkham House, 1945), which he repeatedly asserted (falsely) was a fragment of a novel by Lovecraft that he merely "completed." On top of which, we have a seemingly significant work of biography and criticism—namely, Derleth's *H.P.L.: A Memoir* (Ben Abramson).

From nearly every perspective, however—beginning with its

misleading title—this work is a dismal failure. Even for its time, it is an unsatisfactory account of Lovecraft's life and work, from a writer who preened himself as Lovecraft's disciple, editor, and publisher, but who couldn't find the time or take the trouble to write such a monograph with any degree of care or detail.[24] It is all of 122 pages (including index) and is divided into three parts: "The Facts of Biography," "The Man," and "The Work." The first part is an acceptable outline of the basic course of Lovecraft's life, although Derleth peppers the texts with lengthy footnotes quoting extensive portions of Lovecraft's letters (many of them to himself) verifying the points he makes in the text. This practice becomes more egregious in "The Man," which purports to be an analysis of Lovecraft's character. Here the quotations from letters are dumped right into the text; but even so, Derleth cannot remain focused on a systematic study of Lovecraft's personality; instead, he probes random and inessential elements, such as an eight-page discussion of Lovecraft's relations to music (surely not a very significant phase of his character, but one that Derleth found meaningful to himself), or a nine-page disquisition (mostly made up of quotations) on Lovecraft's views on dialect and nomenclature. It is of some significance that nowhere is there a mention of one of the central features of Lovecraft's philosophical thought—his atheism. There is also no discussion at all of Lovecraft's racism, even though by this time Derleth must have known about it from his accumulation of letters to various individuals. (The subject does not come up very often in letters to Derleth himself.)

As for the discussion of "The Work," it is predictably focused

---

24. It may be mentioned that 1945 was probably the pinnacle of Derleth's own reputation as a mainstream writer, as signalled by Sinclair Lewis's article "The Sac of Fortune" (*Esquire,* November 1945). Even this article, however, chastised Derleth for writing too much and dissipating his energies on too many projects.

on the Cthulhu Mythos, while an extended discussion of Lovecraft's theory of the weird is taken almost entirely from his letters. We then discover a fourth section to the book—namely, a 24-page "Appendix" in which Derleth reprints two entire stories ("The Cats of Ulthar" and "The Festival"), the unidentified fragment "Does 'Vulcan' Exist?,"[25] some of Lovecraft's juvenilia, and the brief essay "Rudis Indigestaque Moles," his notorious panning of T. S. Eliot's *The Waste Land.*

But what turned 1945 into an *annus horribilis* was the review that Edmund Wilson wrote of several of these books in the *New Yorker* (24 November 1945), under the derisive title "Tales of the Marvellous and the Ridiculous." Wilson was a leading critic and reviewer of mainstream fiction, and was also something of a political radical in his early years (Lovecraft, in occasional letters of the 1930s, remarks on Wilson's advocacy of socialism). But he exhibited, in extreme form, the standard mainstream critic's scorn of genre fiction. He had already written two grand nose-thumbings of the detective story ("Why Do People Read Detective Stories?" [*New Yorker,* 14 October 1944]; "Who Cares Who Killed Roger Ackroyd?" [*New Yorker,* 20 June 1945]), and would later give J. R. R. Tolkien a swift kick in the pants ("Oo, Those Awful Orcs!" [*Nation,* 14 April 1956]). For these and other reasons, both contemporary and later critics have questioned whether Wilson really deserved his eminent status in American literary criticism.[26]

Only the previous year, Wilson had written "A Treatise on

25. Derleth identifies it as coming from the *Providence Journal* (1906); but unless this is an unlocated letter to the editor, it cannot be part of an astronomy column, since HPL wrote no such columns for the *Journal.*

26. See René Welleck, "Edmund Wilson (1895–1972)," *Comparative Literature Studies* 15, No. 1 (1978): 97–123. Welleck concludes: "There are definite limits to the reach of [Wilson's] mind."

Tales of Horror" (*New Yorker,* 27 May 1944), which reviewed several collections and anthologies of horror tales, including the Wise and Fraser anthology. His contemptuous attitude is prevalent throughout. Expressing surprise that anyone could still be interested in, and frightened by, "ghost stories" in an age of Nazi horrors,[27] Wilson toys with assembling his own anthology that would be for adult readers instead of ten-year-olds. His prejudice toward mainstream fiction and what might be called symbolic horror are evident in some of his suggestions: Melville's "Bartleby the Scrivener," Conrad's *Heart of Darkness,* Gogol's "Viy," the tales of Walter de la Mare and Franz Kafka. It was, in fact, readers' complaints about the omission of Lovecraft from this article that led Wilson to write "Tales of the Marvellous and the Ridiculous."

The hostile passages from Wilson's review of Lovecraft—later collected in *Classics and Commercials: A Literary Chronicle of the Forties* (1950)—are notorious and familiar:

> I regret that, after examining these books, I am no more enthusiastic than before. . . . these stories were hack-work contributed to such publications as *Weird Tales* and *Amazing Stories,* where, in my opinion, they ought to have been left.
>
> The only real horror in most of these fictions is the horror of bad taste and bad art. Lovecraft was not a good writer. The fact that his verbose and undistinguished style has been compared to Poe's is only one of the many sad signs that almost nobody any more pays real attention to writing. . . .
>
> But the Lovecraft cult, I fear, is on an even more infantile level than the Baker Street Irregulars and the cult of Sherlock Holmes.[28]

---

27. HPL had already responded to this line of thought: "The physical horrors of war, no matter how extreme and unprecedented, hardly have a bearing on the entirely different realms of supernatural terror. Ghosts are still ghosts—the mind can get more thrills from unrealities than from realities!" ("The Defence Reopens!" [1921]; *CE* 5.49).

28. "Tales of the Marvellous and the Ridiculous"; rpt. in Joshi, *H. P. Love-*

This certainly sounds damning, although Lovecraft himself surely cannot be held responsible for the excesses of the "cult" that grew around him, if it could be called that. But what is interesting is how often, and almost in spite of himself, Wilson finds things to admire in Lovecraft. He declares that "Lovecraft himself . . . is a little more interesting than his stories"; that "his long essay on the literature of supernatural horror is a really able piece of work"; that his "stories do show at times some traces of his more serious emotions and interests," noting that "The Colour out of Space" "more or less predicts the effects of the atomic bomb" and that "The Shadow out of Time" "deals not altogether ineffectively with the perspectives of geological eons and the idea of controlling time-sequence."

As for Wilson's criticisms: his comment about comparisons of Lovecraft to Poe sounds magisterial, as if he and he alone is fit to gauge whether Lovecraft's prose is similar to his mentor's; Wilson actually finds it "terrifying" that T. O. Mabbott has enjoyed every word of Lovecraft's stories, apparently failing to acknowledge that Mabbott knows a whole lot more about Poe than he (Wilson) does and might be in a better position to gauge the accuracy of such claims. Wilson's annoyance that Lovecraft uses overt terms such as "horrible," "hellish," and so forth ("Surely one of the primary rules for writing an effective tale of horror is never to use any of these words") is confounded by their liberal use in Poe, Machen, and numerous other undoubted classics of the genre. And Wilson's clear prejudice against *any* material appearing in the pulp magazines is evident in his diametrically wrong belief that Lovecraft's stories were "hack-work" designed specifically to appear in these venues. Whatever the merits of Lovecraft's tales, it should have been ob-

---

craft: Four Decades of Criticism 46–49.

vious even at this juncture that he wrote his tales out of a sincere attempt to convey certain philosophical and aesthetic conceptions clamouring for expression; he was, temperamentally, antipodal to the mindset of the "hack writer," who calculatingly fashions formula matter for a specific market. But Wilson couldn't wrap his mind around the fact that not all work that appeared in pulp magazines need have been written in that manner.

What is even more interesting is that, decades later, Wilson came around to a significantly different view, although he never uttered it in print. He read *Selected Letters I* (1965) soon after it was published; and, according to a friend of Wilson's, had enjoyed it. Even more remarkably, in the very year that *Classics and Commercials* appeared, Wilson published a play, *The Little Blue Light,* that has some definitely Lovecraftian touches. One character, M. S. Ferguson, writes horror stories for a magazine called *Grewsome Tales* (it is unlikely that Wilson knew that this was the title under which "Herbert West—Reanimator" appeared in *Home Brew*). Ferguson has devised a cosmic entity called Shidnats Slyme. The protagonist, named only Frank, asks at one point:

> Say, tell me: what happened to that chemistry professor when he finally got hold of the formula so that he could summon up Shidnats at will? Was he so scared by what happened the first time that he never tried it again or did he turn the demons loose on the academic cabal that was trying to block his promotion?[29]

Clearly there is a liberal dose of parody here, but the play in general does not in fact treat Ferguson purely as a figure of jest, and there is a definite attempt to create a sense of weird atmosphere not entirely dissimilar to what Lovecraft was attempting to do.

---

29. Quoted in L. Sprague de Camp, "H. P. Lovecraft and Edmund Wilson," *Fantasy Mongers* No. 1 (1979): 5.

IV. The Beginnings of Worldwide Dissemination (1946–1959)

There is some doubt as to the extent to which Wilson's blast really coloured mainstream critics' opinions on Lovecraft. Only two years later, J. O. Bailey published the first critical study of science fiction, *Pilgrims through Space and Time* (1947). But this work was written—or, at least, begun—long ago; in fact, Lovecraft himself corresponded briefly with Bailey in 1930 as he was doing research for his treatise, which had begun life as two separate academic papers: a master's thesis (1927) and a doctoral dissertation (1934) written at the University of North Carolina. In any event, Bailey discusses Lovecraft in several pages of his book, although the bulk of his discussion constitutes merely a plot synopsis of *At the Mountains of Madness* and "The Shadow out of Time." But he concludes: "These stories by Lovecraft mediate a combination of the measureless past of geology and astronomy, some grotesque suggestions from the theory of evolution, and ideas from various mythologies. They are splendid examples of scientific fiction turned to the uses of the tale of terror" (*WW* 213).

Much more significantly, an article by Richard B. Gehman—whose chief claim to fame was the editing of the *Oak Ridge Journal* (1943–48), the official weekly of the atomic bomb project—entitled "Imagination Runs Wild" (*New Republic,* 17 January 1949) speaks very positively about Lovecraft, even though Gehman commits the gaffe of referring to him as "Howard

Phelps Lovecraft." The article is mainly about "science-fantasy" and its popularity both before and after the dropping of the atomic bomb. Beginning his survey of the field with the Gothics and Poe, Gehman declares:

> Lovecraft is notable, however, for the tremendous influence he exerted over other writers. In creating the *Cthulhu Mythos,* a series of legends concerned with cosmology and prehistoric races, he provided himself and other writers with material to draw upon for years to come. The *Mythos* was taken up, expanded and enlarged by Clark Ashton Smith, Frank Belknap Long, Robert Bloch, Henry Kuttner, August Derleth and others. (*WW* 218)

It is true that reviews of Lovecraft's books declined in number—and in the prestige of those writing them—in the later 1940s and 1950s; but that was in large part because August Derleth, annoyed at what he believed to be the patronizing reviews of books by Lovecraft, Clark Ashton Smith, and others that he received in the mainstream press, essentially ceased to send out review copies to such venues, relying on word-of-mouth and notices in the fantasy and science fiction fan press to drum up interest in the books and generate sales.

And yet, the fan world remained quite active at this time as far as discussions and debates about Lovecraft are concerned. This is the "Lovecraft cult" that Edmund Wilson referred to in passing, although it is highly unlikely that he really knew much about this phenomenon—assuming there even was such a thing. One commentator who apparently did think there was, and who deprecated it, was Lovecraft's old friend W. Paul Cook, who wrote an article, "A Plea for Lovecraft," in his own amateur magazine, the *Ghost* (May 1945). It is a most curious piece. Cook claims to have come upon a fan who declared, "Lovecraft is almost a god to me," leading him to urge Lovecraft devotees to "get at least one foot on the ground" (*WW* 148). This is all well and good—but Cook goes on to make some very strange judgments regarding the merits of Lovecraft's work. Astonishingly, he agrees with a reviewer of Derleth's anthology *Sleep No More* (1944) who declared that "The Rats in the Walls" is "pure clap-trap."[1] It does not help much that Cook qualifies this judgment by declaring: "Superb clap-trap, it may be, but clap-trap none the less" (*WW* 148). Since neither the reviewer nor Cook define what "clap-trap" means in this context, it is difficult to understand the thrust of the remark. Cook goes on to say that the second Lovecraft omnibus (*Beyond the Wall of Sleep*) "should never have been published" (*WW* 149). With friends like this, Lovecraft doesn't need any enemies! It should be noted that Cook's disdain for Lovecraft's later, quasi-scientific writing (especially *At the Mountains of Madness*) had much to do with the discouragement he felt toward the end of his life as to the progress of his work.

P. Schuyler Miller, a well-known science fiction fan of the period, specifically addressed Edmund Wilson's review in "Let's All Jump on H.P.L." (*Cepheid,* Winter 1945–46). Miller dismisses the chief daggers that Wilson directed toward Lovecraft, but he does acknowledge that Lovecraft's Mythos has become a kind of secret code that only the initiated will understand, leaving others (even other devotees of weird fiction) out in the cold. I doubt the validity of this criticism, for it would suggest that Lovecraft was not attracting new readers, which he clearly was even at this early stage.

Ray H. Zorn—who, like several other figures in this period, straddled the worlds of fantasy fandom and amateur journalism—issued three slim issues of the *Lovecraft Collector* (January, May, and October 1949), each consisting of only four pages.

---

1. The review has not been located.

But he did publish David H. Keller's significant article "Lovecraft's Astronomical Notebook" (October 1949), the only account of the notebook that Lovecraft kept during the years 1909–15 that we had until the notebook itself surfaced recently and was posted online. Keller had earlier created controversy with the article "Shadows over Lovecraft" (*Fantasy Commentator,* Spring 1948), claiming that Lovecraft had congenital syphilis. Kenneth Sterling wrote a rebuttal in *Fantasy Commentator* (Winter 1951–52), but the definitive overthrow of Keller's conjecture had to come decades later, in the early 1990s, when Dr. M. Eileen McNamara consulted Lovecraft's death certificate and saw that he had been given a Wassermann test for syphilis upon his admission into Jane Brown Memorial Hospital on March 10, 1937; it was negative.

But an indication that at least some elements of the fan world were beginning to turn against Lovecraft—perhaps because he was being overly lauded by others—can be found in Francis T. Laney's obscure article "Lovecraft Is 86" (*Sky Hook,* Autumn 1948), a kind of condensation of Laney's pungent autobiography, *Ah! Sweet Idiocy!* (1948), where he expresses disdain and mortification at his own fan activity of previous years. These sentiments caused him to seize upon Lovecraft as a kind of scapegoat for what he perceived to be his own juvenility and uncritical attitude as a fan. He can now find no virtues in Lovecraft at all: he was largely an artistic failure because he knew little about real life and therefore could not portray his settings realistically (Laney does not seem to have any admiration even for Lovecraft's topographical realism); he does not "play other than fumblingly on the strings of terror"; his stories are weakened by "his almost consistent telegraphing of the punch line" (*WW* 162); and so on. Laney concludes:

> Why should any fanzine ever again publish anything by Love-

> craft, or even about him? If fanzines more or less drop HPL from consideration, and if Derleth and one or two other pros stop beating the drums for Lovecraft for even as little as one year, HPL will drop back to his proper status in American literature—almost completely unknown and forgotten. (*WW* 163)

But Derleth was in fact not inclined to "stop beating the drums" for Lovecraft, even after Edmund Wilson's screed. He had already begun getting random stories by Lovecraft back into print through his various anthologies, beginning with *Sleep No More* and continuing on through the early 1950s; he even reprinted *The Case of Charles Dexter Ward* in *Night's Yawning Peal* (1952). Anthologies by other editors followed suit—notably Donald A. Wollheim's *Avon Fantasy Reader* series—and the largely reprint magazines *Famous Fantastic Mysteries* and *Fantastic Novels Magazine* reprinted several Lovecraft stories in the 1940s and 1950s. Another paperback volume, *The Lurking Fear* (Avon, 1947), appeared and was reprinted as late as 1960 under the lurid title *Cry Horror!*

Derleth generated another "stopgap" volume, *Something about Cats and Other Pieces* (Arkham House, 1949)—the last such volume for a decade. It is not quite as noteworthy as *Marginalia,* but has some fine material in it: the title essay (Derleth's regrettable mistitling of "Cats and Dogs") along with six others; five revised or ghostwritten tales (also Robert Bloch's "Satan's Servants," which Lovecraft commented on at length); thirteen poems (two of which, "Death" and "The American Flag," proved to be spurious);[2] insightful memoirs by Rheinhart Kleiner, Samuel Loveman, Sonia H. Davis, Derleth, and E. Hoffmann Price; and Fritz Leiber's pioneering critical essay "A Literary Copernicus."

The Sonia Davis piece is worth noting chiefly because it was

---

2. See Chapter III, n. 3.

first shepherded into print by Winfield Townley Scott, whom we have already mentioned as the author of the landmark biographical article "His Own Most Fantastic Creation" and the keen but brief article "Lovecraft as a Poet." Scott's interest in Lovecraft dates to at least 1943, when he wrote "The Case of Howard Phillips Lovecraft of Providence, R.I." (*Providence Sunday Journal,* 26 December 1943), a general overview of Lovecraft's life, stressing his ties to Providence. Elsewhere[3] Scott reports that this article led various acquaintances of Lovecraft to contact him, leading directly to the writing of the biographical piece. That article shows Scott doing exhaustive research among Providence sources (including records at Butler Hospital regarding Lovecraft's mother, subsequently destroyed), interviews with Lovecraft's childhood friends, and so on. It still contains material that is available in no other work.

Scott discussed Lovecraft repeatedly in his "Bookman's Gallery" column in the *Providence Sunday Journal* in the years 1944–46. It was in 1947 that he came into contact with Frank Belknap Long, from whom he learned that Lovecraft's widow, Sonia H. Davis, was still living in California. Sonia had, incredibly, not learned of Lovecraft's passing until 1945; but after about a year of correspondence with Scott she sent him a lengthy memoir, "The Private Life of H. P. Lovecraft." Scott published only about half of it (while also rewriting other parts) in the *Providence Journal* (22 August 1948), and subsequently in *Books at Brown* (February 1949); Derleth then reprinted it, with further cuts, as "Lovecraft as I Knew Him" in *Something about Cats.* Mercifully, Scott deposited the full version of the memoir in the John Hay Library.

Sonia's piece, even in its truncated form, is bracing. She dis-

---

3. "Foreword" to Davis's "Howard Phillips Lovecraft as His Wife Remembers Him," *Books at Brown* 11, Nos. 1 & 2 (February 1949): 1–2.

cusses the monetary support she lent to Lovecraft during their marriage, her attempts to dress him more fashionably, and, of course, the grim scenario where, at some point after Lovecraft's return to Providence in 1926, he sat down with his aunts to discuss what place—if any—she had in the household, and their rejection of her offer to set up a hat shop in Providence ("The aunts gently but firmly informed me that neither they nor Howard could afford to have Howard's wife work for a living in Providence. That was that. I knew then were we all stood").[4] But it has to be stated that the full memoir, poorly written and even at times incoherent as it is, paints a far more detailed and poignant picture of this fundamentally misaligned couple.

Leiber's "Literary Copernicus" deserves discussion all on its own. It may still be the finest single general article on Lovecraft. It is a revision and expansion of at least two earlier pieces, "The Works of H. P. Lovecraft: Suggestion for a Critical Appraisal" (*Acolyte,* Fall 1944) and "Some Random Reflections about Lovecraft's Writings" (*Acolyte,* Winter 1945). Its celebrated opening paragraph remains as true today as when it was first written: "Howard Phillips Lovecraft was the Copernicus of the horror story. He shifted the focus of supernatural dread from man and his little world and his gods, to the stars and the black and unplumbed gulfs of intergalactic space. To do this effectively, he created a new kind of horror story and new methods for telling it."[5] Leiber goes on to discuss Lovecraft's philosophical stance—materialism and atheism—and its literary corollary, cosmicism. He studies the possible symbolic significance of the various "gods" of Lovecraft's myth-cycle (in the course of which he delivers a pointed rebuke to August Derleth, without naming him: "I believe it is a mistake to regard the beings of the

4. *Something about Cats* 244 (also *AV* 139).

5. *Something about Cats* 290. Further citations will occur in the text.

Cthulhu Mythos as sophisticated equivalents of the entities of Christian demonology, or to attempt to divide them into balancing Zoroastrian hierarchies of good and evil" [294]), and devotes some valuable paragraphs to certain aspects of Lovecraft's prose style and story construction, emphasising the notion of "*confirmation* rather than revelation" (297) and proposing the idea of the "terminal climax": "the story in which the high point and the final sentence coincide" (297). A final section somewhat whimsically supplies a kind of chronology of the key events in Lovecraft's major tales, set mostly in the 1920s and 1930s.

Something about Cats received a predictably favourable review from Vincent Starrett (*Chicago Sunday Tribune,* 18 December 1949) and, more surprisingly, from Joseph Henry Jackson, a longtime book reviewer for the *San Francisco Chronicle* who wrote a mixed but generally positive review (6 January 1950; *WW* 221–22). He expresses disappointment in Sonia's memoir but finds much value in Leiber's essay. Since he recognises that the material actually by Lovecraft in the book is generally of secondary importance, he directs readers to the two earlier Lovecraft omnibuses (although by this time they were out of print).

The 1950s were a lean period both for Arkham House (which published only fourteen books—several of them slim volumes of poetry—during the decade); but the situation for Lovecraft took a surprising turn. Although the fourth printing of the World *Best Supernatural Stories* (1950) was still in print early in the decade, many of his stories were difficult to find in the United States. But he suddenly became available in England when a leading publisher, Victor Gollancz, issued *The Haunter of the Dark and Other Tales of Horror* and the first separate publication of *The Case of Charles Dexter Ward,* both in 1951.

Derleth had previously sold reprint rights to *The Lurker at the Threshold* to a small British firm, Museum Press, which brought out the book in 1948. Around that time, Victor Gollancz himself, visiting New York, established contact with Derleth and negotiated for the rights to the two books. *The Haunter of the Dark* contains ten stories, most of them among his best. According to an illuminating article Derleth wrote late in life, the book was reviewed widely and positively in British newspapers, including favourable reviews by two noted detective writers, Francis Iles (the pseudonym of Anthony Berkeley Cox) and Edmund Crispin.[6] One of the reviews of *The Case of Charles Dexter Ward* is notable—not because it is favourable or even particularly enthusiastic, but because it was written by the distinguished novelist Anthony Powell. It was published in the prestigious *Times Literary Supplement* (22 February 1952), where it appeared (as all reviews in that paper did at the time) anonymously. Powell, in a one-paragraph review, notes: "Mr. Lovecraft supplies a wealth of eighteenth-century pastiche in building up his chronicle of reincarnation and unspeakable wickedness. In fact he rather overloads the canvas. There are, however, undeniably some eerie moments among the corpses" (*WW* 223).

The Haunter of the Dark was reprinted sporadically over the next twenty-six years. I am not aware that *The Case of Charles Dexter Ward* was reprinted by Gollancz itself, but it appeared in a frequently reprinted Panther paperback in 1963.

Even more remarkably, the Gollancz editions—as Derleth notes[7]—led directly to the first book publication of Lovecraft in another language.[8] Editions Denoël brought out *La Couleur*

---

6. August Derleth, "H. P. Lovecraft: The Making of a Literary Reputation, 1937–1971," *Books at Brown* 25 (1977): 13–25 (see p. 19). In a note prefacing the essay, Barton L. St. Armand reports that Derleth had sent the essay to him "only a few months before his death."

7. Ibid., 19.

8. I am discounting the Spanish translation of *The Lurker at the Threshold* as *El que acecha en el umbral* (Buenos Aires: Editorial Molino, 1946).

tombée du ciel, translated by Jacques Papy, in 1954. This was followed in quick succession by *Dans l'abîme du temps* (Denoël, 1954), *Démons et merveilles* (Deux Rives, 1955), and *Par delà le mur du sommeil* (Denoël, 1956).

French interest in Lovecraft canonically dates to 1948, when the first mention of him appears—in, of all places, François Le Lionnais's anthology *Les Grands Courants de la pensée mathematique,* in connexion with a rather complex mathematical equation. But Lovecraft was apparently being bruited about in intellectual circles at least a few years before this. André Breton and other surrealists may have known about Lovecraft, even if indirectly, in the 1940s. Two of them, Gérard Legrand and Robert Benayoun, discussed Lovecraft in extremely brief articles (each consisting of only two paragraphs) in the magazine *Médium* (November 1953), nearly a year before the first Denoël edition. Legrand maintains that Lovecraft's "mythology reflects an authentic occult knowledge, treated with entire freedom." Benayoun stated: "Mr. Lovecraft—in his displaced prose, forged in the furnaces of the alchemy that he venerated—announced the occult return of the Ancient Ones."[9] It is possible that these writers were influenced by an article a decade earlier by an American critic, Robert Allerton Parker, who had discussed Lovecraft in the course of an article, "Such Pulps as Dreams Are Made On," in the surrealist journal *VVV* (March 1943; *WW* 184–92).

But the first two Denoël editions clearly led to significant commentary. *Couleur* contained a brief and rather tendentious introduction by Jacques Bergier, who went on to become one of the most prominent French commentators on Lovecraft over the next several decades; but Bergier's "take" on Lovecraft was sig-

9. The two articles were translated as "H.P.L." and the Black Moon," *Cultural Correspondence* Nos. 10–11 (Fall 1979): 16.

nificantly coloured by his own devotion to occultism, primitivism, and interest in UFOs. As the French Lovecraft critic Michel Meurger wrote, "According to Jacques Bergier, the horror in Lovecraft's work does not stem from literary artifice, but from the degree of hidden reality it is capable of expressing. From here it is only a step to the consideration of the New England author's work as a warning to mankind."[10] Bergier's colleague Louis Pauwels followed suit, writing a review of *Couleur* (*Carrefour,* 6 October 1954) in which he maintained: "For H. P. Lovecraft, intelligences from other planets are preparing to destroy the Earth."[11]

Not quite as irrationally but just as tendentiously, Claude Ernoult, in a pioneering article, "Lovecraft ou la mythe en révolution" (*Les Lettres Nouvelles,* November 1954), apparently abolished the distinction between Lovecraft's fiction and his philosophy (based on rationalism and atheism) by portraying him as manipulating the genre of science fiction to effect a renewal of our belief in the myths of witchcraft and alien incursion. (The issue containing Ernoult's article also contained a translation of a small portion of "The Dreams in the Witch House.")

There was a brief notice, in English, of *La Couleur tombée du ciel* by the distinguished writer Jean Cocteau, as part of a symposium in the London *Observer:* "Mr. Lovecraft, who is American, invents a terrifying world of space-time; his somewhat loose style has gained by translation into French."[12] It is unclear whether Cocteau really read Lovecraft in English; but his com-

10. Michel Meurger, "'Retrograde Anticipation': Primitivism and Occultism in the French Response to Lovecraft 1953–1957," tr. S. T. Joshi, *Lovecraft Studies* Nos. 19/20 (Fall 1989): 11.

11. Quoted in Meurger 11.

12. "Books of 1954: A Symposium," *Observer* (London) (26 December 1954): 7.

ment is true in the sense that Jacques Papy deliberately simplified Lovecraft's sentence structure and actually omitted words and paragraphs that he believed would not translate well into French. It took decades for these inaccurate translations to be replaced.

Lovecraft appeared in Dutch as early as 1949, when "The Thing on the Doorstep" was translated in B. Jessurun Lobo's anthology *Voor en na middernacht.* He appeared in Swedish as early as 1955, when Torsten Jungstedt included "The Picture in the House" in his anthology *Mannen i svart*. Jungstedt included "In the Vault" and "The Colour out of Space" in *Stora skräckboken* (1959). But book publications of Lovecraft's work in Swedish had to wait until the 1970s. "The Rats in the Walls" was translated in a Danish anthology, Tage La Cour's *Spøgelses historier fra hele verden* (1957), as well as in a Dutch anthology, A. De Bruijn and A. van der Hoek's *Griezelverhalen* (1958). "The Shadow over Innsmouth" was serialised in the Polish magazine *Przekrój* from December 1959 to 17 January 1960.[13]

The first Spanish book of Lovecraft's stories was *El color que cayó del cielo* (Ediciones Minotauro, 1957), translated by Ricardo Gosseyn; but "Cool Air" had appeared in the magazine *Los Cuentos Fantasticos* as early as 15 August 1949; this may in fact be the first appearance of a Lovecraft work in a foreign language, assuming it preceded the Lobo anthology. Translations into Italian, German, and other languages did not become widespread until the 1960s or later.

The first Portuguese edition of Lovecraft is worth noting: *Os mortos podem voltar* (Lisbon: Livros do Brasil, [1955]), a translation by Silas Cerqueira of *The Case of Charles Dexter Ward* (the title translates to "The Dead Can Return"). The publisher's name suggests that the book was destined for distribution in

---

13. "The Colour out of Space," "Cool Air," and "The Dunwich Horror" also appeared in this magazine, but their dates of appearance are unknown.

Brazil, but I have no idea of the extent of the volume's circulation either there or in Portugal.

In the United States, the 1950s were a slow period. As mentioned, Arkham House published only fourteen titles in that decade. Several of these had some relation to Lovecraft, even if tangentially. Derleth reprinted the three tales ghostwritten for Zealia Bishop as *The Curse of Yig* (1953), also soliciting a memoir of Lovecraft (highly erroneous in spots and poorly written overall) by Bishop. He published the first book of his "posthumous collaborations" with Lovecraft as *The Survivor and Others* (1957), and the first volume of his own Lovecraft pastiches, *The Mask of Cthulhu* (1958).

Lovecraft continued to appear in anthologies, by Derleth and others. One of the more notable was Groff Conklin's *Omnibus of Science Fiction* (1952), containing "The Colour out of Space"; it was reprinted numerous times and in various abridged versions over the next two or three decades, and introduced many readers to that imperishable story. Even more surprisingly, "The Music of Erich Zann" was reprinted in a textbook, *The Short Story* (Macmillan, 1956), edited by James B. Hall and Joseph Langland, complete with study questions at the end for those wishing to write a term paper on the story. It would be quite a few years before Lovecraft appeared again in a textbook, either at the high school or at the college level. The appearance of an entry on Lovecraft in the "first supplement" (1955) of the well-known reference work *Twentieth Century Authors,* edited by Stanley J. Kunitz, is a notable achievement.

From a very different direction, the men's magazine *Zest* included, in its January 1956 issue, an abridged and partially rewritten version of "The Rats in the Walls," liberally illustrated with photographs of mostly naked ladies. And we need hardly take notice of another edition of Lovecraft issued at this time,

The Dream-Quest of Unknown Kadath (1955), issued by Shroud Publishers (Buffalo, New York). This was the brainchild of Kenneth J. Krueger; but all he did was to take the four-part serialisation of the novel in the *Arkham Sampler* (Winter 1948–Autumn 1948) and duplicate it in an ungainly paperback edition, with a brief introduction by George T. Wetzel. A small number of copies were bound in hardcover.

A significant contribution to Lovecraft criticism from an academic source was the admirably perspicacious discussion of his work in Peter Penzoldt's *The Supernatural in Fiction* (Peter Nevill, 1952). This acute study, at least partially inspired by the author's friendship with Algernon Blackwood, contains wide-ranging discussions of numerous important weird writers of the nineteenth and twentieth centuries. Penzoldt was a Swiss scholar, and his book was originally a Ph.D. dissertation submitted to the University of Geneva in 1949, when the author was only twenty-four years old. Lovecraft is included in a section on "The Pure Tale of Horror" (by which Penzoldt refers to such authors as Machen and F. Marion Crawford, who eschew the conventional ghost or haunted house for more overt horrific scenarios). It is a penetrating study that takes Lovecraft seriously both in regard to his pioneering motifs as well as to his prose style, which Penzoldt regards as well suited to the subject-matter of his tales.

In the fan world, Lovecraft continued to be discussed—but there were an increasing number of dissenting voices among those who seemed to take offence, as Edmund Wilson and others did, at the perceived "Lovecraft cult" that was lauding him to the skies. Two years before its demise in 1954, *Weird Tales* featured a debate in its letter column. It was sparked by one Joseph V. Wilcox, apparently in response to a wealth of letters praising Lovecraft—including those by Robert E. Briney (later to be one of Lovecraft's bibliographers), John Taylor Gatto (who, two decades later, would write a Cliff Notes–style book on Lovecraft), and others—in the May and July issues. In September 1952, Wilcox channelled Wilson in writing:

> Excepting some stories, and I by no means intend a blanket indictment of all of Lovecraft's work, I think that his style is prolix, affected, turgid,[14] and labored. It is full of obvious and ill-concealed strivings for effect—"posing," it might be called. Lovecraft apparently lacked the ability to tell a plain tale and tell it straight. He lacked the clarity and objectivity of a writer such as Ambrose Bierce, who evoked horror by a direct, clear, impeccable prose and added to its effect by a matter of fact detachment.
>
> Not even the most enthusiastic followers of Lovecraft, in Sauk City or elsewhere, can claim for him reticence and detachment. These two qualities, in my mind, are necessary for a good "ghost story," and Lovecraft lacked both completely. He always indicated the feeling supposed to be evoked in the reader with the use of the adjectives "terrible," "horrible," etc., on every page, and his style is so difficult to follow in many cases that one is often at a loss to know what is supposed to have taken place. (WW 107)

These comments are sufficient to indicate Wilcox's biases and presuppositions. Like so many others in an era where the austerity of Ernest Hemingway, Sherwood Anderson, James T. Farrell, and others had become blindly accepted as the only kind of prose a "serious" writer would use, Wilcox entirely overlooks a countervailing tradition—what is called the "Asianic" style, as opposed to the spare "Attic" style—going back to at least the sixteenth century and embodied in particular by such writers as Samuel Johnson, Edward Gibbon, Thomas De Quincey, and

---

14. This is exactly the adjective that Gilbert Highet used in a dismissive comment on HPL in his book *A Clerk of Oxenford* (New York: Oxford University Press, 1956), 9. Highet was once a highly regarded American critic and classical scholar, but is now largely forgotten.

many others; in particular, the weird tradition features just such "Asianic" writers as Poe, Machen, Dunsany, and countless others. Moreover, Wilcox's smallness of vision sees in Lovecraft a bumbling writer of the conventional "ghost story" rather than a pioneer who sought to fashion an entirely new kind of weird tale—and succeeded in doing so.

Wilcox's letter was rebutted by James Wade in the November 1952 issue:

> Mr. Wilcox objects to Lovecraft's style as "affected, turgid, and labored." That is to say, it was complex and dense. So was that of Poe. Lovecraft belongs among writers who cultivated a special manner consciously. As time passes, such writers tend to refine their style until an almost esoteric effect is produced. This makes for difficult reading, but if the style is warranted by the effect, it is certainly permissible. I feel that in the main Lovecraft justified his mannerisms by employing them skillfully and controlling them judiciously.
>
> If H. P. L. "lacked the ability to tell a plain tale and tell it straight," so did Machen, Conrad, Faulkner, and Dickens, to name just the first to come to mind. Neither clarity nor objectivity is necessary in the dream-like effect Lovecraft sought. (*WW* 108)

Wilcox, in a reply in the January 1953 issue, was not particularly convinced. But he doesn't help his cause by saying: "When Lovecraft was good, he was very, very good. I have never denied that he was. But when he was very, very good, as a general rule, he was writing more traditional stories: 'In the Vault,' for example" (*WW* 109). I fear that Mr. Wilcox will join the resident of Sauk City, but not very many others, in thinking that tale one of Lovecraft's best.

It is important to note that weird fiction, strictly considered, was both in short supply and underwent significant alterations in theme and focus during this period. The demise of the pulp magazines (*Weird Tales* finally folded in 1954), and the advent of the digest-sized magazine and the paperback book, resulted in an explosion of writing in the fields of mystery, suspense, and science fiction—but not weird fiction. What weird fiction did appear was far different from the cosmic horror of Lovecraft and his disciples, whether it be the intense focus on personal relationships we find in the work of Shirley Jackson (and, a bit later, Robert Aickman) or the fusion of genres we find in Ray Bradbury, Richard Matheson, Charles Beaumont, and others, much of which was explicitly non- or even anti-Lovecraftian.

And yet, Bradbury, whose earliest stories did appear in *Weird Tales* and whose first volume, *Dark Carnival* (1947), was published by Arkham House, retained a devotion to Lovecraft, even if his own work was almost entirely devoid of Lovecraftian influence. And it is notable that in such tales as "Usher II" (in *The Martian Chronicles,* 1950) and "The Mad Wizards of Mars" (*Maclean's,* September 1949; retitled "The Exiles," *Fantasy and Science Fiction,* Winter–Spring 1950), Lovecraft himself appears as a character, or is at least cited as taking his place with Poe, Hawthorne, Bierce, and other canonical writers of weird fiction.

But the hostility shown to Lovecraft at this time is exemplified by another controversy that broke out in 1956 when John Brunner, then a young British science fiction writer who had published the first few of his many notable novels, took aim at Lovecraft in his column "Rusty Chains" (*Inside and Science Fiction Advertiser,* March 1956; *WW* 164–70). It is a very odd article. Rambling from one subject to the next, Brunner starts by saying, "My claim is merely that he is an overrated and generally bad writer." He admits to a personal distaste for Lovecraft ("I so dislike the man that I haven't a single work of his in my collection of around 900 science fiction and fantasy magazines and books"), then ventures into an unfocused history of weird fiction from a largely sociological perspective. He praises Poe, apparently on the grounds that he dealt with madness and psychological aberration, but avers that this was a "narrow, unrewarding and repetitive" subject, so that it was difficult for later writers to expand upon it. He then goes on to say that "Lovecraft was a throwback, an atavism, deliberately cultivating the modes and manners of an earlier and vanished day"—but here Brunner, like so many other science fiction writers and critics, confuses Lovecraft's *style* with his *subject-matter,* which is forward-looking in its cosmicism and its very fusion of weird fiction and science fiction. The science fiction field, even more so than mainstream literature, was at this time fixated on a relatively simple and straightforward prose expression: its focus was entirely on *ideas* rather than *mode of expression.* Hence Brunner condemns Lovecraft for his richly textured idiom:

> Drunk on the splendor of words and feverishly seeking to capture the unreal weirdness of an opium dream, he was harried by black demons of his own invention to wander among imagined realms of evil whose only existence lay in the bewildering wood of dislocation produced by his use of obsolete terms without meaning to his readers, when on his and every one's doorstep the true terrors waited patiently for someone to notice them.

That sentence itself is unwittingly Lovecraftian in its density and elaborateness!

The September 1956 issue of *Inside* featured a series of rebuttals by Sam Moskowitz, Fritz Leiber, and Edward Wood, with a further note by Brunner (*WW* 170–76). Moskowitz stresses Lovecraft's mingling of horror and science fiction, although he awkwardly admits that he, like Brunner, has been unable to finish *At the Mountains of Madness.* Leiber's rebuttal is surprisingly ineffective, since he admits that many readers who have heard of Lovecraft being highly praised come away disappointed when actually reading him; but he chides Brunner for his "expression of the rather pampered modern distaste for any writing that is slow or difficult, that has not been carefully pruned and speeded up by clever, up-to-the-minute editing."

Wood simply declares that Brunner is expressing a subjective dislike of Lovecraft and trying to translate that into a critical condemnation. Brunner, in his response, refuses to yield on any point, although he claims that a colleague will pass on some Lovecraft texts that he might actually like. Whether that person ever did so, and whether Brunner ever revised his opinion of Lovecraft, is unclear.

But the fan world did more than just debate the value of Lovecraft's work. Several fans, in spite of the limited resources (and, I am sorry to say, limited education and expertise) at their disposal, did yeoman's work in gathering up Lovecraft's fugitive work or in charting his literary output. The chief figure in this movement was George T. Wetzel, who burst on the scene with a seven-volume mimeographed series that he published himself, *The Lovecraft Collectors Library* (SSR Publications, 1952–55). These booklets range from 23 to 42 pages. The first five reprint rare Lovecraft texts: two volumes of "selected essays" (although, oddly enough, the stories "Poetry and the Gods" and "The Street" are included); two volumes of "selected poetry"; and a volume of writings on amateur journalism. These volumes were the product of Wetzel's bibliographical researches, which had apparently begun in the 1940s, especially at the Fossil Collection of Amateur Journalism (then housed in the Philadelphia Free Library) and resulted in volume 7 of the series, "Bibliographies," where Wetzel charted Lovecraft's "amateur press works" and Robert E. Briney catalogued his "professional works and miscellany." Volume 6 was a slim collection of "commentaries"—essays and memoirs mostly taken from the Summer 1940 issue of the *Olympian*.

Wetzel had been writing on Lovecraft since the mid-1940s. One of his earliest pieces was "Some Thoughts on the Lovecraft Pattern," published in *Fantasy Commentator* (Fall 1946), an impressive fanzine edited by A. Langley Searles, who long remained a vital presence in weird fiction fandom. Wetzel's "Genesis of the Cthulhu Mythos" (*Fantastic Story Mag,* March 1954) was one of several thoughtful articles on Lovecraft's pseudomythology that he eventually fashioned into "The Cthulhu Mythos: A Study," published in volume six of the *Lovecraft Collectors Library* and later (as "Notes on the Cthulhu Mythos") in *The Shuttered Room and Other Pieces.*

But Wetzel's bibliographical work is his signal contribution to Lovecraft studies. Finding the Laney-Evans bibliography of 1943 woefully inadequate, he spent years combing through amateur journals and turning up all manner of works by Lovecraft (including many published under pseudonyms) that had not been known before. Understandably, there are errors and omissions, but Wetzel had now established Lovecraft bibliography on a sound footing, and it required only a more scholarly approach to bring his work to fruition. Briney's task in charting Lovecraft's professionally published works was substantially easier, as he had little trouble locating *Weird Tales* and other pulp magazines and anthologies where Lovecraft's work had appeared.

Another pioneering scholar, although he wrote only a few articles, was Matthew H. Onderdonk, whose "The Lord of R'lyeh" first appeared in *Fantasy Commentator* (Spring 1945) and was reprinted in volume six of *The Lovecraft Collectors Library.* This article studied Lovecraft from a philosophical perspective, proposing that the entities in Lovecraft's Mythos were not supernatural but "supernormal." Fully aware that Lovecraft was a materialist and atheist, Onderdonk read his fiction as an instantiation, not a defiance, of that outlook. A later article, "Charon—in Reverse, or, H. P. Lovecraft versus the 'Realists' of Fantasy" (*Fantasy Commentator,* Spring 1948), stress that the "gods" of the Mythos are "not evil in the narrow human sense except as their manifestations interfered with the small purposes of man. . . . The activity of these forces is beyond good and evil, absolutely amoral." It would be decades before these provocative ideas were further developed.

Wetzel, Leiber, and Onderdonk were the leading "fan" critics of the period, but others contributed their mite. The young Lin Carter, finding a fascination with Lovecraft's Mythos, produced two interesting if error-filled compilations, "H. P. Lovecraft: The Books" (*Inside and Science Fiction Advertiser,* March, May, and September 1956) and "H. P. Lovecraft: The Gods" (*Inside Science Fiction,* October 1957), charting both the real and imaginary books in Lovecraft's tales and the "gods" in his pseudomythology. In the amateur world, Willametta Keffer wrote "Howard P(seudonym) Lovecraft: The Many Names of HPL" (*Fossil,* July 1958). She was the first to suggest that Lovecraft was the author of two articles signed "El Imparcial" in the *United Amateur* in 1915–16; August Derleth rejected the conjecture,[15] but Keffer turned out to be right.

As an indication, however tenuous, of Lovecraft's increasing worldwide celebrity, several fans from Australia and New Zealand began exploring Lovecraft, chiefly from a bibliographical perspective. Leon Stone wrote a column, "Lovecraftiana," in his amateur periodical *Koolinda* that extended from April 1948 to December 1952. T. G. L. Cockcroft began his explorations of Lovecraft with "Notes on the Works of H. P. Lovecraft" (*Woomera,* September 1951); he continued his researches sporadically for the next three decades.

Then, out of the blue, came the special Lovecraft issue of *Fresco* (Spring 1958), the student literary magazine of the University of Detroit. The editor, Steve Eisner, thanked George

15. "New HPL Pseudonyms Rejected by Derleth," *Fossil* (October 1958).

Wetzel, August Derleth, and others for their assistance. It was probably Wetzel who persuaded such individuals as David H. Keller, Matthew H. Onderdonk, and others to contribute to it; Derleth may have lured Fritz Leiber, Joseph Payne Brennan, and others. In any case, the issue is a fine compilation, with notable articles both biographical (Leiber's "My Correspondence with Lovecraft"; Samuel Loveman's "Lovecraft as a Conversationalist"; George W. Macauley's "Lovecraft and the Amateur Press") and critical (Onderdonk's "Charon—in Reverse"; Thomas Ollive Mabbott's "Lovecraft as a Student of Poe"; Wetzel's "The Mechanistic-Supernatural of H.P.L.").

Brennan's piece ("H.P.L.—An Informal Commentary") is quite slight, and in this regard it matches his 14-page *H. P. Lovecraft: A Bibliography* (1952) and his 8-page *H. P. Lovecraft: An Evaluation* (1955). Brennan had slightly better success in discussing Lovecraft's poetry and other issues in random brief articles in his journal *Macabre* beginning in the late 1950s and extending into the 1970s.

Fresco went on to serialise James Warren Thomas's "H. P. Lovecraft: A Portrait in Words" (Fall 1958–Summer 1959). This was an abridgement of his master's thesis (the first academic paper ever written on Lovecraft), "Howard Phillips Lovecraft: A Self-Portrait" (Brown University, 1950). Thomas was one of the first to read in detail the letters that Lovecraft wrote to his aunts during his New York period (1924–26), which were still largely uncatalogued in the John Hay Library; but Thomas was so offended by what he believed to be Lovecraft's "snobbishness and race hatred" that he cast unwarranted judgments on Lovecraft's character (he was "narrow and prejudiced and strait-laced and lacking in ordinary human feeling"). There are reports that Derleth attempted to suppress the publication of the thesis by asserting copyright ownership of the Lovecraft letters Thomas liberally quoted in the text; but Thomas at least got it published in *Fresco,* although it did not seem to attract much attention among the Lovecraftian fan community.

Derleth issued his third "stopgap" volume, *The Shuttered Room and Other Pieces* (Arkham House, 1959). It is notable for its inclusion of Lovecraft's very early fictional juvenilia ("The Little Glass Bottle" and so on), the whimsy "Old Bugs," and other curiosities. But Derleth presented a very unsound text of the commonplace book (which he duly "annotated," chiefly by indicating which items he had used to write his "posthumous collaborations"). Of the memoirs, Wandrei's "Lovecraft in Providence" is largely a retread of his piece in *Marginalia;* Derleth's own "Lovecraft as Mentor" is another compilation of extracts from letters; the articles by Dorothy C. Walter ("Three Hours with H. P. Lovecraft") and Alfred Galpin ("Memories of a Friendship") have some value. Derleth also printed some criticism, including Carter's essays on the books and gods in Lovecraft's Mythos and Wetzel's "Notes on the Cthulhu Mythos."

At about the same time, Derleth published a slim pamphlet, *Some Notes on H. P. Lovecraft* (Arkham House, 1959), which dealt not incapably on various "myths" that had accrued about Lovecraft; but its chief value is in printing a truncated version of the notes that R. H. Barlow took during Lovecraft's visit with him in 1934. Because Derleth committed the gaffe of not copyrighting the 43-page booklet, it has been reprinted in facsimile numerous times in the past few decades.

V. Paperbacks and Movies (1960–1971)

No one could have predicted, when the 1960s dawned, that Lovecraft would by the end of the decade become something of a bestselling author. As the decade began, his stories were largely unavailable in hardcover, as the early Arkham House editions of 1939–44 (*The Outsider and Others, Beyond the Wall of Sleep,* and *Marginalia*) were long out of print, and even the numerous anthologies in which they had appeared—by Derleth and others—were difficult to find.

But, even before Derleth undertook the reprinting of the Lovecraft fiction, a surprising development occurred: Lovecraft became something of a media darling. The first media adaptation of a Lovecraft work had occurred all the way back in 1949, when the CBS radio programme *Suspense* broadcast a dramatic reading of "The Dunwich Horror." But then Caedmon—a leader in the realm of spoken-word LPs—brought out an LP featuring Roddy McDowell reading "The Outsider" and "The Hound." McDowell's readings are lively and pungent, as his distinctive voice augments the flamboyance of these early tales.

Three Lovecraft-related films appeared in succession: *The Haunted Palace* (1963), *Die, Monster, Die!* (1965; released in the UK as *Monster of Terror*), and *The Shuttered Room* (1967). The first is an adaptation of *The Case of Charles Dexter Ward,* with a screenplay by noted weird writer Charles Beaumont and with Vincent Price in the starring role, playing both Charles Dexter Ward and his ancestor and lookalike, Joseph Curwen. Lon Chaney, Jr. played Simon Orne in a relatively small role; otherwise, few actors of note appeared. The film appeared as part of Roger Corman's Poe series, since it was believed that Lovecraft's name would not be sufficient to attract a significant audience. But the film now seems cheesy and contrived—a typical B-movie of the period, with crude sets and Price overacting as he customarily does.

Still worse is *Die, Monster, Die!,* based on "The Colour out of Space." This one stars Boris Karloff as Nahum Whitly [*sic*] and Nick Adams as one Stephen Reinhart, who plays the fiancé of Whitly's daughter Susan (played by Suzan Farmer). The film, directed by Daniel Haller and with a screenplay by Jerry Sohl, is set in England. Karloff plays the entire film in a wheelchair. Let us state charitably that the film does not adhere very closely to the story.

The Shuttered Room is, of course, an adaptation of one of the Lovecraft-Derleth "posthumous collaborations." As a film, it may be the most successful of the lot, although the Lovecraftian content is pretty slim. Gig Young, Carol Lynley, and Oliver Reed—all notable actors of the period—do a creditable job in what proves to be a horror-laden domestic melodrama. The film was directed by David Greene, with a screenplay by D. B. Ledrov and Nathaniel Tanchuk.

Derleth does not state that the fees or royalties derived from these films assisted him in the reprinting of the Lovecraft stories that he undertook at this time. I imagine that at least the first of them did come in handy, even if the fee was not especially robust. What Derleth does say is that, when the decision was made to reissue the stories—in *The Dunwich Horror and Others* (1963), *At the Mountains of Madness and Other Novels* (1964), and *Dagon and Other Macabre Tales* (1965)—he had to cut various corners and delay other Arkham House books by several years. One cut corner was his decision to use the plates of the World *Best Super-*

natural Stories volume of 1945 as the basis of *The Dunwich Horror*. The result was a bibliographical anomaly, since the pagination of the frontmatter is confused: Derleth omitted his brief introduction to the World edition and printed a much longer one, taking up pages ix–xx, but the book proper then begins with a blank page 9 (there are no pages 1–8) and the first story ("In the Vault") on page 10. Moreover, he added two stories—"The Shadow over Innsmouth" and "The Shadow out of Time"—but set them in the usual Garamond font used in other Arkham House books, even though the World edition does not use that font. But no matter. Aside from the first two stories ("In the Vault" and "Pickman's Model") as well as "The Terrible Old Man," the volume could well be said to contain much of the best of Lovecraft's short and novella-length fiction.

At the Mountains of Madness contains all three of Lovecraft's short novels along with several other stories, including three of the four shorter Randolph Carter tales (Derleth, like many others, apparently did not realise that "The Unnamable" was also part of this informal "cycle"). *Dagon* included the balance of the short fiction, as well as the ghostwritten tale "Under the Pyramids" (as "Imprisoned with the Pharaohs") and the collaboration "In the Walls of Eryx." It concludes with "Supernatural Horror in Literature." Derleth's brief introduction includes what purports to be a chronology of Lovecraft's fiction, but it is seriously erroneous, since it merely alphabetises those tales written in a given year. Derleth surely had access to numerous chronologies that Lovecraft himself had prepared and sent to correspondents, but he evidently could not be troubled to unearth any of these.

The three-volume fiction edition—which Derleth vowed to keep in print in perpetuity—was by no means all that he did to bring Lovecraft's work into print through Arkham House. Prior to the series, he had assembled a slim volume called *Dreams and Fancies* (1962), a selection of extracts from Lovecraft's letters where he recounts the bizarre dreams he had over a lifetime. Because he could not find enough such extracts to fill even a small volume, Derleth augmented the book with several short stories based explicitly on those dreams, as well as the novella "The Shadow out of Time."

Then there was *Collected Poems* (1963). The title is highly misleading—or, rather, it takes advantage of the ambiguity inherent in the use of the adjective "collected" in a title: it can either be a synonym for "complete," or it can refer merely to those items that the editor decided to collect for the occasion. It is clearly the latter meaning that is intended here, for the 134-page book contains no more than one-third of Lovecraft's total poetic output, and the poems were largely taken from the poetry sections in *Beyond the Wall of Sleep* and *Something about Cats.* In reality, the volume was a showcase for the artwork of Derleth's Wisconsin colleague Frank Utpatel, and it was delayed for many years while Utpatel slowly worked on the illustrations. But the book was well worth the wait, for these are some of the most evocative illustrations appearing in any Lovecraft edition.

Along the same lines was *3 Tales of Horror* (1967), designed to display the artwork of Lee Brown Coye, who had done the dust jacket illustrations to the three-volume Lovecraft fiction set. Opinions differ on the merits of Coye's work, but he certainly evolved a distinctive and readily recognisable style, and the volume is about as close to a "coffee table book" as Arkham House ever published.

There was also *Autobiography: Some Notes on a Nonentity,* a booklet issued in a run of 500 copies featuring the joint imprint of Arkham House and Villiers Press (London). At only 17 pages, it is merely a bit of ephemera, containing Lovecraft's autobiographical essay of 1933 with not terribly helpful annotations by Derleth.

Two other volumes were much more significant. In 1965 appeared, at long last, the first volume of *Selected Letters,* covering the years 1911–24. The project that Derleth (and especially Wandrei) had conceived almost from the moment of Lovecraft's death had finally begun to come to fruition, although the remaining four volumes would take more than a decade to appear. For all the poor editing, mistranscription (including the repeated misspelling of Rheinhart Kleiner's first name [as "Reinhardt"]), and other blemishes, the volume was notable for its mere existence. Had any other author of weird or science fiction from the pulp era had his letters published? I am not aware of it. The reason for the delay in issuance was obvious: Derleth continued to get more and more letters, over decades, from colleagues, and these documents continually interrupted the chronological sequence that Derleth had decided upon, thereby forcing him back to the drawing board over and over again. Derleth might also have been concerned about the sales potential of the volume. Nevertheless, he persevered and issued the second volume (containing letters of 1925–29) in 1968 and the third volume (containing letters from 1929 to 1931) in 1971, just around the time of his death. That third volume, at 451 pages, is the largest of the set and perhaps the most intellectually substantial: it shows Lovecraft truly coming into his own as a thinker, with long, ruminative letters to Frank Belknap Long, Woodburn Harris, Elizabeth Toldridge, and others. Derleth allowed much of his own correspondence from Lovecraft to be included; but Wandrei, concerned about his privacy, allowed only extracts from ten letters to him to be published.

The other volume to appear was *The Dark Brotherhood and Other Pieces* (1966), the fourth and final "miscellany" volume issued by Derleth. Perhaps the slightest of the four, it nonetheless contains much work of interest. Among the rare works by Lovecraft to be published were *Alfredo* (1918), the charming verse "tragedy" presenting caricatures of Alfred Galpin, Rheinhart Kleiner, Maurice W. Moe, and himself; three of the revisions of C. M. Eddy's tales in *Weird Tales* (the first of the Eddy revisions, "Ashes," was not included, even though Derleth printed in *Selected Letters I* a letter where Lovecraft indicates his revision of the story); and the surviving text (outline and one chapter) of *The Cancer of Superstition* (1926), a volume that Harry Houdini had commissioned Lovecraft and Eddy to write, but which was abandoned upon Houdini's unexpected death.

There is only one memoir—C. M. Eddy's slight "Walks with H. P. Lovecraft"—but several critical essays of much interest. The best of them is Fritz Leiber's "Through Hyperspace with Brown Jenkin," a challenging essay on Lovecraft's contribution to science fiction. William Scott Home's "The Lovecraft 'Books': Some Addenda and Corrigenda" and Andrew E. Rothovius's "Lovecraft and the New England Megaliths" are error-sprinkled and unreliable, but John E. Vetter's "Lovecraft's Illustrators" is a worthy first attempt to chronicle and analyse the artists who had interpreted Lovecraft's work up to that time. Derleth, in his "Final Notes," reprinted the bulk of *Some Notes on H. P. Lovecraft*.

By far the most controversial item in the book was Jack L. Chalker's "Howard Phillips Lovecraft: A Bibliography." In all frankness, this work—first published separately as *The New H. P. Lovecraft Bibliography* (Anthem Press, 1962)—was largely a ripoff of Wetzel's 1955 bibliography, with some minimal updates. It follows the exact sequence of Wetzel's work, with its division between amateur press works and professional publications, and in other ways duplicates Wetzel's work with little acknowledgement. Chalker, a fan of the era who published the magazine *Mirage* (and, surprisingly, in later years became a popular writer of fantasy novels), was not in a position to do much original research on Lovecraft bibliography, and his borrowings from Wetzel are all too apparent.

At the end of the decade, Derleth issued *The Horror in the Museum and Other Revisions* (1970). But this book, appearing at a time when his health was deteriorating, is one of the most error-riddled volumes Arkham House ever published; it looks to be simply a bound set of uncorrected proofs. Among the hilarious errors in the book is the rendering of "Old Ones" as "Old Bones" in "The Mound." The volume merely brings together the revisions published in previous Arkham House volumes, with the addition of R. H. Barlow's "'Till A' the Seas.'"

The signal advantage of Derleth's reprinting of Lovecraft's fiction was that it led to numerous paperback and hardcover reprints, both in the United States and in England. Among the first paperback editions were two volumes by Lancer Books, *The Dunwich Horror and Others* (1963) and *The Colour out of Space* (1964). These volumes essentially constituted a reprint of the Arkham House *Dunwich Horror,* although "The Shadow over Innsmouth" did not appear in either volume. The first went through at least two printings, the second at least four. In England, Gollancz reprinted *At the Mountains of Madness and Other Novels* and *Dagon and Other Macabre Tales* in hardcover in 1966 and 1967, respectively, and issued another volume, *The Shadow out of Time and Other Tales of Horror* (1968), containing stories by Lovecraft as well as ten "posthumous collaborations." The paperback publisher Panther Books issued *The Case of Charles Dexter Ward* (1963), *The Lurking Fear and Other Stories* (1964), *At the Mountains of Madness and Other Tales of Terror* (1968), *Dagon and Other Macabre Tales* (1969—an abridged version of the Arkham House edition), and *The Tomb and Other Tales* (1969).

This set the stage for the so-called Arkham Edition of H. P. Lovecraft, an eleven-volume series issued by Beagle Books (a New York firm headed by fantasy writer Peter S. Beagle). In fact, however, only four of the volumes contained work entirely by Lovecraft: *The Tomb and Other Tales* (1970; a reprint of the Panther volume), *At the Mountains of Madness and Other Tales of Terror* (1971), *The Lurking Fear and Other Stories* (1971), and *The Case of Charles Dexter Ward* (1971). The other volumes of the Arkham Edition were *Nine Stories from The Horror in the Museum and Other Revisions* (1971; in fact, ten stories were included), a two-volume paperback reprint of Derleth's anthology *Tales of the Cthulhu Mythos* (Arkham House, 1969), and five volumes of stories by Derleth, including three volumes of "posthumous collaborations." The Beagle edition was later taken over by Ballantine Books and were kept in print for many years. But because this series could not include the stories in the two Lancer editions (Lancer had exclusive paperback rights to those tales), the Beagle volumes in essence feature lesser tales, with the exception of "The Shadow over Innsmouth" (included in *The Lurking Fear*), as well as two of Lovecraft's three short novels.

To augment the confusion, Lin Carter edited two volumes of Lovecraft's tales for his Ballantine Adult Fantasy series, *The Dream-Quest of Unknown Kadath* (1970) and *The Doom that Came to Sarnath* (1971), in which there was a certain overlap in contents with the Beagle/Ballantine edition. Carter's preference was for imaginary-world fantasy of the Dunsany or Clark Ashton Smith sort, and his volumes are almost entirely made up of Lovecraft's "Dunsanian" fantasies. They are creditable compilations, although the sporadic commentary that Carter has added is not terribly illuminating.

We cannot bypass *The Shadow over Innsmouth and Other Stories of Horror* (1971), edited by Margaret Ronan and issued by

Scholastic Books. Ronan was formerly Margaret Sylvester, a late correspondent of Lovecraft; she does not refer to her association with the author in her brief introduction. Scholastic Books made its paperback books (usually costing 95¢ or less) available to students for purchase through their schools. An anthology by Betty Owen, *11 Great Horror Stories* (Scholastic, 1969), had led off with "The Dunwich Horror."

It is unclear whether all these US and UK editions had anything to do with the translation of Lovecraft's work into numerous other languages—a trend that markedly advanced in the 1960s. Lovecraft had appeared in Italian as early as 1954, when "The Outsider" had been translated in the magazine *Pandora* (January 1954); but his work did not become widely available in Italy until the 1960s. The anthology *Storie di fantasmi* (1960), edited by Carlo Fruttero and Franco Lucentini, contained "The Call of Cthulhu" and "The Dunwich Horror." The magazine *Urania* No. 310 (16 June 1963), edited by Fruttero, was entirely devoted to Lovecraft, containing three stories including "The Whisperer in Darkness."

This set the stage for the first of two competing lines of books from leading Italian publishers: *Le montagne della follia* (Sugar, 1966) and *I mostri all'angolo della strada* (Mondadori, 1966). The former, anonymously edited by Massimo Pini, contained two short novels and two stories; the latter, a volume of some 448 pages edited by Fruttero and Lucentini, contained sixteen of Lovecraft's best stories—or, rather, fifteen, with the unfortunate inclusion of a posthumous collaboration, "The Gable Window." In spite of that, the latter series—issued by what was and is regarded as Italy's most prestigious publisher—is the superior of the two. Sugar followed up its first book with *La casa delle streghe e altri racconti* (1967), also edited by Pini. Many more editions appeared in the 1970s.

In Germany, Lovecraft first appeared not in a magazine or anthology, but in a full-length volume, *12 grusel Stories* (Wilhelm Heyne Verlag, 1965). The book is an abridged translation of the Arkham House *Dunwich Horror and Others* (1963), although anomalously such key stories as "The Rats in the Walls" and "The Call of Cthulhu" were omitted. Heyne was a popular publisher, but three years later a volume of a very different sort appeared: *Cthulhu: Geistergeschichten* (Insel Verlag, 1968). The book, containing six stories (four of which had appeared in *12 grusel Stories*), was translated by H. C. Artmann, a highly regarded poet and novelist whose interest in weird fiction is indicated by novel-length parodies of *Dracula* and *Frankenstein*. Unfortunately, Artmann did not write any preface or introduction to the volume, so we are unable to gauge his opinion of Lovecraft.[1] The book was published in paperback by Suhrkamp and went through many reprintings.

Insel followed up this volume with *Das Ding auf der Schwelle* (1969), part of its extensive Bibliothek des Hauses Usher (Library of the House of Usher) series, which translated many works by English and American weird writers into German. *Berge des Wahnsinns* (1970) and *Der Fall Charles Dexter Ward* (1971; also containing "The Shadow over Innsmouth") appeared in quick succession from Insel and were also reprinted frequently by Suhrkamp.

Denoël continued its publications of Lovecraft volumes in French with *Je suis d'ailleurs* (1961). This book appeared in February; toward the end of the year Jacques Bergier published his influential essay "Lovecraft, ce grand génie venu d'ailleurs" (*Planète,* October–November 1961), which elaborated on his views

1. Artmann later wrote a short play in German (with an English title, all in lower-case), entitled *how lovecraft saved the world.* See *The Best of H. C. Artmann,* ed. Klaus Reichert (Frankfurt am Main: Suhrkamp, 1975), 166–68.

of Lovecraft as a philosophical and psychological outsider. Thereafter there was something of a lag in French book publications, although Lovecraft appeared widely in magazines and anthologies. But toward the end of the decade "Supernatural Horror in Literature" was translated into a foreign language for the first time: *Épouvante et surnaturel en littérature* (Christian Bourgois, 1969). It is quite possible that this appearance influenced Tzvetan Todorov, whose *Introduction à la littérature fantastique* (Editions du Seuil, 1970) appeared the following year, and which cites Lovecraft's treatise sporadically. Todorov's monograph was translated into English in 1973 as *The Fantastic: A Structural Approach to a Literary Genre.* Lovecraft's essay was translated by Bergier and François Truchaud; the latter also translated *Dagon et autres récits de terreur* (Pierre Belfond, 1969).

Translations into Spanish (*Obras escogidas* [Ediciones Acervo, 1966]; *En las montañas de la locura* [Editorial Seix Barral, 1968]), Portuguese (*O que sussurrava nas trevas* [Edições G R D, 1966]), Dutch (*Macabere Verhalen* [Uitgeverij Contact, 1967]; *Het gefluister in de duisternis* [A. W. Bruna, 1968]; *Heksensabbat* [A. W. Bruna, 1969]) also appeared in the course of the 1960s. But one of the most significant volumes was the anthology *Los mitos de Cthulhu* (Madrid: Alianza, 1969), edited by Rafael Llopis. The volume, which was frequently reprinted over the next several decades, contained far more than what are generally considered Lovecraft's Mythos tales (including some, such as "The Doom That Came to Sarnath," that are only tangentially related to Lovecraft's evolving pseudomythology); it also includes tales by such of Lovecraft's predecessors as Poe, Robert W. Chambers, and others. The volume thereby ends up being a much more aesthetically cogent book than Derleth's own *Tales of the Cthulhu Mythos,* published that same year.

Criticism in foreign languages was not extensive in the

1960s, but it is impossible to ignore the appearance of the nearly 400-page special issue of *L'Herne* No. 12 (1969) on Lovecraft. This prestigious French periodical, founded in 1963, had previously devoted special issues to such titans as Borges, Céline, and Dostoevsky, so the mere selection of Lovecraft for such treatment is highly significant. The actual contents of the issue are less spectacular: it features some translations of works by Lovecraft, some translations of articles or memoirs on Lovecraft in English (several of them taken from *The Dark Brotherhood,* published only three years earlier), and some original articles in French.

Borges himself, in collaboration with Esther Zembroain de Torres, wrote a slim treatise, *Introducción a la literatura norteamericana* (1967) that politely discussed Lovecraft in half a paragraph—precisely the same amount given to Hawthorne and other canonical writers. The book was translated into English as *An Introduction to American Literature* (1971).

Then there was a passage in Marc Slonim's column "European Notebook," in which he took note of the numerous French, Spanish, and Italian translations of Lovecraft (which he declares are "mostly very good"), then went on to make the startling assertion that "The Spanish essayist José Luis Garcia recently included Lovecraft in a list of 10 best writers of the world."[2] There are several problems with this comment. First, the essayist in question is José Luis Garci (b. 1944), who, although in his early years he was a film critic and also wrote some science fiction stories, later (subsequent to Slonim's article) became a well-known film director, producer, and screenwriter. His actual statement on Lovecraft has not been unearthed; given that it was uttered

2. Marc Slonim, "European Notebook," *New York Times Book Review* (17 May 1970): 14.

(if indeed it was) by someone who was only twenty-six years old at the time, it may not count for much.

In spite of all these editions, in both the English-speaking world and in foreign languages, Lovecraft criticism in the 1960s was in relatively short supply—and some of it was astonishingly hostile. First there was Damon Knight, a notoriously harsh critic of science fiction who directed two review columns in *Fantasy and Science Fiction* to Lovecraft. The first column, in May 1960, although titled "Iä! Yog-Sothoth! Yah, Yah, Yah!," actually covered Lovecraft only tangentially, disputing the notion (which he attributes to Lovecraft, although it is not clear why he does so) that "'mystery' goes out when the lights go on. Masters of the macabre like H. P. Lovecraft tried so hard (and so successfully) to avoid actually introducing any of their eldritch horrors, that the most dreadful thing about these stories is their tedium."[3] This is an odd thing to say about Lovecraft in particular, since he clearly introduces Cthulhu in "The Call of Cthulhu," Yog-Sothoth (or, at any rate, his offspring) in "The Dunwich Horror," and the shoggoth in *At the Mountains of Madness*—but only after a careful build-up that creates a powerful effect of cumulative horror. But perhaps this is what Knight found "tedious."

Knight's next column, in the August 1960 issue, is explicitly titled "The Tedious Mr. Lovecraft." He reports being taken to task by such critics as Fritz Leiber and James Wade over the notion that Lovecraft's monsters are "inexplicit." Knight actually acknowledges the criticism—but it only gives him more ammunition to attack Lovecraft. Unfortunately, he does so by examining various items in *The Shuttered Room and Other Pieces* and uses as his clinching argument—"The Shuttered Room," a

---

3. "Iä! Yog-Sothoth! Yah! Yah! Yah!," *Fantasy and Science Fiction* 18, No. 5 (May 1960): 80.

"posthumous collaboration" whose writing was entirely by Derleth. After quoting a lengthy passage in which the monster shows itself, Knight concludes:

> Now, this is my real objection to Lovecraft and his imitators (aside from their arthritic styles): the monster does appear, sometimes, but only as a sort of peep-show. It is never brought onstage, as Leiber's and Sturgeon's monsters are, to act and react against the other characters. Thus the story remains in embryo, is never developed . . .[4]

The idea of any of Lovecraft's extraterrestrial entities (or "gods") "acting and reacting" against the human characters is beyond grotesque. In fact, a decade and a half later Knight could have pointed to a Lovecraftian author who did exactly this: Brian Lumley, who in the novel *Beneath the Moors* (1974) has the water-lizard Bokrug (from "The Doom That Came to Sarnath") engage in a genial conversation with the human protagonist, Professor Ewart Masters. For unintentional humour, this passage would be difficult to beat.

Then there was Avram Davidson's exuberantly abusive review of *The Survivor and Others*—a curiously delayed one, appearing six years after the book was published—in *Fantasy and Science Fiction* (May 1963). He begins by delivering a backhanded compliment to Lovecraft—"Howard Phillips Lovecraft, Heaven knows, had a talent for writing which was of no mean proportion; only what he did with this talent was a shame and a caution and an eldritch horror"—and goes down from there, objecting to the "rugous [*sic*], squamous, amorphous nasties" who populate Lovecraft's fiction. And he concludes that "Lovecraft

4. "The Tedious Mr. Lovecraft," *Fantasy and Science Fiction* 19, No. 2 (August 1960): 101. Knight does conclude that "out of this grey figure, through his voluminous letters, flowed an astonishing warmth and generosity toward younger writers. That he was much loved is undoubted" (101–2).

was nutty as a five-dollar fruit cake."[5] Davidson, editor of *F&SF* (1962–64), is emblematic of those science fiction writers who disdain Lovecraft both for his style (it is not up-to-date and lean) and his subject-matter (it is dark and paints an unwholesomely lugubrious portrait of the insignificant role of humanity in the cosmos).

August Derleth was understandably irritated with the review, commenting in a letter to Ramsey Campbell that "Davidson has a phobia—a sick one—about HPL and habitually downgrades and patronizes anything with the Arkham House imprint."[6] Samuel D. Russell attempted a rebuttal of Davidson, Edmund Wilson, and other hostile critics in a two-part article, "Open Season on Lovecraft" (*Haunted,* March and December 1964), but his comments are of little consequence.

The most wide-ranging condemnation of Lovecraft came from Colin Wilson, a British cultural critic who had gained notoriety for *The Outsider* (1956), published when he was twenty-four, and dealing with a wide array of literary figures who were social outsiders. It is clear that Wilson was unaware of Lovecraft at this time. But when he came to write *The Strength to Dream: Literature and the Imagination* (1961), he had remedied the defect—although one rather wishes he hadn't.

Wilson begins his treatise with a ten-page polemic against Lovecraft. He states that "Lovecraft carried on a lifelong guerrilla warfare against civilization and materialism, albeit he was a somewhat hysterical and neurotic combatant" (1). He goes on:

> In some ways, Lovecraft is a horrifying figure. In his "war with rationality," he brings to mind W. B. Yeats. But, unlike Yeats, he is sick, and his closest relation is with Peter Kürten, the Düsseldorf murderer, who admitted that his days in solitary confinement were

---

5. Quoted in de Camp, *Lovecraft: A Biography* 439.

6. Campbell and Derleth, *Letters to Arkham* 213.

> spent conjuring up sexual-sadistic fantasies. Lovecraft is totally withdrawn; he has rejected "reality"; he seems to have lost all sense of health that would make a normal man turn back halfway. (1–2)

Exactly what could have led Wilson to lambaste the inoffensive Lovecraft in this manner is difficult to ascertain. The very fact that he puts quotation marks around "reality" would seem to suggest that Wilson himself is doubtful of what he actually means—and the rest of his account does not clarify the matter.

Wilson is obviously so ignorant of the essentials of Lovecraft's philosophy that he repeats the flagrantly false claim that "What is so interesting about Lovecraft is the extraordinary consistency of his attempt to undermine materialism" (3). Lovecraft himself was a materialist and atheist; if, in his fiction, he seeks to demonstrate that a purely materialistic system is an unsound conception of the universe, it is because Lovecraft is depicting what is frightening to *him* (he himself would have been more disturbed than Wilson to contemplate the downfall or overthrow of mechanistic materialism) and for the sake of imaginative liberation.

Wilson goes on to make a number of anachronistic and misleading comments, such as his observation that "His stories are full of horror-film conventions" (8), although Lovecraft wrote at a time long before such conventions had actually become established. This remark was made as an example of how "Lovecraft is a very bad writer" (7–8). And yet, it is striking that Wilson goes on to say:

> But although Lovecraft is such a bad writer, he has something of the same kind of importance as Kafka. If his work fails as literature, it still holds an interest as a psychological case history. Here was a man who made no attempt whatever to come to terms with life. He hated modern civilization, particularly its confident belief in progress and science. (8)

That final sentence is the key to Wilson's distaste, as we shall see.

It should be apparent that Wilson's screed is a childish whine against a writer with whose philosophical outlook (which, in any case, he fundamentally misunderstands) he does not agree with; all the attendant abuse is designed to justify this disagreement. And yet, to the extent that Wilson mentions Lovecraft in the same breath as Yeats and Kafka, one could say that even this attack elevated Lovecraft by considering him as some kind of canonical author who cannot be merely ignored but has to be combatted with whatever rhetorical weapons are available.

Derleth, understandably, did not take kindly to Wilson's remarks. He forcefully rebutted them in the introduction to *The Dunwich Horror and Others* (1963). More provocatively, he got in touch with Wilson almost as soon as *The Strength to Dream* was published in England, and essentially dared Wilson to write a Lovecraftian novel himself. Wilson eventually complied by writing *The Mind Parasites* (1967), first published in England and published in the US by Arkham House. He followed it up with *The Philosopher's Stone* (1969) and *The Space Vampires* (1976), forming a loose trilogy. It was in a prefatory note to the second volume that he admits to his bias:

> A large part of the book [*The Strength to Dream*] was inevitably devoted to the work of H. P. Lovecraft . . . I pointed out that although Lovecraft possesses a gloomy imaginative power that compares with Poe, he is basically an atrocious writer . . . and his work is finally more interesting as case history than literature.
>
> . . . Lovecraft's novels [*sic*] are not about ideas, but about an emotion—an emotion of violent and total rejection of our civilisation, which I, being rather cheerful by temperament, do not happen to share.[7]

---

7. "Prefatory Note" to *The Philosopher's Stone* 18–19.

That is all one needs to know. And yet, Wilson's polemic had virtually no influence on the subsequent course of Lovecraft criticism, since it was so transparently based upon an idiosyncratic perspective that few shared. Wilson—who subsequently wrote an owlish discussion of the Lovecraft-Eddy story "The Loved Dead" in *Order of Assassins: The Psychology of Murder* (1972) and wrote an error-riddled entry on Lovecraft for E. F. Bleiler's *Supernatural Fiction Writers* (1982)—largely destroyed whatever reputation he had by his credulousness in regard to occult and paranormal phenomena.

By contrast, the otherwise unknown Drake Douglas included a chapter on Lovecraft in his popular history of weird fiction, *Horror!* (Macmillan, 1966). The chapter is flamboyantly praiseworthy of Lovecraft; but throughout his treatise Douglas unwittingly testifies to his mediocrity as a critic and historian, so the praise amounts to nothing.

Quite a bit better is the work of longtime science fiction fan and historian Sam Moskowitz, whose article "H. P. Lovecraft: A Study in Horror," first published in *Science Fantasy* (1960), was included in Moskowitz's widely reprinted *Explorers of the Infinite: Shapers of Science Fiction* (1963). Even though Moskowitz propounded the erroneous conjecture that "The Colour out of Space" was first submitted to (and rejected by) *Weird Tales* before it was sent to *Amazing Stories,* his placement of Lovecraft within the realm of science fiction was significant.

Also significant, brief as it was, was the small entry on Lovecraft in James D. Hart's standard reference work *The Oxford Companion to American Literature* (4th edition, 1965). The entry was expanded in the 1983 edition.

The fan world was not notably active in the 1960s; at any rate, Lovecraft did not come up for discussion to any great extent. We need not pay much attention to Redd Boggs's mimeographed fanzine *The Lovecraftsman,* which published only four issues (each of them two pages long) from May 1963 to Autumn 1965. Perhaps its most notable (?) contribution was a brief piece by Arthur Jean Cox, "Lovecrap" (Spring 1964), which Cox elaborated upon in the article "The Call of Nature: A Note on 'The Call of Cthulhu' by Howard Phillips Lovecraft" (*Science Fiction Review,* October 1970). The title says it all: in Cox's learned estimation, Cthulhu is a big turd.

H. P. Lovecraft: A Symposium (1963) is the transcript of a panel discussion on Lovecraft featuring Fritz Leiber, Robert Bloch, Samuel D. Russell, Arthur Jean Cox, and Leland Sapiro. The discussion is occasionally illuminating. The pamphlet was published jointly by the *Riverside Quarterly* and the Los Angeles Science Fantasy Society; the magazine only began publication the next year, continuing all the way down to 1993, the entire run edited by Sapiro. However, I am not aware of any actual articles on Lovecraft in the magazine.

Still less notable is Jack L. Chalker's *Mirage on Lovecraft: A Literary View* (1965), whose most valuable contributions are reprints of Lovecraft's own essays ("Some Notes on a Nonentity, "Notes on Writing Weird Fiction," and "Some Notes on Interplanetary Fiction"). The actual criticism in the issue—by David H. Keller, August Derleth, and Chalker himself—amounts to little. The pieces were taken from Chalker's small-press magazine *Mirage,* which contained a few additional insignificant pieces on Lovecraft.

Haunted—a fanzine that ran for only three sporadic issues (1963–68) and was edited by Samuel D. Russell—had a few items of note, among them Fritz Leiber's "The Whisperer Re-examined" (December 1964), a keen analysis of "The Whisperer in Darkness"; Arthur Jean Cox's "Some Thoughts on Lovecraft" (December 1964); and Muriel E. Eddy's "Lovecraft's Marriage and Divorce" (June 1968), one of Mrs. Eddy's numerous spinoffs of her original 1945 article on Lovecraft.

Mark Owings compiled a slim volume, *The Necronomicon: A Study* (1967), a superficial study that charted citations of the imaginary book in the work of Lovecraft and others.

In the academic world there were some surprising developments. Specifically, half a dozen scholars wrote theses and dissertations on Lovecraft, some of them of considerable value. Far and away the best is Arthur S. Koki's "H. P. Lovecraft: An Introduction to His Life and Writings" (M.A. thesis: Columbia University, 1962). The title is somewhat misleading, for the bulk of the thesis is a detailed examination of Lovecraft's life, especially in his early years (1890–1914). Koki has consulted numerous primary documents—Lovecraft's will of 1912, birth and death records, records of his divorce with Sonia filed in the Rhode Island county courthouse, and so on—to create a far more accurate presentation of his life than any previous biographer. What literary criticism there is in the thesis is superficial and uncoordinated.

From a very different perspective, Barton L. St. Armand's "H. P. Lovecraft: The Outsider in Legend and Myth" (M.A. thesis: Brown University, 1966) is a pioneering study of Lovecraft's work from a psychological perspective. St. Armand, who went on to gain his Ph.D. at Brown and then spent his entire academic career there, wrote several perspicacious articles on Lovecraft, some of which were drawn from this thesis; but as these were published in the 1970s, a discussion of them will appear in the next chapter.

And we can hardly omit T. E. D. Klein's "Some Notes on the Fantasy Tales of H. P. Lovecraft and Lord Dunsany" (Honors thesis: Brown University, 1969), a discursive study of the one writer's influence on the other. Klein would of course become one of the leading weird writers of his generation, but his lifelong devotion to Lovecraft is signalled by this early work.

Lawrence R. Lynn's "The Cthulhu Mythos in the Writings of H. P. Lovecraft" (M.A. thesis: University of Rhode Island, 1971) deals competently with the influence of Poe and Machen on Lovecraft, but suffers from brevity and an unwise decision to segregate Lovecraft's tales into mutually exclusive categories. Robert Stevens Fish's "The Oral Interpretation of the Horror Stories of H. P. Lovecraft" (M.A. thesis: University of Oklahoma, 1965) and Elaine Gillum Eitel's "The Sense of Place in H. P. Lovecraft" (M.A. thesis: Lamar State College of Technology, 1970) have little to recommend them.

Little is known about Maria Tranzocchi's "H. P. Lovecraft" (Ph.D. dissertation: Rome University, 196-); only a chapter has been seen. Assuming it actually exists, it would be the first Ph.D. dissertation on Lovecraft written by a scholar anywhere in the world.

It is worth devoting some attention to some media adaptations of Lovecraft in the later 1960s, even though there is little of intrinsic interest in them.

We start with the curious film *Curse of the Crimson Altar* (1968; US title *The Crimson Cult*), an uncredited and very loose adaptation of "The Dreams in the Witch House." It would be charitable to call this British production a B-movie, for it is little more than a lurid display of conventional witchcraft, with a certain number of naked ladies exhibiting themselves to no particular purpose. It theoretically stars Boris Karloff and Christopher Lee, but they actually appear on screen relatively briefly.

Not a great deal better, although widely publicised at the time, is *The Dunwich Horror* (1970), a crude rendering of an inferior Lovecraft story. Directed by Daniel Haller and with a screenplay by Curtis Lee Hanson and Henry Rosenbaum, it stars

Dean Stockwell as an implausibly handsome Wilbur Whateley, Ed Begley as Henry Armitage (who, in a scene toward the beginning, is shown casually handing a library assistant a copy of the *Necronomicon* with instructions to put it back in the vault), and Sandra Dee, the obligatory female lead who plays a student who falls under Wilbur's sway. Perhaps the best acting job is Sam Jaffe playing the crazed Old Whateley. The cosmic entities in the story, whom the Whateleys are seeking to restore to rulership of the earth, are depicted as dancing hippies wearing tie-dyed outfits.

An extraordinary development—chiefly because it was so relatively early in terms of Lovecraft's popular recognition—was a Lovecraftian thread in the TV show *Dark Shadows* (ABC, 1966–71). In the fall of 1969 the show began a story line involving a purportedly alien race, the Leviathans (although they looked more or less human, except with green skin), apparently the equivalent of Lovecraft's Old Ones; their properties and intentions, along with the plot development over several episodes, betrays the clear influence of "The Call of Cthulhu" and "The Dunwich Horror," although influences from other literary works are also apparent. But the story line proved unpopular with viewers, so it was abruptly terminated in early 1970.

I suppose I am obliged to discuss, as a token of Lovecraft's ascending fame, the fleeting emergence of the rock musicians from Chicago who called themselves H. P. Lovecraft. This was a "psychedelic rock band," and one of the members, David Miotke (a.k.a. Dave Michaels), provided an explanation for the formation of the group:

> Back in 1967 our two managers were familiar with Lovecraft's writings. After rejecting a whole list of possible group names one evening, we took a break and in collective conversation the name H. P. Lovecraft came up. The name itself, so different and contain-

> ing the word "love" drew us into naming ourselves after the author. One of the managers, Bill Traut, a graduate of the University of Wisconsin, knew the professor/author August Derleth, who was executor [*sic*] of the Lovecraft body of work. Bill contacted professor Derleth and got permission to use the name. Shortly thereafter, I began reading some of Lovecraft's stories. Wow! What a gifted and talented mind to create such "beyond scary" stuff![8]

It is interesting that this band member wasn't even acquainted with Lovecraft's work by the time the name of the band was decided upon, and that the group felt it needed Derleth's permission to use the name.

In any event, the group released its first album, simply titled *H. P. Lovecraft,* in 1967; a second album, *H. P. Lovecraft II,* came out in 1968. These albums have songs entitled "The White Ship," "At the Mountains of Madness," and so on. Derleth was delighted with the formation of the band, for largely pecuniary reasons: "During the years that the records were current, Arkham House received almost daily requests for information about Lovecraft; all such inquiries were answered with a copy of the Arkham House stocklist; and approximately forty percent of those inquirers responded with orders, thus further increasing sales."[9] But the band broke up soon after recording the second album, although their two recordings were later released on CD and a live album also appeared (*H. P. Lovecraft: Live, May 11, 1968,* 2000). Lovecraft's influence on rock music would not become extensive for several more years.

---

8. Gary Hill, *The Strange Sound of Cthulhu* 19.
9. Derleth, "The Making of a Literary Reputation" 23.

VI. The Revival of Scholarship (1971–1979)

August Derleth died on July 4, 1971. He was in the midst of writing another "posthumous collaboration," a novella or novel entitled *The Watchers out of Time,* which was found incomplete on his desk. Two years earlier he had edited *Tales of the Cthulhu Mythos* (Arkham House, 1969), which was widely reprinted and translated and came to be regarded as a definitive anthology of Mythos writing, even though much of the contents was merely pulp hackwork and some of it distressingly amateurish.

But Derleth's death did not stop Lovecraft's work from selling. Each of the three fiction volumes from Arkham House was reprinted several times in the decade and a half after first publication; these reprints were in small numbers (2000 to 4000 copies each), but they kept the bulk of Lovecraft's fiction in print in hardcover. Unfortunately, the two Lancer paperbacks fell out of print sometime after 1971, although *The Colour out of Space* was reprinted by Zebra Books in 1975 and both were reprinted by Jove in 1978. But the Beagle/Ballantine paperbacks were reprinted frequently—indeed, one article maintained that "over 1,000,000 copies" were sold "since 1970 alone."

That article was Philip Herrera's "The Dream Lurker," appearing in *Time* magazine for June 11, 1973.[1] This piece, which purported to review four of the Ballantine editions (three by Lovecraft along with *The Shuttered Room* by Derleth), was by far

1. Philip Herrera, "The Dream Lurker," *Time* (11 June 1973): 99–100.

the most visible notice that Lovecraft had ever received up to this time. Herrera had prestigious academic credentials—a B.A. from Harvard and M.A.s from Cambridge and Columbia—but no obvious connection to the weird or science fiction field. His article is a charming parody of Lovecraft's flamboyant prose; and although he commits the egregious mistake of giving an erroneous death date to Lovecraft (February 17, 1937), he speaks highly of Lovecraft's work:

> Yet Lovecraft had real talent too. After a while his reverberant prose seems mesmeric. Well did he know that true terror lies in the tension between our scientific age's rationalism and our primordial sense of individual powerlessness—of being enmeshed in something vast, inexplicable and appallingly evil. For this reason, he eschewed the stock devices of werewolves and vampires for a more intimate horror. . . .
>
> It is true that some of Lovecraft's stories on [*sic*] the Cthulu [*sic*] Mythos—*The Call of Cthulu, At the Mountains of Madness*—rank high among the horror stories of the English language. But Great Cthulu only knows why perfectly good, independent writers from the late August Derleth to Colin Wilson have seized and elaborated on the Mythos in their work.

The article, however, was clearly written more because of Lovecraft's popularity than of his stature as a purely literary figure. This was the early phase of the horror "boom" of the 1970s and 1980s, when—as a result of the increasing influence of horror and science fiction films from the 1950s onward and of such unexpected bestsellers as Ira Levin's *Rosemary's Baby* (1967), William Peter Blatty's *The Exorcist* (1971), and Thomas Tryon's *The Other* (1971)—horror became, for the first time since the Gothic novels of the later eighteenth century, a popular commodity. Lovecraft both profited from the horror boom and came to be seen as a significant ancestor of it, although few of the bestselling novels of the period were even tangentially Lovecraftian.

Lovecraft was also seen, among the young, as a sort of counter-cultural figure, along the lines of Nietzsche, Camus, Dalton Trumbo, and others who were enjoying popularity in high schools and college campuses. Of course, the engagingly lurid covers of the Beagle/Ballantine paperbacks by John Holmes (which in 1973 replaced less distinctive covers by other artists) didn't hurt.

In England, the Panther paperback editions—both original volumes and reprints of the hardcover Gollancz editions—continued to sell briskly and went through several printings. Panther even issued Lovecraft's revisions in two volumes in 1975.

The *Time* article was, however, a rare notice in the mainstream press during the first half of the decade. The bulk of the attention devoted to Lovecraft was from a suddenly revived fan world, where remarkable things were happening. Indeed, it is safe to say that—for all the significant work of such figures as Fritz Leiber, George Wetzel, Matthew H. Onderdonk, and a few others—the serious study of Lovecraft only began in earnest in the 1970s.

Before we discuss those items, we are obliged to cover Lin Carter's *Lovecraft: A Look Behind the "Cthulhu Mythos"* (Ballantine, 1972). This was an obvious attempt to capitalise upon the growing interest in Lovecraft and his disciples and successors. Carter—who had previously written a book on Tolkien's *Lord of the Rings* very much along the same lines—takes what might charitably be called an inclusive view of the Mythos, welcoming all and sundry additions to Lovecraft's pseudomythology and passing little critical judgment as to their quality or their fidelity to Lovecraft's own work. Carter, a prolific fantasy writer of the period, was anything but a trained literary critic, and it shows.

In regard to the issuing of Lovecraft's work, several publications displayed the fan world's interest in exploring the lesser-known aspects of Lovecraft's literary output. Roy A. Squires, a specialty publisher in California who was for many years the literary executor of the estate of Clark Ashton Smith, issued a series of four exquisite pamphlets—with handset type and quality paper—of Lovecraft's *Prose Poems* (1970), in editions of 125 copies. He followed these up with *Hail, Klarkash-Ton!* (1971), a pamphlet transcribing nine postcards from Lovecraft to Smith; a lettered edition of nine copies contained an original postcard.

Gerry de la Ree, a bookseller in New Jersey, issued *E'ch-Pi-El Speaks: An Autobiographical Sketch* (1972)—a long extract of a letter to an unknown correspondent (only recently has this person been identified as one Mr. Michael). The next year he published *The Normal Lovecraft,* consisting of an interesting memoir by Wilfred B. Talman, along with other matter. In 1975 de la Ree issued *The Occult Lovecraft,* edited by Anthony Raven, which printed another long extract of a Lovecraft letter purporting to explain the Hebraic-Greek incantation (which Lovecraft had lifted from the *Encyclopaedia Britannica*) in "The Horror at Red Hook." But Raven's attempts to portray Lovecraft as an occultist are unconvincing, and he further commits the gaffe of printing a vicious attack on Lovecraft by the ageing Samuel Loveman, who accused his old friend of hypocrisy for concealing his anti-Semitism from him.

Only a year after Derleth's death, Meade Frierson III and his wife, Penny, issued a 143-page publication—one can either consider it a one-shot magazine, like W. Paul Cook's *Recluse* (1927), or an anthology—simply called *HPL.* Just under half the issue was devoted to articles and memoirs, by such figures as Robert Bloch, E. Hoffmann Price, Joseph Payne Brennan, J. Vernon Shea, George T. Wetzel (the definitive revision of his essay "The

Cthulhu Mythos: A Study"), Fritz Leiber, and a number of fan writers who would continue to do good work in the future. Few articles are of towering importance in themselves, but collectively they bespeak a new, deeper approach to the study of Lovecraft the man and writer. The rest of the issue is devoted to Lovecraftian fiction and a fine portfolio of Lovecraftian art.

But *HPL* would be notable had it published nothing but Richard L. Tierney's one-page article, "The Derleth Mythos." Picking up on faint clues in the work of Leiber, Onderdonk, and others, Tierney definitively overthrew Derleth's highly erroneous and tendentious interpretation of the Mythos, especially two main pillars of his argument as: (1) Lovecraft's "gods" are elementals; (2) there is a clear good-vs.-evil scenario in Lovecraft's tales between the "good" Elder Gods and the "evil" Old Ones (Tierney established that there were no Elder Gods at all in Lovecraft, and that the Old Ones could only be considered evil from a limited human perspective). Tierney also declared that it was Derleth, not Lovecraft, who coined the term "Cthulhu Mythos." (Robert Bloch, in his contribution to *HPL,* used the term "Lovecraft Mythos," but this term did not become widespread among critics and scholars for another decade.)

One of the critical issues facing those who wished to disseminate their writings on Lovecraft was the relative dearth of venues for the publication of such work. The artist and publisher Harry O. Morris, Jr. attempted to remedy the situation with the establishment of *Nyctalops* in 1970; he also established the Silver Scarab Press to issue modest booklets of fiction, artwork, and criticism. But *Nyctalops* was hampered by its irregular publication schedule: two issues appeared in 1970, three in 1971, two (including a spectacular 100-page issue on Clark Ashton Smith) in 1972, only one each in 1973 and 1974, and so on. And as time went on, the Lovecraftian focus of the magazine waned as Morris published articles and especially fiction outside the narrow range of Lovecraft and his disciples (he published some of the early work of Thomas Ligotti, and in 1986 issued the first edition of Ligotti's collection *Songs of a Dead Dreamer*).

Nevertheless, *Nyctalops* became a focus for increasingly penetrating discussions of Lovecraft. It published the work of two scholars whose work stands out in the early years of the decade: R. Alain Everts and Kenneth W. Faig, Jr. Everts had begun doing work on Lovecraft in the 1960s, traversing the country in his quest to locate and interview friends and colleagues of Lovecraft (including his ex-wife, Sonia H. Davis). The result was such brief but significant pieces as "The Death of a Gentleman: The Last Days of Howard Phillips Lovecraft" (*Nyctalops,* April 1973), "Mrs. Howard Phillips Lovecraft" (*Nyctalops,* April 1973), and "Howard Phillips Lovecraft and Sex" (*Nyctalops,* July 1974).

Faig had come to Brown University in 1970 as a graduate student in mathematics, but had become so fascinated with Lovecraft that he spent the next two years doing an enormous amount of Lovecraft research; at the end of that time, Brown asked him to leave, but he has continued his research from his home in the Chicago area right up to the present day. One of his early triumphs was "Howard Phillips Lovecraft: The Early Years, 1890–1914" (*Nyctalops,* April 1973 and July 1974), an exhaustive account of Lovecraft's childhood that contained the first attempt to chart Lovecraft's early astronomical publications in the Providence newspapers, among other achievements.

Many of Faig's separate articles on Lovecraft were drawn from a volume he had written, "Lovecraftian Voyages," which was never published at the time but circulated widely in manuscript among devotees and scholars. This work, far exceeding 100,000 words, is not a connected treatise but a series of chapters addressing discrete aspects of Lovecraft's life and work, generally from a biographical perspective: his use of pseudonyms, his commonplace book, Lovecraft's lost or abandoned writings, and so on. All these chapters are thoroughly researched (chiefly from letters and other documents at the John Hay Library) and constitute a marked advance in scholarship from the fan writing that had preceded it.

Aside from *Nyctalops,* other magazines appeared. The *Dark Brotherhood Journal* was edited by George S. Record, who published three issues over a three-year period (1971–73). It did not contain anything of transcendent importance, but did have interesting articles by Faig, R. Boerem, and others. *Whispers* (1973–87), edited by Stuart David Schiff, did feature a number of significant pieces on Lovecraft in its early years, but quickly shifted to a fiction magazine publishing the work of the leading figures in the field.

At this time the phenomenon of the amateur press association took hold in Lovecraft fandom. An amateur press association is a group of individuals who each produce their own fanzines and send a requisite number of copies to an official editor, who then distributes one copy of each member's fanzine to every member at stipulated intervals. In 1972 REHUPA (the Robert E. Howard United Press Association) was established, devoted to the work of that young Texan writer; the next year, the Esoteric Order of Dagon was established by Joseph Pumilia and Roger Bryant; Bryant became official editor and remained in that capacity for several years. The membership of the EOD (which continues to exist today) is theoretically limited to thirty-nine members; on those rare occasions when the membership is full, prospective members are placed on a waiting-list. Throughout its long history, the membership has wavered between twenty-five and thirty-five.[2]

This sounds like a paltry number, but the EOD has had an outsize influence on the development of Lovecraft scholarship, chiefly because it allowed for the initial distribution of material—by such noted figures as Kenneth W. Faig, Jr., Ben P. Indick, T. G. L. Cockcroft, R. Boerem, Peter Cannon, David E. Schultz, J. Vernon Shea, George T. Wetzel, and numerous others—that subsequently achieved much wider dissemination. The "mailing comments" that members wrote in response to various articles published in the a.p.a., especially in the 1970s, created a sense of dynamic ferment that, while at times descending to the petty vindictiveness that has always characterised fandom, was on the whole positive and illuminating.

One of the earliest members of the EOD was Dirk W. Mosig, a professor of psychology at Georgia Southwestern College (subsequently at Kearney State College in Nebraska). An entire volume could be written on Mosig's contributions to Lovecraft scholarship; he is the pivotal figure in the transformation of the field from fannish opinionation to academic rigour. And although his preeminence extended for less than a decade (essentially the period 1973–80), his influence continues to be felt today in the work of those whom he carefully nurtured and tutored.

Because Mosig was a professor of psychology, not English, his critical work can at times seem unrelated to the radical critical theories then embroiling English departments throughout the world, notably structuralism, poststructuralism, semiotics, and so forth. Instead, Mosig puts his own discipline to use (he was

2. Another a.p.a., purportedly reflecting a somewhat higher level of scholarship, was the Necronomicon, whose official editor was R. Alain Everts. It lasted only a few years.

himself a behaviourist, although he found great interest in Jung's theories of the collective unconscious) in examining Lovecraft's work from a psychological perspective. But Mosig's chief virtue was an admirably broad and detailed knowledge of Lovecraft's life and work, derived from careful examination of original sources and of lesser-known bodies of Lovecraft's writing, including unpublished essays and poetry. And if Mosig at times defended Lovecraft—both the man and the writer—with the passion of a devotee, his writings were always well argued and could not easily be dismissed as merely the adulation of a fan.

The earliest article by Mosig that I can find—outside of his contributions to the EOD, for which he edited his notable journal, the *Miskatonic* (1973–79)[3]—is "Toward a Greater Appreciation of H. P. Lovecraft: The Analytical Approach," published in abridged form in *Whispers* (July 1973); it gained much wider distribution when it was reprinted in Gahan Wilson's *First World Fantasy Awards* (1977). Here, as in "The Four Faces of 'The Outsider'" (*Nyctalops,* July 1974) and "'The White Ship': A Psychic Odyssey" (*Whispers,* November 1974), Mosig draws deeply upon his academic knowledge of psychology in examining Lovecraft's work through a variety of perspectives. A later article, "Lovecraft: The Dissonance Factor in Imaginative Literature" (*Platte Valley Review,* 1979), reads Lovecraft by way of the notion of cognitive dissonance.[4]

One of Mosig's great virtues was the contacts he established with other scholars, both in the United States and worldwide, in promoting and disseminating Lovecraft's work. His work with the Italian editors Gianfranco de Turris and Sebastiano Fusco is especially notable. These editors worked for Fanucci, which emerged as yet another competitor to Sugar and Mondadori in

3. See the facsimile reprint (Glenview, IL: Moshassuck Press, 1991).

4. For a collection of most of Mosig's writings on HPL, see *Mosig at Last.*

publishing Lovecraft's work in Italian. Sugar had issued a large 900-page omnibus, *Opere complete* (1973). Fanucci responded with a two-volume set, *Nelle spire di Medusa* and *Sfida dall'infinito* (both 1976), which consisted chiefly of translations of the revisions in *The Horror in the Museum and Other Revisions;* but for the latter volume Mosig passed on the text of the Lovecraft-Barlow collaboration "The Night Ocean" (he had discovered Lovecraft's hand in the story from an unpublished letter to Hyman Bradofsky); and that volume also contained several important memoirs. Curiously enough, Mosig does not seem to have had any input in the German translations of Lovecraft in the 1970s. I shall discuss these and other translations elsewhere.

Mosig's true influence, however, lay in the patient tutelage he lent to such scholars (or budding scholars) as Peter Cannon, David E. Schultz, and myself. For much of the decade, it was widely held that Faig and Everts were the leading biographers of Lovecraft, and Mosig was the leading literary critic and scholar. It was only a matter of time, given Lovecraft's increasing popularity, that scholarship on his work would gain a wider audience.

But no one could have predicted the explosion of interest that occurred in 1975, which was truly an *annus mirabilis* for Lovecraft. This was when three books appeared: L. Sprague de Camp's *Lovecraft: A Biography* (Doubleday); Frank Belknap Long's *Howard Phillips Lovecraft: Dreamer on the Nightside* (Arkham House); and Willis Conover's *Lovecraft at Last* (Carrollton-Clark).

De Camp's book was, perforce, the most notable of these, by virtue of its being issued by a major New York publisher and receiving very wide distribution. De Camp was a prolific writer of science fiction and also science fact. He had not written a biography of this length and scope before, and it was not obvious that he was the best candidate to write the first full-length biography of Lovecraft; he exhibited far greater interest in Robert E. Howard, as he prepared numerous editions of Howard's work and also wrote dozens of pastiches (he would go on to co-write a full-scale biography of Howard in 1983). He states in his preface that he knew that Derleth was planning on writing such a biography, so he held off; but when Derleth died without having produced the work, he plunged in. De Camp refers to an unfinished manuscript by Derleth, "H. P. Lovecraft: Notes toward a Biography," that still exists among Derleth's papers at the Wisconsin Historical Society. I have not read this text, but I doubt that Derleth—especially at a time when his health was failing and when he was still preoccupied with a plethora of other literary projects while continuing to run Arkham House—could have produced a satisfactory work.

De Camp goes on to say: "It appeared to me that, even if I had not known Lovecraft, I had one advantage over Lovecraft's friend Derleth. Whereas Derleth admired Lovecraft to the point of idolatry, I felt that I could approach my subject more objectively. Whether I was right in so thinking is for the reader to judge" (xii). De Camp is exaggerating a trifle. While of course admiring his friend, Derleth had the habit of delivering backhanded compliments to Lovecraft, as when he wrote: "his place as a major writer in the minor macabre division of literature is secure."[5] Derleth is clearly making a contrast to himself, who was—in his estimation, at any rate—a major writer in the major division of mainstream literature.

But de Camp's 500-page work is actually not notable for its "objectivity." Although it is clearly the most detailed and comprehensive biographical account of Lovecraft published up to that time, it is crippled by numerous biases that render many of

---

5. "H. P. Lovecraft and His Work," in *The Dunwich Horror and Others* xx.

de Camp's value judgments on Lovecraft all but worthless. He admits forthrightly that "I saw in him certain of my own shortcomings, in what I hope is exaggerated form. To read of his many mistakes and misadventures gives me a 'there-but-for-the-grace-of-God' feeling" (xii). Two particular biases call for discussion.

The first is de Camp's impatience in regard to Lovecraft's "amateur" stance. De Camp believes this stance was wrongheaded and resulted in Lovecraft's failure to attain greater celebrity and material success in his life. What de Camp fails to grasp is that this aesthetic integrity, although it did cause hardship, is a large part of the reason why we read and remember him today, as opposed to such more "successful" hacks as Seabury Quinn or E. Hoffmann Price. De Camp seems unaware—although it should have been obvious from a reading of Lovecraft's letters, of which de Camp read thousands—that Lovecraft's attitude was derived from the eighteenth-century ideal of writing as an "elegant amusement," enhanced by his later absorption of the "art-for-art's-sake" manifesto of such writers as Pater and Wilde; it was, indeed, a chief reason why Lovecraft was so devoted to the cause of amateur journalism, which he (perhaps tendentiously) believed to embody his ideals of non-remunerative self-expression.

The other bias de Camp exhibits is in his account of Lovecraft's racism. Although this phase of Lovecraft's thought had been known (at least among his colleagues) since the 1940s, it had not been widely publicised until de Camp's volume. But his treatment of the subject is full of difficulties. He is content to quote long passages in which Lovecraft exhibits such prejudice—such as a lengthy screed against Jews as found in a letter to Lillian D. Clark of 11 January 1926—without noting that such passages are actually quite rare in his correspondence and are usually a response to some comment by his correspondent. In general, de Camp has simply failed to do research on the history of American racism and therefore has failed to provide a proper understanding of where Lovecraft's views fit in with the culture of his times, the scientific research on the subject available to Lovecraft, and other such factors.

This points to a broader failure in de Camp's biography: his lack of attention to Lovecraft's overall philosophical thought—presumably as a result of his own lack of knowledge of the history and theory of philosophy. By reading de Camp's biography, one would never know how vigorously and cogently Lovecraft debated such subjects as atheism, mechanistic materialism, the relativity of values, the aesthetics of literature (especially weird fiction), and on and on and on—subjects that take up a substantial portion of the correspondence to such colleagues as James F. Morton, Maurice W. Moe, Alfred Galpin, Frank Belknap Long, and many others. De Camp does take note of Lovecraft's late conversion to moderate socialism and his support of Franklin D. Roosevelt, but even here he is deaf to the true bases of Lovecraft's support:

> Now, how could a man support Roosevelt, call himself a liberal Democrat [Lovecraft in fact never called himself that], praise Norman Thomas, speak of the inevitability of Socialism, and at the same time apologise for Hitler and write: "I am an unreserved fascist" and "I believe some form of fascism to be the only sort of civilised government possible under the industrial economy of the machine age?"
>
> The answer is that Lovecraft called himself all sorts of things without much regard for consistency. (375)

No, that is not the answer. In fact, Lovecraft promoted his view of "fascistic socialism" (a perhaps unwise formulation) by propounding the notion that economic wealth should be spread to the many (socialism) but that voting rights should be restricted to those who could pass certain intellectual and civic tests ("fascism," although it is anything but that). It is actually a sound if unorthodox political stance, and one that had some support among other thinkers of the period; but to de Camp it is simply a bundle of contradictions.

De Camp's book is also hampered by extreme naïveté when it comes to the assessment of Lovecraft's work. He was not a trained literary critic; and the best thing he can say about a story is that it is a "rousing good yarn" or some such formulation. His ludicrous contention that Lovecraft bungled "The Shadow over Innsmouth" by "putting the climax [i.e., the narrator's pursuit by the hybrid aliens] in the middle" (354) has provoked endless amusement among subsequent scholars: de Camp is oblivious to the plain fact that the quieter but infinitely more affecting realisation on the narrator's part that he is related to the aliens has so vigorously combatted is the true climax of the tale.

De Camp's book is also full of mistakes large and small—a product of his "Johnny-come-lately" approach to Lovecraft and his attempt to digest an enormous mass of primary data in a relatively short period of time. His method of citation is infinitely confusing, making it difficult to ascertain the sources for any given piece of information in his book.

And yet, *Lovecraft: A Biography*—which appeared around February 1975—is notable largely because it is a large and seemingly exhaustive biographical account that was issued by a major publisher, Doubleday, and hence received wide distribution and garnered many reviews. I have counted sixty-three reviews—in magazines, newspapers, and the weird fiction small press, as well as several reviews in overseas venues. Some reviewers—such as Ursula K. Le Guin (*Times Literary Supplement,* 26 March 1976) or Larry McMurtry (*Washington Post Book World,* 17 February 1975)—simply used the book as an excuse to vent their own disdain of Lovecraft. But many others celebrated the mere existence of the book as a signal of Lovecraft's ascending fame.

The book went through three hardcover printings with Doubleday and was then reprinted in an abridged and slightly revised paperback (but with the notes and index omitted) by Ballantine in 1976. A Spanish translation appeared in 1978, a French one in 1988, and two different German translations (the first abridged, the second unabridged) in 1989 and 2002.

It is not surprising that Long's *Dreamer on the Nightside* appeared in the same year—apparently at the very end of the year—as de Camp's biography; for it was written as a direct refutation of some of the central aspects of de Camp's work. Long had seen some chapters of de Camp's book as they were being written, and the portrait of Lovecraft that was emerging from them so disturbed him that he decided to write what amounted to a book-length refutation, although de Camp himself is never mentioned in the text.

But Long's memoir largely fails in its purpose, simply because he waited far too long to write the book. Even his early memoir in *Marginalia* (1944) contains some dubious reminiscences; and this flaw is multiplied many times over in his book. For someone who knew Lovecraft for the better part of seventeen years and met him on an almost daily basis in New York in the years 1924–26, the recollections he provides are thin and insubstantial. And Long does not do himself any favours by conducting, toward the end, a posthumous interview of Lovecraft in which the responses are not at all acute or convincing.

Toward the end of his book Long quotes several paragraphs of a statement on Lovecraft's racism by Dirk W. Mosig. This statement was subsequently elaborated as "H. P. Lovecraft: Rabid Racist—or Compassionate Gentleman?" (*Xenophile,* October 1975). But Mosig addressed the failings of the de Camp biography more generally in a bracing review, "Lovecraft: A Parody"

(*Fantasy Crossroads,* August 1975). This led to a series of letters between de Camp and Mosig in the next several issues of *Fantasy Crossroads.* As late as 1978, in "Sesquithoughts on Lovecraft" (*Nyctalops,* March 1978), de Camp was still defending his approach to Lovecraft; but by this time it had become widely accepted amongst fans and scholars that the biography was seriously flawed.

The third book that came out in 1975, around May, elicited nothing but praise. This was *Lovecraft at Last,* which actually carried a joint byline—"by H. P. Lovecraft and Willis Conover." Conover was a youth of fifteen when he had come in touch with Lovecraft in July 1936; hence their correspondence lasted only about eight months, ending when Lovecraft weakly scribbled a response to a postcard by Conover as he was about to enter the hospital on March 10, 1937. But this brief association was of immense significance to Conover, who carefully preserved all his letters from Lovecraft (and himself transcribed them for the *Selected Letters* project).

Conover went on to become a significant figure in the Voice of America and was also a noted collector of early jazz albums. He established his own publishing company, Carrollton-Clark, in Arlington, Virginia. He anticipated *Lovecraft at Last* by issuing, in 1974, a booklet, *Supernatural Horror in Literature as Revised in 1936,* consisting of a typescript Lovecraft had prepared—a synopsis of the first eight chapters of "Supernatural Horror in Literature"—when Conover had expressed interest in reprinting that essay, or rather the balance of it from the point where the revised serialisation had ceased in the *Fantasy Fan.* But this item is slight as compared with *Lovecraft at Last,* which is a monument to book production—and to friendship—of the most affecting sort.

Conover has spared no expense in presenting facsimiles of

portions of Lovecraft's handwritten letters in the exact colour of ink in which they were written, as well as entire postcards, the handwritten draft of "History of the 'Necronomicon,'" and numerous other documents. There are numerous illustrations of all sorts, from covers of *Weird Tales* to a facsimile of F. Lee Baldwin's "H. P. Lovecraft: A Biographical Sketch" (*Fantasy Magazine,* April 1935). All this material is interweaved into a poignant narrative of the courtesy and respect accorded by a dying legend of weird fiction toward an enthusiastic young amateur. It is no wonder that Conover remembered his association with Lovecraft for the remainder of his life.

This book was also extensively reviewed—I have located twenty-six reviews of it, in the *Atlantic Monthly, Library Journal, Publishers Weekly,* and other popular or prestigious periodicals. Without any attempt at being any kind of "rebuttal" to de Camp's book (of which Conover presumably had no knowledge prior to writing his own), it presents a far more convincing alternative to the portrait that had emerged from *Lovecraft: A Biography.*

Conover also issued a revival of his old fanzine, *Science-Fantasy Correspondent* (1975). He may have intended this to become an ongoing if irregular periodical, but in the event only this issue ever appeared. But it would be notable if only for its superlative design and for Kenneth Sterling's vibrant memoir "Caverns Measureless to Man," a long rumination on Lovecraft's scientific background.

The year 1975 concluded triumphantly with the First World Fantasy Convention, held in Providence in October. This event was the brainchild of the agent Kirby McCauley, and some unsympathetic commentators believed it was little more than a forum to show off his own clients; but that is an unfair assessment. Whether the convention was explicitly designed to celebrate

Lovecraft is also a matter of doubt, although its setting in Lovecraft's hometown, its numerous events—from panel discussions to a reading of "The Haunter of the Dark" by Fritz Leiber to the appearance of many of Lovecraft's friends and colleagues, from Robert Bloch to Frank Belknap Long, as well as scholars such as Mosig—certainly point in that direction. It was at this venue that the World Fantasy Award—fashioned by Gahan Wilson in a not particularly attractive caricature of Lovecraft's face—was displayed, with the awards going to the authors of the best novel, short story, and so on of the preceding year, as determined by the World Fantasy Committee. The event clearly electrified the attendees and engendered ongoing interest in Lovecraft by devotees and scholars alike.

One of those who was fired with enthusiasm, although he did not attend the convention, was Marc A. Michaud, who at this time was still in high school and lived in West Warwick, Rhode Island. In working for a local newspaper, he stumbled upon Lovecraft's early astronomy articles in the *Pawtuxet Valley Gleaner* of 1906. After approaching Arkham House about issuing them as a book and being turned down, Michaud decided to reprint the articles himself. The result was the first publication by Necronomicon Press: *First Writings: Pawtuxet Valley Gleaner* (1976). The book is of course very crudely produced—the text typed on a typewriter and run off on only one side of the page, fastened with heavy staples—but Michaud had managed to secure a preface by up-and-coming British writer Ramsey Campbell (whose first volume—issued by Arkham House when Campbell was about the same age as Michaud, *The Inhabitant of the Lake and Less Welcome Tenants* [1964]—was a collection of Lovecraft pastiches).

This book attracted little attention, but Michaud's next publication—*The Conservative: Complete 1915–1923*—was a very different proposition. An ungainly mix of transcribed text and poorly reproduced facsimiles, it printed the complete run of the thirteen issues of Lovecraft's amateur periodical. But it quickly came under fire from Tom Collins, a Lovecraft scholar in New York, who claimed that Michaud had stolen his research. The case was implausible—the issues of the *Conservative* were available for anyone's consultation in a large collection of amateur journals at the New York Public Library—but the litigation dragged on for years. Collins did not prevail, but Michaud did issue a peculiar "second edition" in 1977 in which Collins's assistance was acknowledged.

Later in 1976 Necronomicon Press issued a much more impressive volume, *Writings in the United Amateur: 1915–1925,* consisting almost entirely of facsimile reprints and with an illuminating introduction by T. E. D. Klein. Michaud's career as the leading small-press publisher of Lovecraftiana was now off to a good start, and he followed this volume up with another set of facsimile reprints, *The Californian: 1934–1938* (1977), as well as a facsimile reprint of the *Home Brew* appearances of "Herbert West—Reanimator" and "The Lurking Fear" (both 1977).

Necronomicon Press gained greater scholarly credibility with the issuance of *Uncollected Prose and Poetry* (1978), edited by Marc A. Michaud and myself and featuring the first of many cover illustrations by Jason C. Eckhardt. The book, although crudely produced (typed out on a typewriter, reproduced by offset printing, using 8½ × 14 pages folded in half and stapled at the side), was notable including the first American reprint of the Lovecraft-Barlow collaboration "The Night Ocean." (As a result of this appearance, it was subsequently reprinted in Lin Carter's *Weird Tales* No. 2 [1980].) Otherwise, it contained essays from a wide variety of sources (including the lengthy "Lucubrations Lovecraftian," which had incredibly never been identified as a work by Lovecraft) that I had unearthed in the course of my bibliographical researches. Two further volumes were issued in 1980 and 1982.

In 1979 Michaud and I edited *H. P. Lovecraft in "The Eyrie,"* a volume of letters by and about Lovecraft in the letter column of *Weird Tales.* We were obliged to hand-copy the material from the fragile copies in the John Hay Library. The volume illuminated the differing responses to Lovecraft in the magazine that was the chief venue of his weird fiction during his lifetime.

Arkham House was struggling to regain viability after Derleth's death. Initially, co-owner Donald Wandrei took over, issuing a peculiar catalogue (which, according to his colleagues, he referred to as "my latest work of fiction") listing a great many new projects, many of them his own or his brother's. Few of these have appeared, at least not through Arkham House; and soon thereafter Wandrei became embroiled in litigation with the August Derleth Estate on various issues.

At this point Roderick Meng—who had, essentially, been Derleth's office boy—took over as managing editor, and did manage to bring out several volumes that had been much delayed, including Ramsey Campbell's landmark second short story collection, *Demons by Daylight* (1973). But it was clear that Arkham House needed an editor who actually had experience in editing and book production, so around 1975 James Turner was hired. This was a brilliant move, as Turner was an impeccable editor as far as text editing, book design, and other elements were concerned; he did engender controversy by shifting Arkham House's focus to contemporary science fiction, although it is an exaggeration to say that he discounted weird fiction altogether. And he did keep up the Lovecraft program.

Turner brought out the final two volumes (four and five) of *Selected Letters* in 1976. They were quite large, and appear to be based upon typescripts that Wandrei had produced. They were a welcome culmination to the series, as they had far fewer typographical and textual errors than the previous volumes. But the series lacked an index. Turner announced that an index would be forthcoming, as well as a sixth volume of supplementary letters, but neither of these volumes ever appeared.

Meanwhile, others were getting into the business of dredging up Lovecraft's lesser-known writings and making them available to a steadily increasing cadre of devotees. De Camp followed up his biography with the compilation *To Quebec and the Stars* (Donald M. Grant, 1976), whose chief inclusion was Lovecraft's previously unpublished travelogue of Quebec—the longest single work he ever wrote. Even though de Camp received assistance from a French-Canadian colleague, M.-Louis Paré, there are still numerous errors in the transcription. Otherwise, the volume contained miscellaneous essays on science, literature, philosophy, and other subjects, mostly from amateur journals.

Stuart David Schiff's Whispers Press issued *A Winter Wish* (1977), a volume of uncollected poetry assembled by Tom Collins. But Collins was very careless in the preparation of the texts, making dozens of errors and failing to systematise usage throughout the volume. In one particularly egregious instance, he noticed that a line was missing in the published version (in a Providence newspaper) of "An Elegy on Phillips Gamwell, Esq."; so he wrote a line on his own initiative, failing to notify readers of his act. To add to his discomfiture, he failed to notice that a clipping of the appearance existed at the John Hay Library, where Lovecraft himself had written in the missing line—which bore little resemblance to Collins's fabrication.

I was just beginning my textual researches into Lovecraft's work at this time and was appalled at the errors in the volume. I prepared a long errata list, with some prefatory commentary, that appeared in Mosig's *Miskatonic* (May 1978), creating a furore that lasted for well over a year. Collins had numerous colleagues and supporters in the Lovecraft community who took umbrage that a young man not quite twenty years of age had dared to criticise him in what they believed to be an abusive manner; and the fact that I had already become associated with Collins's nemesis, Marc A. Michaud (whom I had first met in the fall of 1976), added to the outrage. But Mosig stood by us. The book, which the publisher optimistically printed in an edition of 2000 hardcover copies, sold relatively poorly.

But the slow transformation of fans into scholars was in the process of occurring. Mosig wrote a bracing essay, "H. P. Lovecraft: Myth-Maker," first published in Italian in the anthology *I miti di Cthulhu* (Fanucci, 1975); it appeared in English in Mosig's *Miskatonic* (February 1976), then in *Whispers* (December 1976) and numerous other venues. This piece, taking up the conclusions found in Tierney's "The Derleth Mythos," was possibly the first adumbration of Lovecraft's philosophy of materialism and atheism and its application to his fiction. Mosig was harsh in dealing with Derleth, condemning Derleth's numerous errors in assessing Lovecraft's work and his mediocre pastiches and "posthumous collaborations," which (as we have seen from Damon Knight's review, among others) cast Lovecraft's own work in a bad light. Mosig also challenged the existence of a key statement that Derleth attributed to Lovecraft (the so-called "black magic quotation"), and which he used as support for his interpretation of the Mythos. Without actually coming out and saying it, Mosig suggested that Derleth had fabricated the quotation. It would be several years before its true source was discovered.

Barton L. St. Armand, an actual academic, had preceded Mosig in the scholarly study of Lovecraft with two scintillating papers. The first, "Facts in the Case of H. P. Lovecraft" (*Rhode*

Island History, February 1972), was a searching analysis of *The Case of Charles Dexter Ward* and its ties to Providence history and culture. The other, "H. P. Lovecraft: New England Decadent," appeared in the French journal *Caliban* No. 12 (1975) and was subsequently reprinted as a booklet (Silver Scarab Press, 1979). While this is a profound study of Lovecraft's fusion of Puritan morality and Decadent imagery in his philosophy and fiction, St. Armand appears to overlook the fact that the Decadent phase in Lovecraft's thought and work was of relatively brief duration, giving way to the "cosmic regionalism" (as it has been called) of his final decade of writing.

St. Armand then published a monograph, *The Roots of Horror in the Fiction of H. P. Lovecraft* (Dragon Press, 1977)—a title that is somewhat misleading, as the bulk of the 102-page treatise deals with "The Rats in the Walls." It is chiefly a psychological analysis of the story, using the theories of C. J. Jung.

Other academics—or academics in the making—were appearing. The 1970s saw a total of nine theses or dissertations on Lovecraft. Those by Elaine Gillum Eitel and Lawrence R. Lynn early in the decade have already been cited. The most superficially impressive work was John Lawson McInnis III's "H. P. Lovecraft: The Maze and the Minotaur" (Ph.D. diss.: Louisiana State University, 1975), an extensive philosophical and psychological study; but its central thesis—that the symbol of the maze, as found in the Lovecraft-Sterling collaboration "In the Walls of Eryx"—is central to Lovecraft's work is partially vitiated by the fact that it was Sterling, and not Lovecraft, who devised the maze motif in that story. Another work, Mark James Estren's "Horrors within and without: A Psychoanalytic Study of Edgar Allan Poe and Howard Phillips Lovecraft" (Ph.D. diss.: State University of New York at Buffalo, 1978), has a long chapter on Poe's influence on Lovecraft and on Lovecraft's mythos.

Peter Cannon established his bona fides as a Lovecraft scholar with two papers, "A Case for Howard Phillips Lovecraft" (honours thesis: Stanford University, 1973) and "Lovecraft's New England" (M.A. thesis: Brown University, 1974). The former is an interesting if somewhat insubstantial defence of Lovecraft's literary importance, but the latter is a worthy contribution assessing his use of New England history and culture in his work. Roy M. Poses's "The Psychology of Fear: Horror and Terror in the Works of H. P. Lovecraft" (independent studies paper: Brown University, 1974) has some points of interest in regard to Lovecraft's principles of weird fiction, but is now largely outdated. Other papers written at this time are of no particular account.

In terms of published work, we can take note of Philip A. Shreffler's *The H. P. Lovecraft Companion* (Greenwood Press, 1977). Shreffler was, at this time, a professor of English at St. Louis Community College and a devotee of Sherlock Holmes. The book is not, strictly speaking, academic, but rather a popular study in which, after an introductory chapter on "Lovecraft's Literary Theory," Shreffler provides plot synopses of the stories, an encyclopaedia of characters and "monsters," a separate chapter on "The Mythos Monsters," and so on. Much of the value of the book comes from its numerous photographs and illustrations; the text itself, when not erroneous, is superficial.

And I suppose we are obliged to John Taylor Gatto's *The Major Works of H. P. Lovecraft* (Monarch Press, 1977). The Monarch Notes (of which this is no. 00982 [*sic*]) are a poor relation to Cliff Notes, those handy cribs for the lazy or overworked undergraduate who wants a quick summary of a literary work. Gatto's little book (all of 100 pages) begins by getting Lovecraft's death date wrong (using the date—February 17, 1937—cited in the *Time* magazine review-article of 1973) and goes downhill from there. Among other things, he proposes that "The Whisperer in Darkness" is a covertly pornographic story.

As an indication that the fan world had not fully converted to scholarship, we can point to Darrell Schweitzer's *The Dream-Quest of H. P. Lovecraft* (R. Reginald/Borgo Press, 1978), a sadly superficial and error-riddled account of Lovecraft's life and work. Much superior is Schweitzer's anthology of criticism, *Essays Lovecraftian* (T-K Graphics, 1976), containing Leiber's "A Literary Copernicus," Mosig's "The Four Faces of 'The Outsider,'" Tierney's "The Derleth Mythos," and numerous other valuable papers. Still earlier, Schweitzer had written a moderately interesting booklet, *Lovecraft in the Cinema* (T-K Graphics, 1975), that investigated Lovecraft adaptations in film and television.

Somewhat better is Henry L. P. Beckwith, Jr.'s *Lovecraft's Providence and Adjacent Parts* (Donald M. Grant, 1979), a cursory survey of Lovecraft-related sites in Providence and surrounding areas, with numerous photographs.

In England, several critics continued to display doubts of Lovecraft's merits, or even his competence as a writer. Brian W. Aldiss, in *Billion-Year Spree: The True History of Science Fiction* (1973), betrayed the science fiction community's prejudice against Lovecraft by declaring that he had a "ghastly" prose style.[6] And one Glen St. John Barclay, in a superficial and error-riddled chapter on Lovecraft in *Anatomy of Horror* (1978), appears to believe that Lovecraft is essentially an insane person, all apart from the literary "sins" he presumably commits on every page of his work.

Lovecraft was now appearing frequently in general histories or studies of weird fiction, but critics' and historians' verdicts on him were still quite mixed. David Punter's *The Literature of Ter-*

---

6. L. Sprague de Camp (*Lovecraft: A Biography* 440) quoted Isaac Asimov as saying that HPL was a "sick juvenile"; but he provides no citation for the comment.

ror (1979) speaks of Lovecraft with a marked lack of enthusiasm as merely the "inheritor of Gothic traditions." (Punter revised his book into a two-volume edition in 1996, but his discussion of Lovecraft remained unchanged, in spite of the massive amount of scholarship that had been done in the intervening two decades.)

Far superior is the sensitive and error-free chapter on Lovecraft in Les Daniels's *Living in Fear: A History of Horror in the Mass Media* (1975). The chapter ("The Bizarre World of H. P. Lovecraft") had first appeared in the magazine *Fusion* (12 November 1971). Also of interest are two articles written by leading British fantaisiste Angela Carter, "The Hidden Child" (*New Society,* 6 March 1975), which attempts to draw out the covert sexual imagery in some of Lovecraft's tales, and "Lovecraft and Landscape" (in George Hay's *Necronomicon* [1978]), a rumination on Lovecraft's imaginary realms. Little influence of Lovecraft has been detected in Carter's own fiction.

A most curious indication of Lovecraft's ascending fame is the interest shown by occultists and other eccentrics in his work. This is not at all surprising, since even in his day Lovecraft was beset by crackpots such as William Lumley, who was convinced that Lovecraft was writing the "truth" about the ancient gods in his fiction without knowing it. He was, in Lumley's view, serving as a channel for the gods' mental communication with humans. Lovecraft was also questioned by various individuals about the reality of the *Necronomicon*. The young James Blish wanted Lovecraft to write the *Necronomicon* himself, but Lovecraft demurred: given that he had cited from p. 751 of the work, the actual composition of it would have been an arduous enterprise.

The British occultist Kenneth Grant first spoke briefly of Lovecraft in his encyclopaedia, *Man, Myth & Magic* (1970), and somewhat more extensively in *The Magical Revival* (1972). Soon thereafter, several books purporting to be the *Necronomicon* appeared. The first of them was an obvious hoax. *The Necronomicon* (Owlswick Press, 1973) was the work of George Scithers and featured a deadpan introduction by L. Sprague de Camp. This claimed to be the Arabic text, and the whole book was indeed in Arabic; but in fact the book consisted of a small number of pages repeated over and over again—something that non-Arabic-speaking readers were not likely to detect.

The most superficially imposing was a *Necronomicon* (1977) written by someone calling himself Simon. Simon was a practising occultist, and his *Necronomicon* is actually full of various spells that he maintained were efficacious. The volume was reprinted in paperback by Avon (1980). Much more impressive, if only as a hoax, is the *Necronomicon* edited by British writer George Hay (Neville Spearman, 1978). This purported to be a transcript of John Dee's English translation of the *Necronomicon,* which is said to survive only in partially burned fragments in the British Library. The reproduction of a few pages of the manuscript was quite convincing, and the book features a long, meandering introduction by Colin Wilson along with several tolerably sound essays on Lovecraft. This book was translated into Italian (1979) and French (1979).

In a class by itself is H. R. Giger's *Necronomicon* (1977), the first major publication of this pioneering Swiss artist's work. It was first published by Sphinx Verlag in Switzerland and appeared in a UK edition later that year. A US edition from Morpheus International was published in 1991. Giger handed the book to director Ridley Scott, who hired him to do the set designs for his film *Alien* (1979), with the result that those designs are markedly Lovecraftian, as is the general tenor of the film. A second *Necronomicon* volume of Giger's artwork appeared in 1984.

And one can certainly not bypass the eccentric Anton LaVey, founder of the Church of Satan, who in *The Satanic Rituals*

(1972) has two brief chapters on Lovecraft, the latter of which ("The Call to Cthulhu") is apparently meant as an actual spell to summon the baleful entity.

In the realm of general literature, note should be taken of James Schevill's surrealist play *Lovecraft's Follies* (1971). Schevill was a longtime professor of English at Brown University, so his familiarity with Lovecraft is not unexpected. The play was performed at the Trinity Square Repertory Company in Providence, under the direction of Adrian Hall, in March and April of 1971.

Far more impressive is Jorge Luis Borges's short story "There Are More Things," dedicated "to the memory of H. P. Lovecraft." The story appeared in Spanish in Borges's *El libro de arena* (1975) and in English in the *Atlantic Monthly* (July 1975) and in *The Book of Sand,* translated by Norman Thomas di Giovanni (1977). It is an evocative piece about a man who explores a house in Buenos Aires (formerly belonging to his uncle and subsequently renovated by the new owner) that appears to habour an alien presence, perhaps from outer space: "What would the inhabitant be like? What could it be looking for on this planet, no less hideous to it than it to us? From what secret regions of astronomy or time, from what ancient and now incalculable dusk can it have reached this South American suburb and this particular night?"[7] In an afterword to *The Book of Sand,* Borges states that he has "perpetrated a posthumous story by H. P. Lovecraft" and goes on to refer to Lovecraft as "an unconscious parodist of Poe."[8]

Stephen King, in the early years of his popularity, wrote an informal and impressionistic view of horror fiction in *Danse Macabre* (1979). Some of his off-the-cuff comments on Lovecraft have been quoted ad infinitum on book jackets, even though he

7. Jorge Luis Borges, "There Are More Things" (tr. Norman Thomas di Giovanni), *Atlantic Monthly* 236, No. 1 (January 1975): 29.

8. Jorge Luis Borges, *The Book of Sand* (New York: E. P. Dutton, 1977), 124.

makes numerous silly errors, such as "the Plains of Leng" (84, 102), "Elder Gods" (188—as if they have any existence in Lovecraft, as opposed to the pastiches of August Derleth), *The Strange Case of Charles Dexter Ward* (332), and so on.

In the realm of pop culture or media adaptations, some interesting developments occurred in the decade. There were no major motion pictures based on Lovecraft's work, but it is arguable that Peter Weir's evocative film *The Last Wave* (1977) owes a great deal to "The Shadow out of Time." No credit is given to Lovecraft in the film, and I am not aware of any instance where Weir has admitted such an influence.[9] Alain Resnais's eccentric film *Providence* (1977) appears to draw upon some Lovecraftian elements: a few glimpses of the city of Providence as well as certain aspects of Lovecraft's own character, twisted out of all recognition in the figure of Clive Langham, played by Sir John Gielgud. Resnais later admitted that Lovecraft was an inspiration for the film; he went so far as to instruct his set designer to read Lovecraft so that Langham's house would be suitably spooky.[10]

In television we had two adaptations appearing back-to-back on *Rod Serling's Night Gallery* (NBC). "Pickman's Model," aired on December 1, 1971. It was directed by Jack Laird and with a screenplay by Alvin Sapinsley, starred Bradford Dillman as Pickman. The story is for no apparent reason set in the nineteenth century, but is otherwise an able adaptation of the tale. The next week, on December 8, an adaptation of "Cool Air" ap-

9. There was a 50-minute TV movie in Germany, *H. P. Lovecraft: Der Schatten aus der Zeit* (1975), directed by George Moorse, based on "The Shadow out of Time." And an Italian film, *L'isola degli uomini pesce* (Dania Film, 1979), released in the US as *Screamers,* directed by Sergio Martino, is a loose and uncredited adaptation of "The Shadow over Innsmouth." I have not seen either of these films.

10. See Robert Benayoun, *Alain Resnais* (Paris: Editions Ramsay, 2008), 240–41.

peared. This was directed by Jack Laird, with a teleplay by Serling himself and starring Henry Darrow as Dr. Muñoz. In spite of the fact that the place of the (male) narrator in the story was filled by a woman, named Agatha Howard and played by Barbara Rush, this adaptation was also reasonably effective, fusing terror with poignancy. Both stories were subsequently reprinted in *Rod Serling's Night Gallery Reader* (1987), edited by Carol Serling and others.

Lovecraft became a presence in comic books at this time. Some Lovecraftian elements, including the *Necronomicon,* had been cited as early as the DC comic *Justice League of America* No. 10 (March 1962); but it was Marvel Comics' *Tower of Shadows* No. 3 (January 1970) that featured the first explicit adaptation of a Lovecraft story—"The Terrible Old Man," written by Roy Thomas and illustrated by Barry Smith (later Barry Windsor-Smith). Issue no. 9 of the same comic (January 1971) adapted "Pickman's Model," while *Chamber of Darkness* No. 5 (June 1970), also a Marvel comic, adapted 'The Music of Erich Zann" (as "The Music from Beyond"). An underground comic, *Skull* Nos. 4 and 5 (1972), adapted five Lovecraft stories as well as the poem "To a Dreamer." But the most notable comic adaptation of the period was "The Dunwich Horror," published in the US in *Heavy Metal* (October 1979). This was a reprint from a Spanish publication, *Los mitos de Cthulhu* (1973), in which several Lovecraft stories were adapted by the noted Argentine illustrator Alberto Breccia, with text by Norberto Buscaglia. This work rises to the level of a true "graphic novel," and Breccia's artwork is polished, evocative, and highly sensitive to the source material.

But Lovecraft's infiltration of comic books was far greater than this, and would become even more extensive in the decades to follow.[11] For example, "Arkham Asylum" was first cited in

---

11. For two good surveys, see Will Murray, "Lovecraft in the Comics,"

Batman No. 258 (October 1974) and thereafter became a regular feature of that comic. A Lovecraftian story appeared in *Swamp Thing* as early as issue no. 8 (February 1974) and was followed by numerous others. The highly visual quality of Lovecraft's tales—especially their "monsters"—has proved alluring to comic artists, who can render these images in a way that can be digested without the dense language that surrounds them in the stories.

Foreign interest in Lovecraft continued apace in this decade. In France, Christian Bourgois published a two-volume edition of Lovecraft's revisions and collaborations, *L'Horreur dans la musée,* taken pretty directly from the Arkham House *Horror in the Museum.* More interestingly, Yves Rivière translated a slim selection of letters (taken from the first two volumes of *Selected Letters*) as *Lettres d'Arkham* (Editions Jacques Glénat, 1975). The selections are extremely brief, and the dates of writing and addresses are almost never identified. Much more impressive is *Lettres, Volume 1 (1914–1926),* translated by Francis Lacassin (Christian Bourgois, 1978). Derleth and Wandrei are, anomalously, listed as the actual editors of the volume, although the book is only a selection of volumes 1 and 2 of *Selected Letters.* Lacassin has added extensive annotations. I was informed that the volume sold so poorly that the publisher abandoned the project (it is unclear how many volumes it would have extended to). Also notable is the first complete translation of *Fungi from Yuggoth,* appearing in the magazine *Ides . . . et Autres* (April 15, 1978). This was a prose translation.

In Germany, Insel Verlag issued *Stadt ohne Namen* (1973), later reprinted in paperback by Suhrkamp. Suhrkamp continued

---

Crypt of Cthulhu No. 30 (Eastertide 1985): 35–38; and James Ambuehl, Boyd E. Pearson, and Dan Ross, "Cthulhu in the Comics," *Parts* No. 15 (May 1999): 28–33.

to reprint other Insel Verlag volumes throughout the 1970s, signalling a clear demand. An illustrated edition of "The Dreams in the Witch House" appeared as *Träume im Hexenhaus* (Anabis Verlag, 1971), with illustrations by Peter Collien. The edition was limited to 470 copies. A prospectus for a twelve-volume edition of Lovecraft's letters—possibly a complete translation of *Selected Letters*—was issued in 1975 by Verlag Claus Neugebauer, but never appeared because of insufficient finances. Around the same time this same publisher announced a volume of criticism devoted to Lovecraft, *Howard Phillips Lovecraft: Materialien zu seinem Leben und Werk,* edited by Hans Joachim Alpers, but this volume also never appeared.

Spanish-language editions, both in Spain and in Latin America, became widespread. *Viajes al otro mundo,* edited by Rafael Llopis and translated by F. Torres Oliver (Madrid: Alianza, 1971), was a volume of four of the five Randolph Carter tales ("The Unnamable" was overlooked). It went through many printings in the 1970s and 1980s.

The Barcelona publisher Barral Editores issued numerous small paperbacks of Lovecraft's tales in the early 1970s. Ediciones Acerto finally followed up its first volume of *Obras escogidas* with a second volume in 1974. Editorial Bruguera (Barcelona) got into the act with two volumes of stories in 1977. The Barcelona journal *Nueva Dimensión* published translations of many Lovecraft stories in the 1970s. I have already discussed the Italian editions of this period above. Fanucci also published a translation of Derleth's *Tales of the Cthulhu Mythos* as *I miti di Cthulhu* (1975).

In Holland, A. W. Bruna & Zoon issued four additional volumes of stories in the 1970s. The first Norwegian book of Lovecraft stories was published as *Tingen på terskelen og andre hårreisende historier* (J. W. Cappenels Forlag, 1973), translated by Øyvind Myhre and Einar Engstad. Around the same time, a Swedish volume of stories, *Skräkens labyrinter* (Askild & Karnekull, 1973), edited and translated by Sam J. Lundwall, appeared. *Gengångaren* (Delta Forlags, 1975), a translation of *The Case of Charles Dexter Ward* by Gunnar Gällmo, also appeared.

It is difficult to trace the first appearance of Lovecraft in Japanese. There are reports that Lovecraft's work appeared in the magazine *Hoseki* as early as the later 1940s, but these reports have not been confirmed. Otherwise, we know that "The Outsider" appeared in Edogawa Ranpo's anthology *Kaiki shosetsu kessakushu 1* (Sogensha, 1957). The editor's real name is Taro Hirai (his pseudonym is "Edgar Allan Poe" rendered into Japanese), a significant figure in the development of mystery fiction in Japan. "The Dunwich Horror," "The Shadow over Innsmouth," and "The Rats in the Walls" were translated in the anonymous anthology *Sekai kyofu shosetsu zenshu 5* (Sogensha, 1958). Hiroshi Aramata translated "The Quest of Iranon" in *Little Weird* No. 6 (August 1967); a translation of "Polaris" appeared in the March 1968 issue, and a translation of "The Colour out of Space" appeared in the November 1968 issue. Aramata is a widely published Japanese author of fantasy and science fiction, with a particular interest in older imaginative literature. *Hayakawa's Mystery Magazine* (more or less an equivalent to *Ellery Queen's Mystery Magazine*, although of course the latter published no weird fiction) translated several Lovecraft tales in the 1970s.

The first volume of Lovecraft's work in Japanese appeared as *Lovecraft kessakushu: Angoku no higi* (Sodosha, 1972), translated by Katsuo Jinka. Sodosha attempted to follow this up with a four-volume series, *Lovecraft zenshu* (1975–78), but only volumes 1 and 4 appeared. These volumes were translated by Hiroshi Aramata. Another publisher, Sogensha, issued a two-volume set, *Lovecraft kessakushu* (1974–76), translated by Tadaaki Onishi and Toshiyasu Uno.

One baffling item is a supposed Bengali translation of *The Case of Charles Dexter Ward* that purportedly came out in 1976, as listed in the *Indian National Bibliography.*[12] But in spite of attempts by numerous scholars—including some in India—to locate this item, it has not been found.

In the realm of criticism from overseas, one volume deserves unstinted praise. The French scholar Maurice Lévy wrote a dissertation on Lovecraft, "L'Univers fantastique de H. P. Lovecraft," for the Sorbonne (1969).[13] This volume, somewhat revised, appeared as *Lovecraft ou du fantastique* (Christian Bourgois, 1972). A penetrating study of Lovecraft's literary work, the treatise explores his fiction as the author's search for a "cure" for his various psychological ailments, but nonetheless finds great power in his writing overall. It may well remain the finest general study of Lovecraft ever written. Lévy, a longtime professor at the University of Toulouse, went on to write shorter pieces on Lovecraft that are also illuminating.

The Buenos Aires newspaper *La Opinión,* in its cultural supplement for August 1, 1973, was entirely devoted to Lovecraft. It contained translations of "The Picture in the House," "The Terrible Old Man," and a Lovecraft letter, along with a translation of a portion of Derleth's "H. P. Lovecraft and His Work" and his "The Making of a Hoax" (from *The Dark Brotherhood,* concerning Lovecraft's creation of the *Necronomicon*), along with a few other articles.

---

12. The translator was listed as Adris Bardhan and the publisher was Granthaprakash (Calcutta).

13. French Ph.D. candidates are obliged to write two dissertations, a lengthy one and a shorter one. This is the shorter one. Lévy's lengthier one was the landmark volume *Le Roman "gothique" anglais, 1764–1824* (1968).

Much of the interest in Lovecraft in foreign countries was at this time fueled by appearances of his work, as well as articles about him, in such small-press magazines as *Quarber Merkur, Ganymed Horror, Simplizissimus,* and *Weird Fiction Times* (Germany), *Genso to Kaiki, Little Weird,* and *Crypt Horror Tales* (Japan), *Drab* (Netherlands), *Il Re in Giallo, Oltre in Cielo,* and *Galassia* (Italian), *Nova* (Norwegian), *Blagdaross* (Spanish), and others.

Even more notable as a token of Lovecraft's ascending fame overseas was the H. P. Lovecraft International Symposium, held in Trieste, Italy, on June 11–12, 1977. Dirk W. Mosig was in attendance, as was Alfred Galpin (who had resided in Italy for many years), along with numerous scholars and critics from all over Europe. It would be more than a decade before anything comparable to this event was held in the United States.

VII. Looking toward the Centennial (1980–1990)

In the summer of 1980, my critical anthology *H. P. Lovecraft: Four Decades of Criticism* appeared from Ohio University Press. It was the first book on Lovecraft published by a university press. Right from the time I began compiling the anthology in the summer of 1975, I had specifically eschewed approaching the numerous small presses in the field that might have been interested, recognising that an important step in Lovecraft's recognition was to bring his work to the attention of the academic community. Because of the demise of the "public intellectual" (such as Edmund Wilson [!]), the canonisation of literature is in the hands of academics; the work they choose to study, and to assign to their students, is in large part what comes to be regarded as "canonical."

It took more than thirty queries among academic presses, several of whom saw portions of the book but ultimately turned it down, before Ohio University Press accepted the book in the fall of 1978. The book was in part meant as a kind of history of Lovecraft criticism up to this time; hence the inclusion of the early notices by T. O. Mabbott, Edmund Wilson, Winfield Townley Scott, and others. Otherwise, it featured Fritz Leiber's two most important pieces ("A Literary Copernicus" and "Through Hyperspace with Brown Jenkin"), Mosig's "Myth-Maker" article, Wetzel's "The Cthulhu Mythos: A Study," St. Armand's "Facts in the Case of H. P. Lovecraft," and others.

And it also included several unpublished pieces—two by Peter Cannon, J. Vernon Shea's long and discursive study of literary influences on Lovecraft, and others.

One interesting piece was Paul Buhle's "Dystopia as Utopia: Howard Phillips Lovecraft and the Unknown Content of American Horror Literature" (*Minnesota Review*, Spring 1976). This was a rare article in the academic press on Lovecraft at this time, and it was a perspicacious study of Lovecraft's work in the context of the political, social, and economic tendencies of the time.

Four Decades of Criticism was an unusually long time in production, but when it finally did appear it created something of a sensation. It received fifteen reviews, an unusually large number for an academic-press book; many of these were in the fantasy or science fiction press, but a number of them were in academic venues relating to these genres, such as *Extrapolation*, *Gothic*, and *SFRA Newsletter*, as well as in such standard periodicals catering to academic and public libraries as *Library Journal* and *Choice*. Most of these reviews were favourable (although there was an inexplicably hostile one by Lincoln Van Rose in *Fantasy Commentator*, Winter 1982).

But the most surprising review came a full year after publication—nothing less than a review spanning the first two pages of the *Times Literary Supplement* (London). It was titled "Allurements of the Abyss" and was written by S. S. Prawer, a professor of German at Oxford who had previously written a book on the horror film. The review of the book itself was somewhat mixed, but Prawer's interpretation of Lovecraft's work is sensitive and penetrating. Taking note of Edmund Wilson's hostile criticism, he concludes:

> I venture to prophesy that *The Case of Charles Dexter Ward*, *The Colour out of Space*, *The Haunter of the Dark* and other fictions discussed in the volume under review will remain in print, and be read with fascinated appreciation, longer than that famous essay in *Classics and Com-*

> *mercials* which has induced many a literary jury to return a negative verdict in the case of Howard Phillips Lovecraft.[1]

H. P. Lovecraft: Four Decades of Criticism sold out its hardcover printing and went through two or three paperback printings, remaining in print for well over a decade.

About a year after the *Four Decades* appeared, Kent State University Press published my *H. P. Lovecraft and Lovecraft Criticism: An Annotated Bibliography*. This volume had also been long in the works; I had begun the compilation in the spring of 1976, after I heard from an editor at Kent State (whom I had queried about the *Four Decades*) that a new bibliography of Lovecraft might be in order. This was certainly the case. Although Mark Owings and Jack L. Chalker and issued *The Revised H. P. Lovecraft Bibliography* (Mirage Press, 1973), presenting some minimal revisions to the Chalker bibliography in *Dark Brotherhood* (which, as I have mentioned, was largely taken from Wetzel's earlier compilation), the whole field of Lovecraft bibliography needed to be overhauled and brought to a professional level. Under tutelage from the Kent State editors, I learned the art of descriptive bibliography, and the book ended up exceeding 500 pages. Some years later, Leigh Blackmore and I assembled a large supplement to the bibliography (Necronomicon Press, 1984).

A good deal of the work was done by other hands. As early as 1976, David E. Schultz had prepared an exhaustive list of Lovecraft's appearances in anthologies. In the summer of 1977 I visited Dirk W. Mosig in Georgia, as he had the most extensive private collection of foreign Lovecraftiana in the world. The John Hay Library, of course, was invaluable as a resource, and I studied its holdings with care. Under Mosig's advice, I rejected

1. "Allurements of the Abyss," *Times Literary Supplement* (18 June 1981): 688.

the Lovecraft–Derleth "posthumous collaborations" as work by Lovecraft, placing them in a category of "Apocrypha and Other Miscellany." The section on Lovecraft criticism—especially in regard to book reviews and academic papers—was almost entirely original.

This work also received largely favourable notices in the press, although as a reference work it was not likely to generate reviews that presented any sort of assessment of Lovecraft himself. Even so, it garnered twelve reviews, including those by Roger Schlobin in *Science Fiction and Fantasy Book Review* (January 1982) and A. Langley Searles in *Fantasy Commentator* (Winter 1983).

Another reference work I had produced earlier was *An Index to the Selected Letters of H. P. Lovecraft* (Necronomicon Press, 1980). Almost simultaneous with this was my *Lovecraft's Library: A Catalogue* (Necronomicon Press, 1980), compiled with Marc A. Michaud. We had discovered a list of Lovecraft's library prepared by Mary Spink at the behest of Annie E. P. Gamwell shortly after Lovecraft's death; she had contemplated selling the books. Spink's listing (both a typescript and, more valuably, a handwritten draft in a ledger book) was unearthed at the John Hay Library, but it provided very little in the way of bibliographical information. We fleshed out this skeletonic listing by means of the *National Union Catalog*, the *British Library Catalog*, and other reference works. Lovecraft himself had prepared a list of "Weird &c. Items in Library of H. P. Lovecraft," which he would circulate to colleagues who wished to borrow books from his library. This work engendered additional studies of literary influences on Lovecraft, as it included such works as Henri Béraud's *Lazarus* (1925), Barry Pain's *An Exchange of Souls* (1911), and other items that played a previously unidentified role in the genesis of his fiction and other work.

The scholarly revolution of the 1980s had to proceed without its chief representative up to that time—Dirk W. Mosig. Because of various personal and other difficulties, he was compelled to bow out of active participation in Lovecraftian work, with calamitous results to those (such as myself) who had relied upon his patience and expertise in guiding us toward a sounder view of Lovecraft. Two projects in particular were left uncompleted by Mosig: a brief study of Lovecraft for the Starmont Readers Guides series (being published in Mercer Island, Washington, by Thaddeus K. Dikty, a longtime devotee of science fiction) and, much more significantly, a book on Lovecraft for Twayne's United States Authors series.

I was assigned the Starmont book and produced it in short order in the summer of 1981; it appeared in 1982. In a small space (the book was only 83 pages) I attempted a synthesis of Lovecraft's life, work, and thought. The book was on the whole well received, although it received a hostile review in *Modern Fiction Studies* (Summer 1984); it was translated into French by Joseph Altairac as *Clefs pour Lovecraft* (Encrage, 1990).

The Twayne project was far more significant. This series—encompassing compact studies of authors of American, British, and world literature—had commenced in the 1960s (one of the earliest volumes, peculiarly enough, was on Arthur Machen, a superlative study written by Wesley D. Sweetser and published in 1964), and by this time there were hundreds of volumes available. To a significant degree, these volumes constituted an informal canonisation of the authors it covered, since the very fact that an author was chosen for study—as well as the fact that the books were widely purchased by academic libraries—suggested the author's high standing in literature.

Upon Mosig's departure, Donald R. Burleson offered to take up the Twayne project. I myself felt that he was an excellent choice. He had already collaborated with Mosig on several essays on Lovecraft for Frank N. Magill's *Survey of Science Fiction Literature* (Salem Press, 1979), and would himself write three fine pieces for Magill's *Survey of Fantasy Literature* (Salem Press, 1983). But Burleson was passed over, perhaps because, as a professor of mathematics, he did not conform to the publisher's view of what an author of one of their books should be. The assignment was instead given to Barton L. St. Armand, who was certainly an unexceptionable choice. But St. Armand, amidst a shifting of his literary interests toward Emily Dickinson and other authors, did not complete—and perhaps did not even begin—the treatise. So it passed to yet another scholar, as I shall relate presently.

Meanwhile, Burleson went on to write the essential equivalent of a Twayne monograph, *H. P. Lovecraft: A Critical Study* (Greenwood Press, 1983). Quite a bit larger than the usual Twayne book, it is an exemplary introduction to Lovecraft that retains much of its value today. The fact that only six years separated Shreffler's essentially amateurish *H. P. Lovecraft Companion* from this work issued by the same publisher shows how remarkably Lovecraft studies had progressed in that short period of time.

The autumn before the publication of the *Four Decades of Criticism,* Necronomicon Press published the first issue of *Lovecraft Studies.* Marc A. Michaud and I had lamented the increasing difficulty of getting the growing amount of Lovecraft criticism and scholarship published in such venues as *Nyctalops* or *Whispers,* which were either becoming more and more irregular in their issuance or veering away from criticism toward original fiction. Moreover, we felt that a journal that embodied a high level of scholarly rigour was now needed. At first we attempted to negotiate with an official at Brown University for university sponsorship of the journal, but our talks came to nothing; we were, in any case, doubtful that Brown would entrust the editing of such a journal to a pair of undergraduates. It made eminent sense to publish it through Necronomicon Press, as this publisher had already become well established as the leading small press for Lovecraftiana.

One of the things we prided ourselves on was that, in the nearly thirty years of the magazine's run, we managed to stick to a regular schedule, coming out in spring and fall with content that averaged about 20,000 words per issue and included articles, reviews, and rare works by Lovecraft. There was a brief hiatus between issue nos. 7 (Fall 1982) and 8 (Spring 1984), as personal difficulties by Michaud caused the press to go largely into abeyance (indeed, that Spring 1984 issue was guided through the press by Jason C. Eckhardt, whose covers graced every single issue of the journal); but thereafter, we kept up a regular pace until the early 2000s.

Donald R. Burleson, well before the publication of his *Critical Study,* now emerged as a leading voice in Lovecraft scholarship. His "Humor Beneath Horror: Some Sources for 'The Dunwich Horror' and 'The Whisperer in Darkness'" (Summer 1980) is a landmark piece studying the topographical and historical sources for these two major stories. "The Mythic Hero Archetype in 'The Dunwich Horror'" (Spring 1981) is a pioneering essay interpreting the Whateley twins as the true "heroes" of the tale, using the mythological theories of Joseph Campbell and others.

With "'The Terrible Old Man': A Deconstruction" (Fall 1987), Burleson began a series of articles using advanced literary theories to study Lovecraft. The value of such an approach is debatable, but there is no question that the articles analysed Lovecraft's work in minute detail. Burleson's "Lovecraft and the World as Cryptogram" (Spring 1988) provided insights into

Lovecraft's use of cryptography in "The Dunwich Horror" and other tales.

I myself began writing critical studies that I trust have some value. The first issue (Autumn 1979) contained "Autobiography in Lovecraft," an examination of the autobiographical portrayals in the fiction, in which I dispute the facile assumption that Randolph Carter is an unequivocal stand-in for Lovecraft. "'Reality' and Knowledge: Some Notes on the Aesthetic Thought of H. P. Lovecraft" (Fall 1980) attempted to build upon the work of Matthew H. Onderdonk (whose "Charon—in Reverse" was reprinted in the issue) in studying Lovecraft's theory of weird fiction and its application to the fiction. In "Textual Problems in Lovecraft" (Spring 1982) I attempted a preliminary survey of the textual errors besetting Lovecraft's fiction and outlined a methodology for the establishment of the soundest text of a given story. In a several-part series that spanned the issues from Spring 1984 to Fall 1985 and was later collected as "The Development of Lovecraftian Studies, 1971–1982," I examined in detail the manner in which the dissemination and study of Lovecraft's work had progressed in the period in question.

Robert M. Price contributed the valuable article "Higher Criticism and the *Necronomicon*" (Spring 1982), examining the way in which Lovecraft's imaginary tome underwent significant alterations of focus over the course of his work. Still more valuable was "Demythologizing Cthulhu" (Spring 1984), in which Price established that the "gods" of Lovecraft's mythos had evolved from supernatural entities to space aliens.[2]

Steven J. Mariconda, who became one of the acutest analysts of Lovecraft in the succeeding decades, introduced himself with

---

2. In a later article, "The Last Vestige of the Cthulhu Mythos" (Spring 1991), Price argued compellingly that this "demythologising" had been apparent right from the beginning, with "The Call of Cthulhu."

a scintillating article, "H. P. Lovecraft: Consummate Prose Stylist" (Fall 1984), an incisive study of the meticulous manner in which Lovecraft utilised prose rhythm to create his horrific effects—a direct challenge to those numerous commentators who maintained that Lovecraft was a poor manipulator of prose. He followed this article with "Notes on the Prose Realism of H. P. Lovecraft" (Spring 1985) and "Lovecraft's Concept of 'Background'" (Spring 1986), both highly insightful. "On the Emergence of 'Cthulhu'" (Fall 1987) is a detailed examination of the sources Lovecraft drew upon to write "The Call of Cthulhu."[3]

Peter Cannon contributed a number of short but illuminating pieces, among them "Lovecraft and the Mainstream Literature of the Day" (Fall 1982) and "The Late Francis Wayland Thurston of Boston: Lovecraft's Last Dilettante" (Fall 1989).

Will Murray began writing articles generally focused on the details of the Mythos, such as "The Dunwich Chimera and Others" (Spring 1984) and "On the Natures of Nug and Yeb" (Fall 1984). "An Uncompromising Look at the Cthulhu Mythos" (Spring 1986) was a purportedly iconoclastic examination of how Lovecraft "lost control" of the Mythos early on by allowing other writers to contribute to it. Murray's conclusions were somewhat overblown, and he was rebutted by David E. Schultz in "Who Needs the 'Cthulhu Mythos'?" (Fall 1986)—but Schultz went to the opposite extreme, fueled by his distaste for the egregious distortions of the Mythos effected by August Derleth, and maintained implausibly that the Mythos is unnecessary in the analysis of Lovecraft's work. This line of thought culminated in "What Is the Cthulhu Mythos?" (Spring 1987), a transcript of a panel discussion at the World Fantasy Convention in

3. A similar article, "Some Antecedents of the Shining Trapezohedron" (*Etchings and Odysseys,* 1983), studied the possible literary influences on that curious object cited in "The Haunter of the Dark."

Providence in October 1986, featuring Donald R. Burleson, Will Murray, Robert M. Price, David E. Schultz, and myself. The discussion was later translated into French.[4]

With "In Search of Arkham Country" (Fall 1986), and continuing with "In Search of Arkham Country Revisited" (Fall 1989), Murray attempted a revision of the standard view of the locations of Lovecraft's imaginary New England cities, claiming to find evidence that Arkham had initially been in central Massachusetts (Murray believed it to be located in the general area of the actual village of Oakham) and only later moved to the coast to align with Salem; Innsmouth, he maintained, actually drew upon the cities of Gloucester and Rockport. Unfortunately, Murray's interpretation was erroneous, and it was thoroughly rebutted by Robert D. Marten in the next decade. Robert H. Waugh introduced himself to the Lovecraft community with "The Hands of H. P. Lovecraft" (Fall 1988).

The study of Lovecraft's sources and background material was significantly augmented by such articles as Jason C. Eckhardt's "Behind the Mountains of Madness: Lovecraft and the Antarctic in 1930" (Spring 1987), a close study of the effect of Admiral Byrd's Antarctic expeditions on *At the Mountains of Madness*. Norman R. Gayford, in "Lovecraft and James Joyce" (Spring 1989) and "The Influence of Two Dunsany Plays" (Fall 1989), sought to probe literary influences on Lovecraft's work.

With the approach of Lovecraft's centennial, *Lovecraft Studies* issued a pair of double issues, Nos. 19/20 (Fall 1989), commemorating the journal's own decade of publication, and Nos. 22/23 (Fall 1990), which came out just after the centennial. In the first issue, I translated Michel Meurger's penetrating study "'Retrograde Anticipation': Primitivism and Occultism in the

4. *Qu'est-ce que le mythe de Cthulhu?* (Dole: La Clef d'Argent, 1988, 1990, 2000, 2007).

French Response to Lovecraft 1953–1957." Thekla Zachrau's "The 'Cthulhu Mythos': Between Horror and Science Fiction," translated by L. G. Boba and myself, was a chapter of Zachrau's treatise (for which see below). M. Eileen McNamara and I, in "Who Was the Real Charles Dexter Ward?," found evidence that the character in question was based on a figure who lived near Lovecraft's home at 10 Barnes Street. Burleson's "Lovecraft and Romanticism" was brief but insightful, and the issue contained numerous other pieces of value.

The Fall 1990 issue contained various articles of interest, but the chief contribution was Will Murray's "An Interview with Harry K. Brobst," a lengthy transcript of a phone interview of a friend of Lovecraft, now quite elderly, who had met him frequently in Providence during the years 1932–37. Otherwise, the issue had Wheeler Winston Dixon's "Notes on the Cinematic Interpretations of the Works of H. P. Lovecraft," Robert M. Price's "Erich Zann and the Rue d'Auseil," Mollie L. Burleson's provocative "The Outsider: A Woman?," James Anderson's "'Pickman's Model': H. P. Lovecraft's Model of Terror" (a structuralist analysis), and reviews of the burgeoning scholarly treatises on Lovecraft issued around the time of the centennial.

Lovecraft Studies also brought into print for the first time several works by Lovecraft, ranging from frivolities such as "Correspondence Between R. H. Barlow and Wilson Shepherd" (Fall 1986) and "Commercial Blurbs" (Spring 1988) to more substantial pieces such as "Some Repetitions on the Times" (Spring 1986) and "Instructions in Case of Decease" (Fall 1985).

Less than two years after the founding of *Lovecraft Studies,* Robert M. Price established *Crypt of Cthulhu.* Whereas the former, although published by a small press in the horror field, sought to be a scholarly journal in the fullest sense of the term, the latter was avowedly a "fan" publication; and yet, apart from certain deliberately humorous elements (a column featuring autobiographies of Lovecraft devotees, "Fun Guys from Yuggoth"; an advice column, "Advice to the Lovecraft-Lorn," run by a woman disguising herself as "Donna Death"; etc.), the scholarly content of the actual articles in the journal was notably high—not entirely surprisingly, since Price himself, for all his fannish enthusiasm, was a serious scholar in New Testament studies—and as a result there was a dynamic cross-pollination with the material in *Lovecraft Studies.*

Price had initially submitted *Crypt* as a contribution to the Esoteric Order of Dagon amateur press association, but quickly decided to distribute the journal far more widely. The first issue was dated Hallowmas 1981, but within a year Price was bringing out an incredible eight issues a year, thereby bringing into print a quantity of material almost unprecedented in the history of fantasy fandom. Lovecraft was not entirely the focus of the journal; other writers in the Lovecraft tradition were also covered, and Price was an unapologetic supporter of the "Cthulhu Mythos" in its broadest sense.

It would be cumbrous to attempt any comprehensive survey of the contents of *Crypt of Cthulhu,* but some note should be made of its more significant items. Price's own innumerable articles took center stage in many early issues, ranging from "Lovecraft's Concept of Blasphemy" (Hallowmas 1981); "Genres in the Lovecraftian Library" (Candlemas 1982); "The Cosmogony of Azathoth" (Eastertide 1982); "Lovecraft's Use of Theosophy" (Roodmas 1982); "The Lovecraft-Derleth Connection" (St. John's Eve 1982); "The Revision Mythos" (Candlemas 1983); "Brian Lumley—Reanimator" (Candlemas 1984); and "H. P. Lovecraft and the Cthulhu Mythos" (Hallowmas 1985).

Several articles probed literary influences on Lovecraft. The entire issue no. 49 (Lammas 1987) focused on this issue, with penetrating articles by Marc A. Cerasini (on the influence of Poe's *Arthur Gordon Pym* and Melville's *Moby-Dick* on *At the Mountains of Madness*), Peter Cannon, and others. Mike Ashley contributed "Lovecraft and Blackwood: A Surveillance" to the Hallowmas 1987 issue. Among the interesting essays on later writers of Lovecraftian fiction are "The Transition of Colin Wilson" by Charles Hoffman and Marc A. Cerasini (Lammas 1982) and "The Cthulhu Mythos Fiction of Robert Bloch" by Randall D. Larson (St. John's Eve 1986—the entire issue was devoted to Bloch).

I myself contributed several papers that appeared in *Crypt* (sometimes in abridged form), including "Lovecraft's Other Planets" (Eastertide 1982); "Lovecraft's Revisions: How Much of Them Did He Write?" (Candlemas 1983); "The Dream World and the Real World in Lovecraft" (Lammas 1983); "Lovecraft's Alien Civilizations: A Political Interpretation" (St. John's Eve 1985); "The Structure of Lovecraft's Longer Narratives" (Candlemas 1986); and "A Look at Lovecraft's Letters" (Eastertide 1987). Otherwise, *Crypt* published many articles by Will Murray, David E. Schultz, William Fulwiler, Peter Cannon, Steven J. Mariconda, and others.

Some special issues call for notice. Issue no. 10 (1982) included several revisions ("Ashes," by C. M. Eddy, Jr.; "The Sorcery of Aphlar" and "Dreams of Yith" by Duane W. Rimel) that had not been previously reprinted, along with the original versions of stories by William Lumley, Adolphe de Castro, and E. Hoffmann Price that Lovecraft later revised or entirely rewrote. No. 13 (Roodmas 1983) compared the Lovecraft circle with the Inklings (Tolkien, C. S. Lewis, and Charles Williams). No. 16 (Michaelmas 1983) reprinted lesser-known Lovecraft-influenced tales by Clark Ashton Smith, Robert E. Howard, and others, including the first reprinting of Duane W. Rimel's "The Tree on the Hill," revised by Lovecraft. No. 21 (1984) is my edition of *Saturnalia and Other Poems,* a collection of Lovecraft's previously unpublished poetry; this was followed up by no. 44 (1986), *Medusa and Other Poems,* containing his uncollected poetry. No. 27 (Hallowmas 1984), *Untold Tales,* featured unpublished stories by Clark Ashton Smith. No. 42 (Michaelmas 1986) reprinted several obscure works by Frank Belknap Long. No. 43 (Hallowmas 1986), *The Tomb-Herd and Others,* reprinted early Lovecraftian tales by Ramsey Campbell; No. 50 (Michaelmas 1987), *Ghostly Tales,* printed Campbell's juvenile booklet written when he was eleven years old. Of lesser interest were several issues devoted to the work of Lin Carter, whose literary executor Price became after Carter's death in 1988.

The letters column ("Mail-Call of Cthulhu") frequently contained lively discussion on various contributions to the magazine, engendering vibrant and usually polite debates on a wide array of subjects. Indeed, the sheer frequency of *Crypt of Cthulhu* allowed fans and critics to dwell on the smallest minutiae of Lovecraftian fiction and other areas, with the result that many small but significant points were clarified.

Some important booklets appeared from the small press, augmenting our knowledge of Lovecraft's life and work. Necronomicon Press issued my edition of Sonia H. Davis's *The Private Life of H. P. Lovecraft* (1985). The typescript of Sonia's memoir had been in the John Hay Library for decades, but the memoir was available in print only through the versions heavily edited by Winfield Townley Scott and August Derleth. While it is true that Sonia was not the most gifted writer imaginable, it was felt that the original text of the memoir was important to publish for the light it shed on the critical period of Lovecraft's marriage and life in New York, to say nothing of Sonia's unvarnished attitudes toward her husband.

R. Alain Everts's *The Death of a Gentleman: The Last Days of Howard Phillips Lovecraft* (Strange Co., 1987) was an expansion of Everts's article of 1973 along with other matter—including the first publication of Lovecraft's "death diary" (i.e., R. H. Barlow's incomplete transcript of the notes on his health that Lovecraft took during his final months of life). Peter Cannon's *The Chronology out of Time* (Necronomicon Press, 1986) is a fascinating compilation of dates in Lovecraft's fiction, from remote antiquity to the 1930s—an indication of the precision with which Lovecraft established the verisimilitude of his tales. Darrell Schweitzer significantly expanded his earlier compilation, *Essays Lovecraftian,* retitling it *Discovering H. P. Lovecraft* (Starmont House, 1987).

There was very little criticism of Lovecraft in the general academic community at this time. One curious item was J. L. Meikle's "Other Frequencies: The Parallel Worlds of Thomas Pynchon and H. P. Lovecraft" (*Modern Fiction Studies,* Summer 1981), which made the intriguing speculation that Pynchon's *The Crying of Lot 49* was inspired in part by Lovecraft.

Small-press publishers continued to issue lesser-known work by Lovecraft. Necronomicon Press continued to dominate the field in this regard. It issued my edition of Lovecraft's *Juvenilia: 1895–1905* (1984); *In Defence of Dagon* (1985), containing the three previously unpublished essays of 1921; *Uncollected Letters* (1986), chiefly including published letters during and just after Lovecraft's lifetime; and *The Fantastic Poetry* (1990; rev. 1993), a comprehensive collection of his weird poetry, including one or two unpublished items.

In a class by itself is David E. Schultz's annotated edition of the *Commonplace Book* (1987), issued in two volumes, a monument of scholarship that will only be superseded when Schultz himself issues the revised edition that he has been working on for years. Schultz definitely established the centrality of this humble little notebook to the genesis of Lovecraft's most significant work.

Schultz and I assembled a slim booklet for Necronomicon Press, *Letters to Henry Kuttner* (1990), which constituted the first of our many annotated editions of Lovecraft's unabridged letters.

R. Alain Everts's Strange Company issued numerous booklets of Lovecraft's work, including *The Illustrated Fungi from Yuggoth* (1983) and the poems *An Epistle to Francis, Ld. Belknap* (1987) and *An Epistle to the Rt. Hon*^ble^ *Maurice Winter Moe* (1987). *Ye Obt Servt* (1988) is a slender booklet of some of Lovecraft's postcards to Wilfred B. Talman. Soft Books in Toronto, operated by Joseph Bell, issued *The Young Folks' Ulysses* (1982) and *Cats and Dogs* (1986), among others.

More impressively, Ballantine issued the first trade paperback of Lovecraft stories, albeit under the cringe-inducing title of *The Best of H. P. Lovecraft: Bloodcurdling Tales of Horror and the Macabre* (1982). At long last the exclusive paperback rights to many of Lovecraft's major stories held by Lancer Books had lapsed, so this volume generally did include a great many of Lovecraft's finest tales, with the exception of his three short novels. The book went through many editions, selling in excess of 200,000 copies over the next two decades. In England, Panther Books published *At the Mountains of Madness and Other Novels of Terror* as volume 1 of the H. P. Lovecraft Omnibus. Volume 2 was a reissue of *Dagon and Other Macabre Tales,* and volume 3 was *The Haunter of the Dark and Other Tales of Horror*. All these editions appeared in 1985.

But the most significant editions of the decade were the revised texts of Lovecraft's fiction published by Arkham House—*The Dunwich Horror and Others* (1984), *At the Mountains of Madness and Other Novels* (1985), and *Dagon and Other Macabre*

Tales (1986)—under my editorship. As early as the winter of 1976–77, during my freshman year at Brown, I had begun examining the manuscripts and early printed appearances of Lovecraft's fiction with a view to ascertaining the accuracy of the current Arkham House editions. I was appalled when, in comparing the text of *At the Mountains of Madness* with the surviving typescript, I found more than 1500 textual errors in the Arkham House text.

My concomitant work in classical studies aided my Lovecraft work, since an understanding of the means by which Latin and Greek texts had been transmitted to us from antiquity was instrumental in determining the method by which the most accurate text of a given work could be ascertained. This work consumed the next five or six years, all the way till the summer of 1982, when I left Brown for Princeton. In the fall of 1982, I met James Turner at the World Fantasy Convention in New Haven, and we began hammering out the details of a new edition. The matter was complicated by the bad blood existing between Donald Wandrei and the current owners of Arkham House; as a result, we could not present entirely new editions of Lovecraft's stories, arranged chronologically, as I had wished; instead, in order to avoid litigation by Wandrei, we had to go through the charade of declaring these new editions "corrected printings." I grudgingly accepted these terms because of the supreme importance of getting the corrected texts available without delay.

The first volume did get numerous positive reviews in both genre publications (*Fantasy & Science Fiction, Fantasy Review, Science Fiction Review,* and of course *Lovecraft Studies* and *Crypt of Cthulhu*) as well as library journals and major newspapers (*San Francisco Chronicle, St. Louis Post-Dispatch*). Two amusingly contrasting reviews appeared: a favourable capsule review by Edna

Stumpf in the staid *New York Times Book Review* (May 19, 1985) and a flamboyant review by Michael Feingold in the bohemian *Village Voice* (March 19, 1985) that condemned Lovecraft as "trash" but urged readers to buy the new edition in any event. Notices of the second and third volumes were less abundant, but remained politely cordial.

After a three-year hiatus, Arkham House published my corrected edition of *The Horror in the Museum and Other Revisions* (1989). Now that Wandrei had died, it was determined that the volume could be radically reordered: not only by the inclusion of "new" revisions that had been discovered since the publication of the earlier edition (Whitehead's "The Trap," Rimel's "The Disinterment," Barlow's "The Night Ocean," among others), but by a division of the stories into "Primary Revisions" (those stories written almost entirely by Lovecraft) and "Secondary Revisions" (those stories that the collaborator or revision client had initially written but that had been revised, extensively or otherwise, by Lovecraft).

Foreign editions continued apace. In France, the publisher Pierre Belfond issued *Night Ocean et autres nouvelles* (1986), containing numerous relatively little-known tales (both original and revisions), along with a translation of the commonplace book. Still more significant was the first substantial volume of Lovecraft's poetry in a foreign language, *Fungi de Yuggoth et autres poèmes fantastiques* (Nouvelles Editions Oswald, 1987), edited by François Truchaud. This is a bilingual edition, with English and French text on facing pages, and appears to be largely a translation of the Arkham House *Collected Poems*. *Lettres d'Innsmouth* (Encrage, 1989), edited by Joseph Altairac, was a small-press publication that translated several booklets from Necronomicon Press, including *Uncollected Letters* and *In Defence of Dagon.*

German publications were numerous: *Die Katzen von Ulthar*

und andere Erzählungen (1980), *Der Schatten aus der Zeit* (1982), *In der Gruft und andere makabre Erzählungen* (1982), *Das Grauen im Museum und andere Erzählungen* (1984), and *Azathoth* (1989) all appeared in paperback from Suhrkamp, edited variously by two leading German scholars, Kalju Kirde and Franz Rottensteiner. The last volume unfortunately included some of the Derleth "posthumous collaborations," but redeemed itself by including several of Lovecraft's more notable essays. Suhrkamp also issued a *Lovecraft Lesebuch* (1987), edited by Rottensteiner, a selection of tales from previous Suhrkamp editions.

Some small presses joined in the fray. *The Dream-Quest of Unknown Kadath* appeared as *Die Traumfährt zum unbekannten Kadath* (Hobbit Press, 1980). "Supernatural Horror in Literature" appeared as *Unheimliche Horror* (Ullstein, 1987). Verlag Das Neue Berlin issued *Die Farbe aus dem Raum* (1990), a hardcover selection of stories. In a class by itself is *Ex Oblivione* (1989), a slim volume of three prose-poems translated and published by the young Michael Siefener in an edition of ten hardcover copies. Siefener would go on to become a widely published novelist.

Italian publications were also numerous, although several of them were repackagings by Sugar (now SugarCo) of some of its earlier volumes. A more pretentious item was *Tutto Lovecraft* (Fanucci, 1987–93), a twelve-volume series edited by Gianni Pilo and Sebastiano Fusco, which not only included most of the original fiction, revisions, and some poetry, but also selected critical articles on Lovecraft by Wetzel, Faig, Mosig, Leiber, and others, as well as some memoirs. Volume 11 was, anomalously, a translation of the George Hay *Necronomicon*. Considerably more valuable as a scholarly endeavour was Giuseppe Lippi's edition of *Tutti i racconti* (Mondadori, 1989–92), in four volumes. This edition translated from my corrected texts, as the Pilo–

Fusco edition did not, and included much bibliographical and other information. It intermingled the original fiction and revisions, producing an interesting reading experience. Lippi edited a popular edition of the series, *I miti dell'orrore* (Mondadori, 1990).

Malcolm Skey edited a translation (by Silvia Roberti Aliotta) of "Supernatural Horror in Literature," as *L'orrore soprannaturale in letteratura* (Edizioni Theoria, 1989). Curiously, he edited a new translation (by Stefania Censi) of the same work a few years later (Edizioni Theoria, 1992).

Nearly a dozen Spanish translations appeared in the decade, including *El horror de Dunwich* (1980), *En la cripta* (1980), *En las montañas de la locura y otros relatos* (1981), *Dagón y otros cuentos macabros* (1982), and *El clérigo malvado y otros relatos* (1983), all published by Alianza (Madrid). This publisher also translated "Supernatural Horror in Literature" (1984). Another leading publisher, Luis de Caralt (Barcelona), published *La maldición de Sarnath* (1981), while Valdemar Ediciones (Madrid) published a volume of poetry, *Hongos de Yuggoth y otros poemas fantásticos* (1988).

A large Dutch volume edited by Erik Lankester appeared as *Griezelverhalen* (Loeb, 1982), with translations mostly derived from previous Dutch editions; it was followed by *Het gefluister in de duisternis: Griezelverhalen* (Loeb, 1984). Several Swedish volumes appeared, including the two-volume *Cthulhu* edited by Sam J. Lundwall (Delta Forlags, 1988), containing most of Lovecraft's Cthulhu Mythos tales.

Lovecraft appeared in Catalan (a language independent of Spanish that is spoken in the area around Barcelona and elsewhere) for the first time in *A las muntanyes de la follia* (Laertes, 1985), *El cas de Charles Dexter Ward* (Edicions de Mall, 1985), and *L'ombra sobre Innsmouth* (Els Libres de Glauco, 1987).

Lovecraft exploded into modern Greek with ten separate volumes between 1986 and 1990. Most were published by Aiolos. Three of these volumes were part of an omnibus series, *Hapanta* (1990); a fourth volume was issued by a different publisher, Kaktos (1990?). "The Music of Erich Zann" appeared in an Icelandic anthology, Alfred Flóki's *Hrollvekjur: Átta sögur* (Idunn, 1982)—the only known appearance of Lovecraft in that language to date.

The first volume of Lovecraft in Polish was *Zew Cthulhu* (Czytelnik, 1983), containing several major stories. *At the Mountains of Madness* was translated as *W górach szaleństwa* (As-Editor, 1990). Toward the end of this period Lovecraft appeared in a Czech volume, *Necronomicon* (CAD Press, 1988), although this was a samizdat edition that was probably issued in no more than a few hundred copies. A more standard edition was the three-volume series "Spisy H. P. Lovecraft" (Zlatý Kun, 1990), edited by Pavel Nosek and including a substantial proportion of Lovecraft's shorter fiction; two further volumes were announced but did not appear. Several Lovecraft stories were included in the anthology *Galaktika 40* (Mozmosz-Könyvek, 1980), marking his first appearances in Hungarian. Two volumes of Lovecraft appeared in Serbo-Croatian, one translating *At the Mountains of Madness* (*Planine ludila* [1986]) and the other a selection of short stories (*S onu stranu sna* [1989]).

In Japan, the publisher Kokushi-Kankohkai took the lead. It first issued a ten-volume edition of Cthulhu Mythos tales by various hands, *Shin Cthulhu Shinwa Taikei* (1983), of which volume five was entirely by Lovecraft. The publisher then worked with me to issue an eleven-volume edition of Lovecraft's complete fiction, revisions, selected poetry, selected essays, and even two volumes of letters (1984–85). I provided my corrected texts; in some cases (as with the revisions), the texts appeared in

Japanese before they appeared in English. The publisher also translated my *H. P. Lovecraft: Four Decades of Criticism* in two volumes. This prestigious and attractive edition, with each volume enclosed in a slipcase, featured translations supervised by Kozaburo Yano. Each volume's slipcase features an illustration from Giger's *Necronomicon*.

Foreign interest in Lovecraft can also be gauged by the increasing quantity and sophistication of scholarship the decade produced. Hans Joachim Alpers edited a critical anthology, *H. P. Lovecraft: Der Poet des Grauens* (Corian Verlag Heinrich Wimmer, 1983), featuring a miscellany of Lovecraft letters, criticism from German and American critics, and other matter. Franz Rottensteiner assembled the impressive critical anthology *Über H. P. Lovecraft* (Suhrkamp, 1984), featuring work by French, German, Polish, and American critics, with an exhaustive bibliography of German publications relating to Lovecraft compiled by Kalju Kirde. Thekla Zachrau wrote the impressive monograph, *Mythos und Phantastik: Funktion und Struktur der Cthulhu-Mythologie in den phantastischen Erzählungen H. P. Lovecrafts* (Peter Lang, 1986). In Italy, Claudio De Nardi edited a substantial volume of memoirs of Lovecraft, *Vita privata di H. P. Lovecraft* (Reverdito Editore, 1987).

In Italy, Gianfranco de Turris and Sebastiano Fusco gathered their collected essays on Lovecraft (which had appeared in a wide array of Italian magazines and newspapers) as *L'ultimo demiurgo e altri saggi lovecraftiani* (Marino Solfanelli Editore, 1989). Antonio Cecchi wrote a long M.A. thesis, "Il passato e il suo potere nella narrativa di Howard Phillips Lovecraft" (University of Pisa, 1986), focusing on the use of the past in Lovecraft's work.

The French scholar William Schnabel wrote a substantial M.A. thesis in English, "Narrative Structures in Lovecraft's Works" (Université de Toulouse, 1989), that has much value.

Otherwise, there was not a great deal of critical or scholarly work in France. However, Joseph Altairac did begin issuing *Études Lovecraftiennes* sometime in the decade (the first five issues are undated; issue 6 is dated September 1989). Far from being merely a translation of *Lovecraft Studies* (although some important articles from that journal were translated), *Études Lovecraftiennes* contained an abundance of original material of no little value. The periodical continued till issue 14 (Summer–Autumn 1994).

In popular culture, two transcendent events early in the decade transformed the Lovecraft world and significantly augmented interest in his work worldwide. The first was the issuance of the role-playing game *Call of Cthulhu* from Chaosium in 1982. The role-playing game phenomenon began with the issuance of *Dungeons & Dragons* in 1974. *Call of Cthulhu,* set in the 1920s, made use of many of the elements in Lovecraft's fiction—"gods," characters, settings, and the like—and, more controversially, incorporated elements from other writers of Lovecraftian fiction. In spite (or perhaps even because) of this lack of "purity," the game became an immediate hit. Its various manuals were regularly updated and continue to be so down to the present day; and, interestingly enough, it attracted players whose familiarity with Lovecraft's actual writings was either scant or even nonexistent. Consider the comment of an early reviewer:

> *Call of Cthulhu* is well done. The graphics are of high quality (including a cover illustration by Gene Day); the rules are well written and clear. The sanity rules are an especially nice touch. Though I am only a casual reader of Lovecraft, it seems to me that the designer has a firm grasp of his subject and has made no gross errors regarding the Mythos.[5]

5. Greg Costikyan, Review of *Call of Cthulhu, Lovecraft Studies* No. 7 (Fall 1982): 31.

The overriding issue of whether the generally cerebral work of Lovecraft is even amenable to adaptation into the fundamentally artificial realm of the role-playing game is almost irrelevant; there is such an abundance of striking visual effects and compelling dramatic action in some of Lovecraft's scenarios that they can be manipulated into a wide array of media. It is precisely this that has made Lovecraft, almost uniquely among writers in the entire range of world literature, appealing to both highbrow and popular audiences.

And appeal of a definitely popular sort is exactly what director Stuart Gordon was aiming for in *Re-Animator* (1985), whose opening credits referred to the film as "H. P. Lovecraft's Re-Animator." Gordon, whose sole previous credit had been as writer and director of the film *Bleacher Bums* (1979), co-wrote the screenplay with Dennis Paoli and William J. Norris, and chose the charismatic Jeffrey Combs to play Herbert West. The fact that Gordon chose to adapt what Lovecraft himself regarded as his single worst story was weirdly appropriate; for the over-the-top flamboyance of the film renders it a hilarious parody of the horror film in exactly the same way that the story is in some senses a parody of itself. And the film was in fact more or less faithful to the story, featuring West's sidekick (here named Dan Cain and played by Bruce Abbott), Dr. Halsey, and other figures from the tale. However, West's nemesis becomes a fellow physician, Dr. Carl Hill (David Gale), whose severed but animated head creates difficulties for West.

But the chief point about the film, as far as Lovecraft's popularity is concerned, is its incredibly wide distribution throughout the world, and later its availability as a VHS cassette, DVD, and other formats. It continues to be popular today.

Gordon followed up *Re-Animator* with *From Beyond* (1986), starring Combs as Crawford Tillinghast and Barbara Crampton (who had played Dr. Halsey's daughter in the earlier film) as Dr. Katherine McMichaels. The latter, of course, had no role in the original story, and indeed the idea of making a feature-length film from a story of less than 3000 words strains credulity. Let us say charitably that the adaptation is quite loose, and the film lacks the riotous melding of horror and comedy that distinguished *Re-Animator*. It was not nearly as successful or critically acclaimed as its predecessor.

In *The Curse* (1987) director David Keith has produced an able adaptation of "The Colour out of Space"—although the story is not in fact credited in the film. Although the setting is transferred from Massachusetts to rural Tennessee, the general atmosphere of insidious decay is handled well, with Wil Wheaton, Claude Akins, and other capable actors playing the hapless farming family afflicted with the effects of the alien meteorite. The film is not highly regarded and was not exactly a box-office success, but it could have been far worse; and there are moments of atmospheric tensity that are otherwise rare in Lovecraft films.

Brian Yuzna (who had co-written the screenplay of *From Beyond*) directed *Bride of Re-Animator* (1990), a riotously amusing sequel to *Re-Animator* that premiered at the H. P. Lovecraft Centennial Conference in Providence in August 1990. Understandably, the actual Lovecraft content is vanishingly small, but Jeffrey Combs returns to form as Dr. Herbert West, as do Bruce Abbott as Dan Cain (now a physician himself) and David Gale as Carl Hill. Of *The Unnamable* (1988), written and directed by Jean-Paul Ouellette, little need be said. The connexion to the Lovecraft story is all but non-existent, and the film is little more than a standard young-people-terrorised-in-a-haunted-house scenario that we have seen too many times before.

As we have seen before and will see again in future years,

some of the most interesting nods to Lovecraft came from films or other media that are not explicitly based on his work. If nothing else (and in some cases there is indeed nothing else), these tips of the hat display the degree to which Lovecraft had entered popular culture at this time, with the expectation that viewers would axiomatically pick up on the references without further explanation.

The first two *Evil Dead* films (1981, 1987), directed by Sam Raimi, are infused with Lovecraftian elements. Raimi has admitted that he was inspired by Lovecraft's work in these films, and the first one makes much use of a book (purportedly in Sumerian) that is a clear analogue to the *Necronomicon;* the second film actually features the book (now titled—in bad Latin—*Necronomicon Ex Mortis*), and a prop of this book, sculpted by Russ Lukich, is available for purchase.

Unexpectedly, BBC Radio released a 43-minute documentary, *H. P. Lovecraft: The Young Man from Providence* (1983), directed by Shaun MacLoughlin, consisting of a biographical overview of Lovecraft and readings of extracts from Lovecraft's letters and stories. (The production was in fact a video, not simply an audio recording.) Preceding the first actual Lovecraft documentary by twenty years, it is a surprisingly able venture.

Although this volume does not cover the proliferation of "Cthulhu Mythos" writings by writers succeeding Lovecraft, some attention should be given to authors who use Lovecraft himself as a character in fiction, whether that fiction is supernatural or historical. Of the latter sort is Richard A. Lupoff's *Lovecraft's Book* (Arkham House, 1985), which the publisher attempted to market as a "true" account of an unknown episode in Lovecraft's life. But both the premise of the book—that Lovecraft allowed himself to become enmeshed for a time in a proto-Nazi plot concocted by German-American agitator George Sylvester Viereck (whom Lovecraft despised)—and its execution (Lovecraft resorts to social drinking on numerous occasions, in spite of his known opposition to the consumption of alcohol) leave much to be desired. The book was heavily edited by James Turner of Arkham House; decades later Lupoff published the full version as *Marblehead* (2007), although it retains the objectionable features of the earlier version.

Not much better—in fact, quite a bit worse—is Gahan Wilson's long story "H. P. L." in the anthology *Lovecraft's Legacy* (Tor, 1990), edited by Robert Weinberg and Martin H. Greenberg. This story is painfully inept in portraying Lovecraft's final days, but at least it shows—as later works do—that Lovecraft himself was starting to become an icon in popular culture.

From a more orthodox perspective, an important testament of Lovecraft's ascending critical esteem is the appearance of a single quotation (the first sentence of "The Call of Cthulhu") in the 15th edition of *Bartlett's Familiar Quotations* (1980). One could imagine diligent scholars scouring the totality of Lovecraft's work—essays, poetry, letters—for additional quotations (my favourite is from the *In Defence of Dagon* essays: "The world is indeed comic, but the joke is on mankind").

Lovecraft was now regularly appearing in histories of or monographs on weird fiction. Although he is mentioned only sporadically in Rosemary Jackson's *Fantasy: The Literature of Subversion* (1981), he comes in for extensive discussion in Brian Attebury's *The Fantasy Tradition in American Literature* (1980), where *The Dream-Quest of Unknown Kadath* is examined, and in Terry Heller's *The Delights of Terror* (1987), which dissects *At the Mountains of Madness.* R. D. Stock devotes some luminous pages on demonic figures in Lovecraft in *The Flutes of Dionysus: Daemonic Enthrallment in Literature* (1989).

Noël Carroll's *The Philosophy of Horror* (1990), being more of a theoretical work than a history, cites Lovecraft at random moments, chiefly in regard to his emphasis on cosmic awe. But we reach a nadir in Clive Bloom's "The Revolting Graveyard of the Universe: The Horror Fiction of H. P. Lovecraft," a contribution to Brian Docherty's critical anthology *American Horror Fiction* (1990). Bloom, a British academic, presents a superficial survey of Lovecraft's work but, astoundingly, uses the Derleth "posthumous collaborations" to underscore points about Lovecraft's own writings.

With the advent of the centennial of Lovecraft's birth, a multitude of scholars undertook to produce monographs or other writings to commemorate the event, and a number of important works of scholarship appeared.

My translation of Maurice Lévy's *Lovecraft ou du fantastique* (1972), on which I had been working since 1976, finally appeared as *Lovecraft: A Study in the Fantastic* (Wayne State University Press, 1988). It did well on both hardcover and paperback and received glowing reviews from Neil Barron, Esther Rochon, Barton L. St. Armand, and others. My *Selected Papers on Lovecraft* (Necronomicon Press, 1989) was a collection of five long essays that had appeared in abridged form in *Crypt of Cthulhu*.

Peter Cannon's *H. P. Lovecraft* (1989), for Twayne's United States Authors series, appeared about a year before the centennial. It is in every way a sound and competent study. One wishes the publisher had allowed Cannon slightly more room for analysis (as opposed to plot summary) of the major tales, but the books in the series tend to be of uniform size, so elaborate commentary is not possible. Even so, the book is well structured and presents a sound overview of Lovecraft's life and work. Its greatest virtue, perhaps, is its mere existence in such a prestigious series (although the publisher went out of business early in the twenty-first century and the book is now difficult to acquire). Around the same time, Necronomicon Press issued a slim volume of Cannon's miscellaneous essays, *"Sunset Terrace Imagery in Lovecraft" and Other Essays* (1990), which also contains much good work.

Much more ambitious is Donald R. Burleson's *Lovecraft: Disturbing the Universe* (University Press of Kentucky, 1990), a work that applies deconstructionist methodology to Lovecraft's tales. Whatever one thinks of the value of this critical theory, no one can deny that Burleson has engendered more than a few illuminating insights into Lovecraft's work. Amusingly, it was briefly reviewed in the prestigious journal *American Literature,* the entire review consisting of a single sentence: "It's getting to where those who still ignore Lovecraft will have to go on the defensive."[6]

I myself published two books of some relevance. *The Weird Tale* (University of Texas Press, 1990), even though it contained only a single (long) chapter on Lovecraft, was essentially a kind of dialogue with Lovecraft as both a fiction writer and a critic; specifically, I studied the four "modern masters" of "Supernatural Horror in Literature" (Arthur Machen, Lord Dunsany, Algernon Blackwood, and M. R. James), along with Ambrose Bierce and Lovecraft himself; I not only debated Lovecraft's own evaluations of these authors, but regarded his work as in some senses a culmination of the work of the others. The book sold tolerably well and received wide-ranging and mostly positive reviews.

My *H. P. Lovecraft: The Decline of the West* (Starmont House, 1990) was an attempt at a full-scale treatment of Lovecraft's philosophical thought and its application to the interpretation of

6. *American Literature* 63, No. 2 (June 1991): 374.

his fiction. Since Lovecraft's philosophical thought was not fully expressed in a single treatise, or even in his surviving essays, but rather in his correspondence, it required considerable research to ascertain the details and evolution of his views on the chief philosophical aspects that I studied (metaphysics, ethics, aesthetics, politics). The work came out to be quite a bit longer than expected, and the publisher was compelled to issue it in an ungainly two-column format to save paper.

Robert M. Price assembled many of his essays on Lovecraft in *H. P. Lovecraft and the Cthulhu Mythos* (Starmont House, 1990). David Barker's self-published booklet *The Lovecrafter—100th Anniversary Issue* (1990) and Jon Cooke's *The H. P. Lovecraft Centennial Guidebook* (Montilla Publications, 1990) also feature an array of good work.

The latter publication was specifically designed for distribution at the H. P. Lovecraft Centennial Conference, held in Providence on August 17–20, 1990. It was to be expected that the conference would be organised by myself, with Necronomicon Press taking a leading role; but we were fortunate in securing the backing of Brown University, making it the first academic conference on Lovecraft in the United States. For all the troubles involved in the preparation of the event, it ended up being a triumph in every way. Scholars from around the world were invited, and the six different panels were all lively and cogent. There were walking tours of Lovecraft's Providence, a substantial dealers' room for selling of Lovecraft-related material, and an impressive display of Lovecraft manuscripts and other material at the John Hay Library.

The event received considerable publicity locally as well as internationally, and it culminated with the unveiling of the H. P. Lovecraft Memorial Plaque, on the grounds of the John Hay Library—a project that had been organised by Jon Cooke, Will

Murray, and myself, with funding supplied by a wide array of devotees, including such notables as Peter Straub and Harlan Ellison.

By the end of the year, it could safely be said that Lovecraft was well on the way to critical recognition, and his popular appeal had never been higher. It would take another fifteen years for that recognition to attain full flower, while his popularity continued to surge.

VIII. The Road to Canonisation (1991–2005)

The six panel discussions at the Centennial Conference were recorded on both videotape and audiotape. I secured the audiotapes and spent the next several months preparing transcripts as close to the original presentations as possible, consulting with the various panelists over their individual texts. In the spring of 1991 Necronomicon Press published *The H. P. Lovecraft Centennial Conference: Proceedings* under my editorship, an 80-page booklet of microscopic type. Far more prestigious was the special Lovecraft issue of *Books at Brown,* the occasional publication of the Friends of the Library of Brown University. Edited by John H. Stanley, the curator of the Lovecraft collection, the issue (volumes 38–39, dated 1991–92 but in fact appearing around 1995) included presentations by eleven of the panelists, including my "Concluding Address"; the texts were significantly revised and augmented. In addition, the issue contained the unabridged text of Lovecraft's letters to John T. Dunn (his early colleague in the Providence Amateur Press Association), edited and annotated by David E. Schultz, John H. Stanley, and myself.

A volume that was designed to appear in the centennial year but missed it by a few months was *An Epicure in the Terrible,* edited by David E. Schultz and myself (Fairleigh Dickinson University Press, 1991). We had asked a number of leading Lovecraft scholars to write original essays on central issues in

Lovecraft's life and work, and all thirteen of the contributors came through with brilliant articles, ranging from Jason C. Eckhardt's assessment of Lovecraft as a "cosmic Yankee" to Steven J. Mariconda's study of Lovecraft's cosmic imagery to Schultz's article on the development of Lovecraft's cosmic vision to an investigation by Norman R. Gayford of Lovecraft's relations to Modernism to Barton L. St. Armand's comparison of Lovecraft and Borges. Kenneth W. Faig's essay "The Parents of Howard Phillips Lovecraft," as originally written, was a virtual monograph and had to be cut down radically to be accommodated into the volume; but it contained so many valuable insights that it was published more or less intact by Necronomicon Press (1990).

Some years after the centennial conference, a new convention, the NecronomiCon, began. The first two events (1993 and 1995) were located in Danvers, Massachusetts, the latter three (1997, 1999, and 2001) in Providence. While there were numerous interesting panel discussions (including one on *At the Mountains of Madness* that was later transcribed and published in the Spring 1996 issue of *Lovecraft Studies*), these conventions cannot be considered scholarly; nevertheless, they generated much interest in the Lovecraft and weird fiction community and were customarily attended by many of the leading authorities on Lovecraft.

Scholarly activity was still restricted largely to the small press, although the occasional article appeared in more orthodox scholarly journals. *Lovecraft Studies* maintained a regular sequence of twice-yearly publication throughout the decade, although in the early twenty-first century it became increasingly irregular, finally folding with the issue no. 45 (Spring 2005). But much valuable work appeared in its pages.

Robert H. Waugh began to dominate the issues in which he

appeared with a number of scintillating papers that always contained illuminating insights, ranging from "Documents, Creatures, and History in H. P. Lovecraft" (Fall 1991) to "'The Outsider,' the Terminal Climax, and Other Conclusions" (Spring 1996) to "Lovecraft and Keats Confront the 'Awful Rainbow'" (Fall 1996 & Spring 1997) to "The Outsider, the Autodidact, and Other Professions" (Fall 1997 & Spring 1998) to "The Subway and the Shoggoth" (Summer & Fall 1998).

Steven J. Mariconda continued his penetrating work with "H. P. Lovecraft: Art, Artifact, and Reality" (Fall 1993) and "Tightening the Coil" (Spring 1995), a valuable study of Lovecraft's revision of "The Whisperer in Darkness." Paul Montelone published several papers stressing the ways in which several stories express Schopenhauerian pessimism or other philosophical conceptions, among them "The Rats in the Walls" (Spring 1995), "Ex Oblivione" (Fall 1995), "The Shadow out of Time" (Spring 1996), "The Outsider" (Fall 1996), and "The White Ship" (Spring 1997).

Sam Gafford's expansive essay "'The Shadow over Innsmouth': Lovecraft's Melting Pot" (Spring 1991) is one of the acutest essays on that major story ever published. Will Murray's "Behind the Mask of Nyarlathotep" (Fall 1991) argues convincingly that the figure of Nyarlathotep was at least partially inspired by the eccentric scientist Nikola Tesla.

Anne K. Scargill and Scott D. Briggs translated the first half of Rafael Llopis's incisive introduction to *Los mitos de Cthulhu,* but they never managed to translate the second half. Hubert Van Calenbergh translated the Belgian scholar Hubert Lampo's chapter on Lovecraft from *De zwanen van Stonehenge* (1972). Lampo wrote numerous articles on Lovecraft during the 1970s.

Robert D. Marten destroyed Will Murray's attempt to revise the map of Lovecraft's fictitious New England cities in "Arkham

Country: In Rescue of the Lost Searchers" (Summer 1998), and followed it up with a trenchant essay on the setting of "Pickman's Model" (2004). Kenneth W. Faig, Jr.'s essay on "He" (Fall 1997) was matched by Michael Cisco's close reading of the fragment "The Book" (Autumn 2001).

On the biographical front, Dr. M. Eileen McNamara studied the medical record of Winfield Scott Lovecraft at Butler Hospital (Spring 1991). Mara Kirk Hart, the daughter of Lovecraft's New York friend George Kirk, wrote a substantial memoir, "Walkers in the City" (Spring 1993), largely based on her discovery of her father's letters to his eventual wife. Chris Powell presented a fascinating array of previously unknown information on Lovecraft's sometime collaborator Adolphe de Castro (Spring 1997). Stephen J. Jordan presented a comprehensive study of "H. P. Lovecraft in Florida" (Autumn 2001).

Other fine essays by Stefan Dziemianowicz, Dan Clore, Carl Buchanan, Faye Ringel Hazel, John Kipling Hitz, Esther Rochon, Kieran Setiya, and numerous others appeared.

Crypt of Cthulhu continued its remarkable run, although increasingly it focused on Lovecraftian fiction rather than critical articles. Still, pieces such as Stefan Dziemianowicz's "The Leiber-Lovecraft Connection" (Hallowmas 1990), Donald R. Burleson's "Lovecraft: An American Allegory" (St. John's Eve 1991), Fred Blosser's study of the film *Die, Monster, Die!* (Eastertide 1996), John Shire's "Lovecraft, Lacan, and the Lurking Fear" (Lammas 2000), and numerous others bespeak both the continuing ability of Robert M. Price to secure vibrant and thought-provoking articles.

Kenneth W. Faig, Jr.'s enormous "'The Silver Key' and Lovecraft's Childhood" (St. John's Eve 1992) definitively chronicled how that story emerged out of Lovecraft's visit to ancestral areas in Rhode Island in 1926. Faig followed this up with "The

Friendship of Louise Imogen Guiney and Sarah Susan Phillips" (Hallowmas 1998), along with an article on a highly obscure episode in Lovecraft's involvement in amateur journalism (Hallowmas 1999).

David E. Schultz's "Notes toward a History of the Cthulhu Mythos" (Eastertide 1996) is a fascinating compendium of quotations from Lovecraft and others showing how the Mythos became a kind of shared-world universe. Price himself became a fleeting convert to deconstruction with "The Criticism of Azathoth" (Eastertide 1992), although he eventually snapped out of it and returned to his more fruitful vein of studying Lovecraft through the lens of religious studies. Price also managed to entice Colin Wilson to write an original piece, "H. P. Lovecraft and the Century of Violence" (Michaelmas 1990), although the essay is a trifle confused and unfocused.

Special issues focused on such figures as Duane W. Rimel (Hallowmas 1991), Richard L. Tierney (Eastertide 1994), Peter Cannon (Lammas 1995), August Derleth (Hallowmas 1996—including a complete reprint of Derleth's B.A. thesis, "The Weird Tale in English Since 1890" [1930]), among others.

Crypt of Cthulhu suddenly terminated with issue 107 (Eastertide 2001) and did not resume publication for sixteen years.

Several valuable publications appeared from the small press. Necronomicon Press continued to take the lead, issuing an exhaustively annotated edition of *The Shadow over Innsmouth* (1994; rev. 1997) prepared by David E. Schultz and myself, as well as editions of Lovecraft's letters to Richard F. Searight (1992) and Robert Bloch (1993). Among monographs we can note Richard D. Squires's *Stern Fathers 'neath the Mould: The Lovecraft Family in Rochester* (1995), an exhaustive discussion of Lovecraft's paternal ancestry after the family had emigrated from England to Rochester, New York. My compilation of *H. P. Love-*

craft in the Argosy (1994) presented the complete texts of the letters by Lovecraft and others in the *Argosy* and *All-Story* (1913–14)—the controversy that led to Lovecraft's entry into amateur journalism. *Caverns Measureless to Man* (1996) is a slim collection of Lovecraft memoirs, chiefly from the amateur press. Necronomicon Press also issued a volume of Steven J. Mariconda's essays on Lovecraft, *On the Emergence of "Cthulhu" and Other Observations* (1995), as well as *Mosig at Last* (1997), a collection of Dirk W. Mosig's still valuable papers on Lovecraft, mostly written in the 1970s.

Arkham House briefly returned to the stage by issuing my edition of Lovecraft's *Miscellaneous Writings* (1995). The volume had initially been conceived by August Derleth, although in all likelihood he envisioned only the gathering up of various Lovecraft items published in the previous Arkham House "stopgap" volumes, among others. James Turner then contemplated assembling the book, but amidst his myriad other duties in keeping Arkham House afloat he never got around to it; so he commissioned me to do the job. I asked for as free a hand as possible, and he granted it. After a section containing the remaining scraps of fiction not included in the four previous corrected editions from Arkham House, I arranged the balance of the book (all essays or other nonfiction) into eight categories, ranging from philosophy to literary criticism to amateur journalism to travel and others; a brief section of letters published in his lifetime was also included. The volume constituted the first publication of two major travel essays by Lovecraft ("Travels in the Provinces of America" and "An Account of Charleston"); in many ways it remains the best single volume of Lovecraft's essays published to date.

The Cthulhu Mythos was studied in two penetrating studies by Daniel Harms. The first (co-written with John Wisdom

Gonce III) was *The Necronomicon Files* (Night Shade, 1998), a thorough discussion of Lovecraft's fictitious book in his writings and in those of others. Harms's *Encyclopedia Cthulhuiana* (Chaosium, 1994; rev. ed. 1998) is an exhaustive glossary of the gods, books, places, and other entities in tales by Lovecraft and his imitators.

Not to be overlooked, in spite of its ungainly format, is Kenneth W. Faig, Jr.'s *Some of the Descendants of Asaph Phillips and Esther Whipple of Foster, Rhode Island* (Moshassuck Press, 1993), an extraordinary monument of scholarship providing detailed information on dozens of Lovecraft's maternal ancestors extending back to the eighteenth century. Much shorter but along the same lines is *Devonshire Ancestry of Howard Phillips Lovecraft* (Moshassuck Press, 2003), prepared by Chris J. Docherty, A. Langley Searles, and Kenneth W. Faig, Jr.

The burgeoning biographical work on the most minute details of Lovecraft's life (including his family and more remote ancestry) culminated in the first version of my biography, published as *H. P. Lovecraft: A Life* (Necronomicon Press, 1996). I had spent a full two years (1993–95) on the project, only undertaking it when I determined that several other scholars who might have done the work ably were not in a position to do so. I was determined to correct the errors and misjudgments in de Camp's book, chiefly by presenting Lovecraft's life and work in the context of his historical era and also in light of his philosophical vision. Only by this integrated approach, I believed, could a well-rounded portrait of Lovecraft appear.

I had expected the book to run quite long, given the amount of documentary evidence on Lovecraft now available; I could easily have imagined it running to 250,000 words. But given that the amount of information on the final decade of Lovecraft's life is so abundant, my draft ran to 508,000 words (not including notes, bibliography, and other matter). I made some attempts to secure publication of the book with leading commercial and academic firms; but its length, and the fact that (in spite of my numerous publications with university presses) I myself did not have a lofty reputation, made it impossible for me to find a publisher.

Marc Michaud came to my aid, vowing to publish the book as a kind of public service to the Lovecraft community. But he was unable to publish the book at its full length, and so I abridged it to about 350,000 words. When it appeared, it created as much of a sensation as was possible from a book issued by a small press. The 250-copy hardcover edition sold out in a week, and three paperback editions appeared through 2004. The book was widely and, generally, favourably reviewed, by such critics as Donald M. Hassler (*Extrapolation*), Brian McNaughton (*Deathrealm*), R. D. Mullen (*Science-Fiction Studies*), and numerous others.

But the most surprising review came from Joyce Carol Oates, who wrote an extensive review-article, "The King of Weird," in the *New York Review of Books* (31 October 1996). In all frankness, Oates was using the biography to express her views on Lovecraft, but these views were unfailingly keen and perspicacious. The last two pages of the review covered my book specifically. The prominence of both the author and the venue constituted a notable advance in Lovecraft's recognition. A radically abridged version of the biography appeared in England as *A Dreamer and a Visionary: H. P. Lovecraft in His Time* (Liverpool University Press, 2001).

During the latter stages of my work on the biography, I was asked by Robert Reginald, who had taken over the Starmont House list under his Borgo Press imprint, to write a much expanded version of my Starmont Readers Guide of 1982. I did so, producing *A Subtler Magick: The Writings and Philosophy of H. P. Lovecraft* (1996). The title is the publisher's. While focusing on the work, I believe this monograph also integrates Lovecraft's life, work, and thought in the manner I had attempted in my biography.

An important landmark in the study of Lovecraft's life is Peter Cannon's anthology *Lovecraft Remembered* (1998), which constitutes the last volume by or about Lovecraft to be published by Arkham House, aside from its continued reprints of the corrected fiction volumes I edited in the 1980s. Cannon's book may be open to some small criticism—as in his decision to use the abridged version of Sonia H. Davis's memoir, or to print one of the later versions of Muriel Eddy's memoir, where she seems to have exaggerated the extent of her and her husband's relations to Lovecraft—but overall this volume is a splendid compilation. The memoirs are arranged thematically and present a comprehensive portrait of the man as seen by his friends, colleagues, and disciples.

And we can hardly bypass Cannon's historical novel *The Lovecraft Chronicles* (Mythos Books, 2004), a delightful alternate-history account whereby Lovecraft actually does get a book published by Alfred A. Knopf in his lifetime, thereby catapulting him into celebrity and economic comfort. He lives far beyond the year 1937, migrating to his beloved England and (surprisingly) fending off romantic involvements with a succession of fetching ladies. It is all perfectly captivating.

Publications of Lovecraft's work continued their bifurcation of previous years: major publishers continued to issue his tales in volumes (mostly trade paperbacks) of ever-widening circulation, while the small press focused on issuing lesser-known bodies of his work, especially his letters.

Ballantine Books issued additional trade paperback volumes

of Lovecraft's tales (following the *Bloodcurdling Tales* volume of 1982) with *The Dream Cycle of H. P. Lovecraft* (1995), *The Transition of H. P. Lovecraft* (1996), and *Waking Up Screaming: Haunting Tales of Terror* (2003). The first, aside from featuring an error-sprinkled introduction by Neil Gaiman, contained Lovecraft's Dunsanian tales but also *The Case of Charles Dexter Ward* and others; the second (with an introduction by Barbara Hambly) was essentially a volume of Lovecraft's early macabre tales, concluding with *At the Mountains of Madness;* the third (with an introduction by Poppy Z. Brite) includes "The Shadow over Innsmouth," *The Case of Charles Dexter Ward,* and other miscellaneous tales. All three volumes have sold well and remain in print. None of them used my corrected texts.

Other volumes of Lovecraft's work *did* use my texts. *Tales of H. P. Lovecraft* (Ecco Press, 1997) was a hardcover volume of stories chosen by Joyce Carol Oates, who used her review of my *H. P. Lovecraft: A Life* as the introduction. The book was subsequently reprinted in paperback by HarperCollins (2000) and later in the Harper Perennial Modern Classics series (2007). My *Annotated H. P. Lovecraft* (Dell, 1997) was a volume that contained only four stories, among them *At the Mountains of Madness,* with extensive annotations. The project was commissioned by a book packager and sold quite well—about 25,000 copies over the next several years. There was a follow-up volume, *More Annotated H. P. Lovecraft* (Dell, 1999); but here Peter Cannon did all the annotations except the one for "Herbert West—Reanimator" (which had initially been scheduled for the first volume but had been later removed).

Far more significant for Lovecraft's recognition was the first volume of Lovecraft's tales in Penguin Classics, *The Call of Cthulhu and Other Weird Stories* (1999), in which I edited and extensively annotated the texts. Penguin had apparently been trying to get in touch with me for years about such a project. The book was first published in the Penguin Modern Classics series, with a striking cover by John Martin, the early nineteenth-century painter whose cosmic landscapes Lovecraft admired. Later the book appeared under the standard Penguin Classics imprint. There were two succeeding volumes: *The Thing on the Doorstep and Other Weird Stories* (2001) and *The Dreams in the Witch House and Other Weird Stories* (2004); all three volumes, which contain nearly the totality of Lovecraft's original fiction, have been frequently reprinted and remain in print.

Less creditable is *Black Seas of Infinity: The Best of H. P. Lovecraft* (Science Fiction Book Club, 2001), a volume edited by Andrew Wheeler and containing a rather odd mix of major tales, very minor ones (such as "History of the 'Necronomicon'"), and revisions. My corrected texts were used, albeit without authorisation. Still less reputable—and a sad harbinger of the future—were a series of Lovecraft volumes issued in 2004 by Kessinger Publishing, a print-on-demand publisher in Montana that publishes public-domain material in crude and slapdash editions; one of the Lovecraft volumes consisted only of "The Horror at Red Hook." There was some doubt at the time as to whether Lovecraft's tales—or any other work—really were in the public domain, but Kessinger forged ahead, apparently assuming no estate or agent or other entity would pursue legal action against it. That is exactly what happened, and countless other print-on-demand editions of highly dubious quality have appeared subsequently.

Lovecraft's collected poetry was brought into print at last by Night Shade Books as *The Ancient Track: The Complete Poetical Works of H. P. Lovecraft* (2001), under my editorship. The volume had initially been compiled for Arkham House, but James Turner's departure from the firm around 1995 caused the plan to fall by the wayside. Necronomicon Press then contemplated issuing the book and actually prepared proofs; but Marc Michaud's various difficulties around 1999 once again stymied plans to publish the book. Night Shade secured the proofs from Michaud and issued the book. It contained almost the totality of Lovecraft's poetry, including fragments found in letters, with extensive annotation.

David E. Schultz and I, now in possession of an enormous quantity of Lovecraft's letters, published and unpublished (totalling about 4.5 million words), felt that we could assemble a kind of autobiography—which would also include discussions of Lovecraft's philosophy, aesthetics, and other elements—from this mass of material. We did so in the volume *Lord of a Visible World: An Autobiography in Letters,* published in 2000 by Ohio University Press, which had helped to ignite scholarly interest in Lovecraft twenty years earlier by the issuance of my *Four Decades of Criticism.*

Night Shade also assisted in the quest to bring Lovecraft's letters into print. It issued two volumes edited by Schultz and myself, *Mysteries of Time and Spirit* (2002) and *Letters from New York* (2005). The first was the unabridged joint correspondence of Lovecraft and Donald Wandrei—the first time that both sides of a Lovecraft correspondence had been published. The second volume was an attempt to exhibit the incredible value of the letters that Lovecraft wrote to his two aunts relating to New York, especially during his two-year residency there (1924–26); but because of the enormous quantity of material (the letters from that two-year period come to more than 400,000 words), the letters had to be severely abridged. In any event, this volume appeared at a time when Night Shade was purchased by another company that did not wish to pursue the Lovecraft Letters project, as it was called.

But by this time a new publisher had emerged, Hippocampus Press, in the wake of the decline of Necronomicon Press; indeed, one issue of *Lovecraft Studies* and *Studies in Weird Fiction* actually appeared under the Hippocampus Press imprint before Necronomicon Press, briefly coming back to life, issued the final issues of each publication. Hippocampus Press was the brainchild of Derrick Hussey, a young enthusiast of Lovecraft who had already gained expertise in New York publishing but who was unsatisfied with his advance up the corporate ladder. When I informed him that, if he established a small press devoted to Lovecraft and other authors of weird fiction, I could guarantee an all but endless line of books (I was not referring only to my own projects) that he could publish, he decided to take the plunge.

Hussey began slowly. Securing the assistance of David E. Schultz (who, all apart from his scholarly expertise, evolved into a skilled book designer) and others, he issued my *The Annotated Supernatural Horror in Literature* in 2000. This book had actually been compiled as early as 1981 for Greenwood Press; but the publisher withdrew the offer to publish the book at a later stage. This was Hippocampus's only publication in 2000, but it created a sensation in 2001 when it issued *The Shadow out of Time*.

This was an annotated edition of the story, analogous to the annotated *Shadow over Innsmouth* that Necronomicon Press published in 1994; but the text was nothing less than Lovecraft's original handwritten draft, which he had given to R. H. Barlow as recompense for preparing the typescript. The manuscript had wended its way from Florida to Mexico to Hawaii, where a relative of the woman who owned it, and who had recently died, donated the manuscript to the John Hay Library. I was allowed to consult the item in early 1994, and my impression that the published text was seriously corrupt (albeit not to the degree that *At the Mountains of Madness* was butchered in *Astounding Stories*) was confirmed. James Turner of Arkham House had offered to publish the corrected text and had actually sent me galley proofs of it; but the project collapsed after his departure from the firm. The Hippocampus Press publication finally allowed the unadulterated text to be read by Lovecraft devotees, a full sixty-six years after it had been written.

Hippocampus Press followed up this item with *From the Pest Zone* (2003), a volume of the five stories Lovecraft wrote in New York, extensively annotated by David E. Schultz and myself; and, more significantly, with *Letters to Alfred Galpin* (2003) and *Letters to Rheinhart Kleiner* (2005), the first complete publication of the letters to these two correspondents, again heavily annotated and also presenting a wealth of ancillary documents (mostly by Galpin and Kleiner) to round out the picture of their relationship with Lovecraft. And, as an indication of the extent to which anyone connected with Lovecraft was now achieving a certain celebrity in his own right, Hippocampus issued *Eyes of the God* (2002), a volume of the collected stories and poems of R. H. Barlow, and *Out of the Immortal Night* (2004), the first attempt to collect the poetry and fiction of Samuel Loveman.

Hippocampus's most ambitious project in its early years was its publication of a five-volume set of Lovecraft's *Collected Essays* (2004–06) under my editorship. This is a project I had conceived as early as my undergraduate years at Brown in the late 1970s, when I had come up with a rudimentary prospectus for a "Collected Works of H. P. Lovecraft." Now that the fiction and poetry had been issued in corrected and annotated texts, all that remained (aside, of course, from the immense job of publishing the letters) was the essays. I broke the set down by category—amateur journalism, literary criticism, science, travel, and philosophy (along with autobiography and miscellany). The volumes appeared in hardcover, paperback, and in electronic formats as well.

In the decade and a half covered in this chapter, the flood of foreign translations of Lovecraft's work that we had seen earlier now attained the dimensions of a tsunami, especially in the major European languages.

In France, Francis Lacassin edited an immense three-volume omnibus of Lovecraft in the publisher Robert Laffont's Bouquins series (1991–92), although the volumes contained a fair number of Cthulhu Mythos stories from other hands (many taken from the anthology *Légendes du mythe de Cthulhu* [1975]); but it also included such things as Lovecraft's juvenile stories, story notes, essays, and poetry. Volume three committed the gaffe of including the Derleth "posthumous collaborations," but also included a sheaf of letters (apparently taken from *Dreams and Fancies*) as well as a number of significant memoirs of Lovecraft. But the old translations by Jacques Papy, Paule Pérez, Jacques Parsons, and others were used. These translations continued to be reprinted into the 1990s, including a slim bilingual edition of "The Dunwich Horror" by the prestigious publisher Gallimard (1993); most of the other reprints were issued by the popular paperback publisher J'ai Lu.

In Germany, one of the most distinguished editions of Lovecraft ever issued in any language appeared as *Gesammelte Werke* (Edition Phantasia, 1999–2004), a twelve-volume edition edited by Marco Frenschkowski, Joachim Körber, and Uli Kohnle, and based on my corrected texts. This hardcover edition was limited to 350 copies and presented the original in chronological order (volumes 1–5), followed by three volumes of revisions, and the Derleth "posthumous collaborations" (volumes 9 and 10). The translations were mostly taken from previous editions. Phantasia had preceded this edition with a smaller selection of revisions,

Das Nachtmeer (1995), and a bilingual edition of *Fungi from Yuggoth, Saat von den Sternen* (1999).

Michael Siefener continued his limited editions of Lovecraft with the publication of the poems "Nathicana" (*Nathicana,* 1991; 22 copies), "The City" (*Die Stadt,* 1991; 22 copies), and *Fungi from Yuggoth* (*Pilze vom Yuggoth,* 1992; 20 copies). Franz Rottensteiner edited a new translation of "Supernatural Horror in Literature," *Die Literatur der Angst* (Suhrkamp, 1995), with a translation by Michael Koseler. Suhrkamp also issued a *Best of H. P. Lovecraft* (1996). A new translation of Lovecraft's major works by Florian F. Marzin and others appeared as *Vom Jenseits* (area Verlag, 2005).

In Italy, Giuseppe Lippi's *Tutti i racconti* (1989–92) was twice reprinted by Mondadori (1997–98, 2006–07). Gianni Pilo and Sebastiano Fusco attempted a rival collected edition, *Tutti i romanzi e i racconti* (Grandi Tascabili Economici Newton, 1993; 5 volumes), although this appears to be largely a repackaging of their earlier edition, *Tutto Lovecraft* (1987–93). Both editions were broken down into numerous smaller-scale volumes over the next several years.

Italian editors, unlike those in other countries, made a concerted effort to publish other bodies of Lovecraft's work. SugarCo issued a volume of Lovecraft's literary essays, *In difesa di Dagon e altri saggi sul fantastico* (1994), edited by Gianfranco de Turris, followed by a new translation of "Supernatural Horror in Literature," *L'orrore soprannaturale nella letteratura* (1994). A revised and augmented edition, combining the two volumes, appeared as *Teoria dell'orrore* (Castelvecchi, 2001). Mondadori countered with Lippi's edition of a volume of letters, *Lettere dall'altrove* (1993) and *Diario di un incubo* (1994), a translation by Claudio De Nardi of David E. Schultz's edition of the commonplace book. Lippi also edited a unique volume, *Lovecraft: Le parole, le immagini* (Mondadori, 1994), a volume of photographs of Lovecraft and other images pertaining to his life and work, with brief passages taken from letters and other sources. Sebastiano Fusco edited the first extensive selection of Lovecraft's poetry, *Il vento delle stelle* (Agpha Press, 1998).

Carlo Fruttero and Franco Lucentini, one of the original editors of Lovecraft in Italy, resurrected their volume *I mostri all'angolo della strada* (1966) in an abridged edition, *L'orrendo richiamo: Tutti i mostri del Ciclo di Cthulhu* (Einaudi, 1994). Similarly, Fanucci returned to Lovecraft with *I racconti del Necronomicon* (1995; 2 volumes [reissued in one volume, 2002]), followed by *Incubi dalle tenebre* (1997).

And one cannot bypass *I gatti di Ulthar e altri gatti* (Felinamenta/Publigold, 1993), a slim volume of Lovecraft's stories and poems about cats. A similar volume, *Il libro dei gatti* (Il Cerchio, 1996), edited by Gianfranco de Turris and Claudio De Nardi, included the essay "Cats and Dogs" and passages from several letters. Yet another such volume was *Da Providence a Ulthar* (Yorick Editions, 2005), edited by Pietro Guarriello, one of the leading Italian Lovecraft scholars of the era.

A most peculiar volume was *The Cosmical Horror of H. P. Lovecraft: A Pictorial Anthology* (Bibliotheca L'Enfer de Babel, 1991), edited by Stefano Piselli, Federico de Zigno, and Riccardo Morrocchi, consisting of text and images in Italian, English, and French, and mostly reprinting various comic book adaptations of Lovecraft stories, along with some discussion of Lovecraft-related films.

There were a grand total of fifty-six new editions in Spanish along with continuing reprints of earlier editions. The Argentinian publisher Andrómeda released seven slender volumes in 1991–92, edited and translated by Jon Wakeman. The Barcelona publisher El Observador issued five volumes in the same period. The Madrid publisher Edaf began an extensive publishing programme in 1991, with more than thirty volumes down to 2005, many of them edited by Alberto Santos Castillo. Many of these volumes were then gathered in three different multi-volume editions, *Mitos de Cthulhu* (2003–04; 4 volumes), *Relatos de Terror* (2003–04; 5 volumes), and *Colaboraciones* (2003–04; 8 volumes), the last of course including the revisions and collaborations. These volumes were all part of a Biblioteca H. P. Lovecraft that ran to at least twenty-seven volumes.

The Mexican publisher Fontamara, aside from publishing several volumes of tales, also issued *El horror sobrenatural en la literatura* (1995). A different translation of "Supernatural Horror in Literature" appeared under the same title (Editorial Leviatan, 1998). Edaf issued its own translation of Lovecraft's treatise, along with other essays, as *El horror sobrenatural en la literatura y otros escritos* (2002).

Lovecraft appeared in Galician (a language spoken mostly in northwest Spain) in two volumes issued in 1999. Portuguese publishers, both in Portugal and Brazil, issued five editions of Lovecraft between 1998 and 2005. Lovecraft appeared in nearly a dozen Hungarian editions during this period, beginning with *Cthulhu hívása* (Valhalla Páholy, 1993). The most impressive of these was a three-volume edition, *Összes művei* (Szukits, 2001–05), which contained most of the fiction but also a selection of essays and letters.

The first book publication of Lovecraft in Estonian was *Pimeduses sosistaja* (Elmatar, 1996), a substantial collection of the better-known tales. Polish editions became abundant at this time, with seventeen different editions between 1991 and 2005. Many of the volumes were issued by the Warsaw publisher Wydawnictwo S.R.; others were by Zysk i S-ka and Copernicus Corporation. In nearly every instance the editions contained the original fiction and revisions, although one volume translating

"Supernatural Horror in Literature" did appear (Wydawnictwo, 2000). Lovecraft appeared in Slovak in *Pripad Charlesa Dextera Warda* (Formát, 2001), as well as a translation of "Supernatural Horror in Literature" (Fischer & Formát, 1997). An edition of *Fungi from Yuggoth* in modern Greek appeared as *Hoi mykētes ap' ton Yuggoth* (Aiolos, 1992), followed by a volume of letters, *Epistoles* (Aiolos, 1997).

The first Romanian books of Lovecraft's stories were *Hypnos* (1993) and *Dagon* (1993), both translated by Mircea Opriţă and published by Dacia.[1] Another volume, *Demoni şi miracole* (Leda, 2005), was translated by Traian Finţescu.

The first of seven Danish translations appeared, *Tilfældet Charles Dexter Ward* (Schønberg, 1991). The other six were published either by the Science Fiction Cirklen or Interpresse. The volumes tended to be small, with only a few stories or a single short novel per volume. Two Finnish editions appeared: *Vaeltaja unien portilla* (Science Fiction Seura, 1997), a volume of the Randolph Carter cycle, and *Temppeli, nimeton kaupunki ja muita kertomuksia* (Jalava, 1999), a volume of mostly early short stories, but also including *At the Mountains of Madness*. Three Norwegian editions appeared in the 1990s. In Sweden, Sam J. Lundwall continued his editing and translating of Lovecraft's work with five editions in the 1990s.

The first known appearance of Lovecraft in Russian was a slim booklet, *Khram* (MP Sotsium, 1990), containing only "The Temple" along with Derleth's story "House—with Ghost." *The Case of Charles Dexter Ward* appeared in an anonymously edited anthology in 1992. The first full-scale volume was *Po tu storonu sna* (Terra Incognita, 1991), followed by a two-volume edition,

1. "The Colour out of Space" and a brief extract from "Supernatural Horror in Literature" had appeared in the Romanian magazine *Seculol 20* No. 4 (1973).

Polnoe sobranie sochinenti (Technomark, 1992–93), although this edition included a distressing number of the "posthumous collaborations." But the floodgates were now opened, and fourteen more editions appeared down to 2005. The most impressive of them were *Zov Cthulhu* (Gudial Press, 2001) and the two-volume *Pritaivshiisia uzhas* (TERRA—Knizhnyi Klub, 2001). The publisher Izd-vo "Azbuka-Klasska" issued three volumes of Lovecraft in 2004–05, which included all the major fiction along with *Fungi from Yuggoth.*

Lovecraft appeared in Korean for the first time in *Gwanggiui sanmaeg* (Think North, 2001), a translation of *At the Mountains of Madness. Ch'alsu T'eksut'o Wodu ui pimil* (Yongon Munhwasa, 2003) is a translation of *The Case of Charles Dexter Ward.* Three editions of Lovecraft in Turkish appeared in 2000 and 2001.

And the first known Chinese translations appeared in 2004. The publisher Qi huan ji di chu ban issued two volumes in 2004, *Zhan li chuan shuo* (a translation of *Bloodcurdling Tales of Horror and the Macabre*) and *Kesulu shen hua* (a translation of Derleth's *Tales of the Cthulhu Mythos*—"Kesulu" being the closest the Chinese language can come to "Cthulhu"). Another book appeared in 2005 from another publisher.

Strikingly, a Hebrew edition was published in Tel Aviv, *ha-Tohu ha-mizdahel* (Odise'ah, 2002), translated by Daniyel Barak.

But the full scale of the foreign interest on Lovecraft cannot be captured merely by the number of volumes of his work that appeared; there was also a tremendous explosion of critical and scholarly work. Perhaps most celebrated—and notorious—was Michel Houellebecq's *H. P. Lovecraft: Contre le monde, contre la vie* (1991). This was, in fact, Houellebecq's first published book, but it seemed to constitute an important touchstone of his work when he began publishing an array of novels beginning in the mid-1990s that catapulted him into fame. His little book on Lovecraft (all of 136 pages) was reprinted frequently in French and was translated into Italian (2001), German (2002), English (2005), and Spanish (2006).

To be charitable, the book says a great deal more about Houellebecq than about Lovecraft. He flatly declares that Lovecraft generally scorned "reality"—the same accusation that Colin Wilson made of him in *The Strength to Dream,* although Houellebecq counts it as a point in Lovecraft's favour, stating that his lack of interest in many of the phases of life (money, sex, personal relations, etc.) that are the stuff of mainstream literature lend a particular intensity to his weird fiction. The problem is that a significant majority of weird fiction could be said to do much the same thing.

But Houellebecq gets into trouble when he declares that racism is the dominant feature in the entirety of Lovecraft's thought and fictional work. Here the problem is that Houellebecq doesn't marshal sufficient—indeed, any—evidence to support this controversial claim. There are additional issues with his analysis, and it can hardly be said that Houellebecq has a firm grasp of Lovecraft's overall oeuvre, since he appears to have read his fiction and letters only in French.[2] Houellebecq himself has now been accused of some of the same prejudices—including misogyny, racism, and Islamophobia—as Lovecraft, although he appears to share Lovecraft's atheism.

But French work of considerably higher grade, if less visibility, appeared later in the decade and into the early twenty-first century. Marc Bailly anonymously edited a large anthology, *H. P. Lovecraft: Le Maître de Providence* (1999), chiefly taken from the special Lovecraft issues of the magazine *Phénix* (June

2. See my article "Why Michel Houellebecq Is Wrong about Lovecraft's Racism," *Lovecraft Annual* No. 12 (2018): 43–50.

and September 1986). The volume contained important articles by Maurice Lévy, Jacques Van Herp, Christophe Thill, Denis Labbé, and many others. Another anthology of criticism, *H. P. Lovecraft: Fantastique, mythe et modernité* (2002), is an even more impressive volume, with essays by Lévy, Gilles Menegaldo, Michel Meurger, and others. Meurger had earlier issued a two-volume collection of his Lovecraft essays, *Lovecraft et la S.-F.* (1991–94).

Some interesting monographs appeared. Florent Montaclair's *Fantastique et événement* (1997) is a comparison of Lovecraft with Jules Verne. Patrice Allart's *Guide du mythe de Cthulhu* (1999) is a study of the evolution of the Mythos by Lovecraft and later writers. Guillaume Foresti's *Corman Lovecraft: Le Rencontre fantastique* (2002) examines Roger Corman's film adaptations of Lovecraft's work.

One of the most acute French commentators on Lovecraft was William Schnabel, who published two short treatises, *Masques dans le miroir: Le Double lovecraftien* (2002) and *Lovecraft: Histoire d'un gentleman raciste* (2003). These books were based on research Schnabel had conducted at the University of Tolouse (presumably under Maurice Lévy), resulting in two dissertations, a "short" one ("Narrative Structures in Lovecraft's Works" [1989; 167 pp.]) and a "long" one ("Les Monstres familiers de H. P. Lovecraft" [1995; 668 pp.]).

In Germany, Franz Rottensteiner followed up his earlier anthology, *Über H. P. Lovecraft* (1984), with *Der Einsiedler von Providence* (1992), focusing chiefly on Lovecraft's life and containing translations of important memoirs or biographical essays on Lovecraft, including those by Sonia H. Davis, Winfield Townley Scott, W. Paul Cook, and others. W. H. Müller's *Lovecraft: Schatzmeister des Verborgenen* (1992) is a brief overview of Lovecraft's work, while Susanne Smuda's *H. P. Lovecrafts Mythologie* (1997) is an insightful assessment of the Lovecraft Mythos.

Spanish scholarship on Lovecraft is represented by Juan-Jacobo Bajarlía's *H. P. Lovecraft: El horror sobrenatural* (1996), a somewhat cursory overview of Lovecraft's work published in Buenos Aires. In Spain itself, Teodoro Gómez's *Lovecraft: La antología* (2002) is a broad biographical and critical survey. Claudio De Nardi's *Lovecraftiana* (1996) is a slim volume of Lovecraft memoirs and essays translated into Italian, and Michele Tetro's *H. P. Lovecraft Sculptus in Tenebris* (2001) contains essays on Lovecraft by numerous Italian scholars.

Of the dozen or more dissertations on Lovecraft in foreign languages during this period, we can cite only a few. Massimo Berruti's "H. P. Lovecraft e l'anatomia dell nulla" (M.A. thesis: University of Turin, 2002) introduced this scholar to the world, and he has gone on to write penetrating essays on Lovecraft and other writers, chiefly from a structuralist perspective. Franz Rossnagel's "Typische Strukturelemente und ihre Funktionen in den phantastischen Erzählungen H. P. Lovecrafts" (M.A. thesis: University of Stuttgart, 1990) has some merit, as do two other theses: Marco Mattiello's "The Oldest and Strongest Kind of Fear Is Fear of the Unknown: Howard Phillips Lovecraft, dal romanzo gotico al *Necronomicon*" (M.A. thesis: University of Padova, 2003) and Tomasz Ostafiński's "The Reversal of Values in the Prose of Howard Phillips Lovecraft" (M.A. thesis: Silesian School of Economics and Languages [Katowice, Poland], 2004), the latter written in English.

A number of small-press magazines devoted to Lovecraft appeared at this time: the Italian *Il Circolo di Lovecraft* (1995–2002), edited by Massimo Tassi and Pietro Guarriello; and the Spanish *Los Diletantes de Lovecraft* (1997–98), edited by José Rafael Martínez Pina.

Some scholarly and popular work in English at the turn of the millennium needs to be discussed. Timo Airaksinen's *The*

Philosophy of H. P. Lovecraft (1999) is an imposing work that seems to be a comprehensive assessment of Lovecraft's philosophical thought and its incorporation into his fiction; but it proves to be very much less than this. Airaksinen—a professor of philosophy at the University of Helsinki, Finland—is determined to see Lovecraft as a pure nihilist, but can't understand how in his letters Lovecraft fervently espouses various ethical, social, and political stances that seem to undercut his nihilism. What Airaksinen reveals is a near-total failure to grasp the essentials of Lovecraft's character and even some central aspects of his philosophical thought—chiefly, Lovecraft's oft-stated claim that human values are indeed of no significance in the vast cosmos-at-large but are (legitimately) of relevance on the human scale.

Nonetheless, Airaksinen's book provides occasional insights when he undertakes close readings of some key Lovecraft stories. Even here, however—as in an attempt at a sexual interpretation of "The Colour out of Space"—Airaksinen sometimes descends into unintentional bathos. Given that the author does not even have a high regard for Lovecraft's work ("Even the best Lovecraftian stories are too defective to be part of the literary canon" [90]), one wonders why he even undertook such a laborious study. His confident assertion was of course proven to be false within a decade. Overall, the book's utility to the Lovecraft devotee is minimal.

Some important reference works appeared. Andrew Migliore and John Strysik assembled *The Lurker in the Lobby: A Guide to the Cinema of H. P. Lovecraft* (Armitage House, 1999), a fascinating assemblage of material pertaining to the numerous Lovecraft-related films that had appeared over the past several decades. Migliore had founded the H. P. Lovecraft Film Festival in Portland, Oregon, in 1991, while Strysik had produced a haunting short film, *The Music of Erich Zann* (1981), one of the best and most faithful adaptations of a Lovecraft story ever made. *The Lurker in the Lobby* was published in an extensively updated form by Night Shade (2005).

An H. P. Lovecraft Encyclopedia (Greenwood Press, 2001), by David E. Schultz and myself, attempted to redo Shreffler's *H. P. Lovecraft Companion,* issued by the same publisher twenty-four years earlier, with extensively updated information regarding Lovecraft's life, colleagues, work, and other matters. Anthony Pearsall's *The Lovecraft Lexicon* (New Falcon Publications, 2005) is an enormous volume with entries focused more specifically on elements in Lovecraft's stories. Charles P. Mitchell's *The Complete H. P. Lovecraft Filmography* (Greenwood Press, 2001) provides cast lists and other information on thirty-three film adaptations of Lovecraft.

Scott Connors's *A Century Less a Dream: Selected Criticism on H. P. Lovecraft* (Wildside Press, 2002) attempted a sort of update to my *H. P. Lovecraft: Four Decades of Criticism* (1980) and contained a number of fine essays, many of them taken from *Lovecraft Studies* or *Crypt of Cthulhu.* But the book was hindered by poor distribution from the publisher.

Two unusual volumes need to be mentioned. William Schoell's *H. P. Lovecraft: Master of Weird Fiction* (Morgan Reynolds, 2004) is the first biography of Lovecraft intended for young adults. At 128 pages, it does a serviceable job of presenting the basic facts of Lovecraft's life and work for its chosen audience. Of a very different order is Jason Colavito's *The Cult of Alien Gods: H. P. Lovecraft and Extraterrestrial Pop Culture* (Prometheus Books, 2005), which makes the bold assertion that Lovecraft's work is the unacknowledged source of the "ancient astronaut" craze that began with Erich von Däniken's *Chariots of the Gods* (1973; a translation of *Erinnerungen an die zukunft,* 1968) and its numerous successors and spinoffs. But the best that Colavito can do is to establish an indirect connexion—i.e., via Lovecraft's influence on *The Morning of the Magicians* (1963; a translation of *Le Matin des magiciens,* 1960) by Louis Pauwels (whom Colavito throughout his book misspells as Pauwles) and Jacques Bergier. This book did indeed have some influence on von Däniken's theories. But of course Lovecraft himself drew upon the work of Ignatius Donnelly, the Theosophists, and others who had made roughly similar arguments, and some of the authors Colavito discusses in his book surely came by their views directly from these earlier sources.

While Colavito makes numerous small errors in the treatment of Lovecraft's work (e.g., his erroneous belief that Charles Fort played a role in the composition of "The Call of Cthulhu," whereas Lovecraft had not read Fort at the time he wrote the story), he has written a thoroughly entertaining treatise that incisively dissects the flaws in the work of von Däniken, Robert Temple, Graham Hancock, and a host of other crackpots and charlatans who have propounded arguments on the arrival of space aliens in the remote past, or (à la *At the Mountains of Madness* and, indirectly, "The Shadow out of Time") on the actual creation of the human race by aliens, or (à la "The Whisperer in Darkness") the transportation of human brains throughout the cosmos by aliens.

Theses and dissertations in the US were now becoming frequent, even routine, and we can take note of only a few of them. James Anderson's "Out of the Shadows" (Ph.D. diss.: University of Rhode Island, 1992) is a structuralist approach to Lovecraft, and Anderson went on to publish several articles based on the work. The full dissertation was published as a book in 2011. Bennett Graff did the same with his M.A. thesis, "Horror in Evolution" (City University of New York, 1995), publishing several interesting papers (under the name Bennett Lovett-Graff) in *Extrapolation* and *Journal of the Fantastic in the Arts*. David Cal Clements's "Cosmic Psychoanalysis" (Ph.D. diss.: State University of New York at Buffalo, 1998) was a Lacanian analysis of Lovecraft. Bradley Alan Will's "The 'Supramundane': The Kantian Sublime in Lovecraft, Clarke, and Gibson" (Ph.D. diss.: University of Oklahoma, 1998) is a somewhat recondite thesis, but full of interesting insights.

The Australian scholar Cecelia Drewer wrote "The Literary Manifesto of H. P. Lovecraft" (M.A. thesis: University of New South Wales, 1993) and has gone on to publish several illuminating pieces. Not to be overlooked is Adam L. G. Nevill's "H. P. Lovecraft: 'Aesthetics, Psychoanalysis and Ideology'" (Honours thesis: University of Birmingham, 1990), only because this British author has become one of the most accomplished writers of weird fiction today.

Among shorter papers, we can take note of Victoria Nelson's "H. P. Lovecraft and the Great Heresies" (*Raritan*, Winter 1996), later incorporated into her book *The Secret Life of Puppets* (Harvard University Press, 2001), a psychoanalytic interpretation of Lovecraft, although with some questionable assertions and presuppositions. Faye Ringel has written several illuminating papers on Lovecraft from an historical perspective, one of which is in her treatise *New England's Gothic Literature* (Edwin Mellen Press, 1995). There are two lengthy papers on Lovecraft, both from a philosophical orientation, by James Campbell and myself in Douglas Robillard's critical anthology *American Supernatural Fiction* (Garland, 1996). Timothy Evans is one of the few who have written on Lovecraft's travelogues, his fascination with architecture, and related topics, in two papers, one published in *Extrapolation* (Summer 2004) and the other in the *Journal of Folklore* (January–April 2005).

James Van Hise's self-published anthology *The Fantastic*

Worlds of H. P. Lovecraft (1999) demonstrated that the fan world was not done having its say on Lovecraft. While this volume largely consisted of reprints—some of them quite unfortunate, such as John Brunner's old "Rusty Chains" article and Will Murray's erroneous "In Search of Arkham Country" pieces—other articles by Donald R. Burleson, Peter Cannon, Rusty Burke, and others make this volume not entirely valueless.

As has been suggested above, this period witnessed a tremendous explosion of media adaptations of Lovecraft, especially in film, perhaps inspired by the establishment of the H. P. Lovecraft Film Festival. The database IMDb.com lists fifty-five films during the period covered by this chapter. The great majority of these are short, independent films of no particular account. Even some of the putatively "major" full-length films are largely forgettable, among them *The Unnamable II: The Statement of Randolph Carter* (1992), which has little to do with either story; Juan Piquer Simón's *Cthulhu Mansion* (1992), a wretched hash of Lovecraftian elements; *Necronomicon* (1993), a feeble trilogy of corny Lovecraftian adaptations; *Lurking Fear* (1994), directed by J. Courtney Joyner, a sorry excuse for blood and gore; Eric Morgret's forgettable *The Thing on the Doorstep* (2003); and several others that need not be mentioned.

A few other films are not quite as contemptible. Jeffrey Combs plays Lovecraft himself as a kind of narrator or introducer of three segments (none of them explicitly based on any Lovecraft work) in *Necronomicon: Book of the Dead* (1993). Brian Yuzna directed one more instalment of the Re-Animator series, *Beyond Re-Animator* (2003), where Combs and others are enmeshed in the usual entertaining gruesomeness. Stuart Gordon directed a fair-to-middling hour-long adaptation of "The Dreams in the Witch House" for the TV show *Masters of Horror* (4 November 2005).

Of considerably greater interest is *The Resurrected* (1991), a skilful adaptation of *The Case of Charles Dexter Ward* by director Dan O'Bannon, whose devotion to Lovecraft was of long standing. Chris Sarandon ably plays both Charles Dexter Ward and Joseph Curwen, while John Terry (as "John March") plays the Dr. Willett character. Regrettably, the film was updated to the present day, but nevertheless it contains some fine moments. O'Bannon had intended to title the film *The Ancestor,* and his director's cut (still extant, although without music and some special effects) was edited quite differently.

Bryan Moore's 44-minute version of *Cool Air* (1999) is a splendid and faithful adaptation of the story. He himself stars as the narrator (naming himself Randolph Carter), and he made an excellent decision in selecting veteran actor Jack Donner as Dr. Muñoz. The shooting of the film in black-and-white was an inspired choice.

Stuart Gordon returned to the Lovecraftian realm with *Dagon* (2001). The film is in fact an adaptation of "The Shadow over Innsmouth," but—as Gordon told me—he chose the title of a story that is clearly in the public domain to avoid any copyright issues. There is much to enjoy in this film, even though the setting is updated to the present day and the setting is moved to Spain (where, in fact, the film was shot, probably for budgetary reasons); but toward the end it simply devolves into the standard beautiful-young-naked-woman-threatened-by-evil-monster topos.

Several films released during this period are actually more effective in conveying Lovecraftian terror, precisely because they are not explicit adaptations of a given work. The TV movie *Cast a Deadly Spell* (HBO, 1991) was originally going to be called *Lovecraft;* it stars Fred Ward as the private detective Harry Philip Lovecraft, working in an alternate-world Los Angeles where magic is widely and effectively used. The fusion of hard-boiled crime and the supernatural is notably effective under Martin Campbell's direction. A follow-up, *Witch Hunt* (1994), with Dennis Hopper playing Lovecraft, was less successful.

Also of some note is *Out of Mind: The Stories of H. P. Lovecraft* (1998), directed by Raymond St.-Jean for the Canadian Bravo cable network. While a bit of a mishmash—partly a documentary, partly a re-enactment of scenes out of Lovecraft's stories—the 56-minute program features a mesmerising performance by Christopher Heyerdahl, who manages to look and sound (insofar as it can be determined what Lovecraft's voice sounded like) like Lovecraft in the flesh. Then there was an actual documentary, *The Eldritch Influence: The Life, Vision, and Phenomenon of H. P. Lovecraft* (2003), directed by Shawn Owens, a creditable first attempt at portraying Lovecraft's life, work, and posthumous reputation.

Quite in a category of its own is *Rough Magik* (2000), the pilot for a planned BBC television series that was never made. The director (Jamie Payne) and writer (Stephen W. Parsons) have skilfully utilised Lovecraftian elements in a contemporary setting (the Falkland Islands war of the early 1980s), and it is a shame that the BBC did not follow through on the series. Also worth citing is *The Call of Cthulhu* (2005), a 47-minute silent film written and directed by Andrew Leman and Sean Branney, who founded an H. P. Lovecraft Historical Society to promote the work of Lovecraft in various media. There is considerable panache in the entire production, and the filmmakers have remained true to the story and to the time period in which it takes place.

And we can hardly ignore John Carpenter's *In the Mouth of Madness* (1995). Carpenter's interest in Lovecraft was of long standing, and random mentions of Arkham and other elements from Lovecraft's stories can be found in several earlier films. *The Thing* (1982)—a remake of the 1951 film—clearly incorporated imagery from *At the Mountains of Madness,* especially in the climactic revelation of the alien entity. Both films were of course based on John W. Campbell, Jr.'s novella "Who Goes There?" (1938), itself an apparent attempt to rewrite *At the Mountains of Madness* in a manner Campbell considered more appropriate to the subject. *In the Mouth of Madness* is an entertaining horror film in which the protagonist—a popular horror writer played by Jürgen Prochnow—is a melding of Lovecraft and Stephen King. Some of the scenes toward the latter part of the film manifestly draw upon Lovecraft's aliens. Carpenter gives the game away by having a minor character named Mrs. Pickman.

In the realm of comic books or graphic novels, note must be taken of the British artist John Coulthart, who emerged in the 1980s and has become one of the most accomplished Lovecraft illustrators of his time. *H. P. Lovecraft's The Haunter of the Dark and Other Creative Visions* (Oneiros Books, 2000) features some of his best work. Coulthart also appears in a curious volume, *The Starry Wisdom: A Tribute to H. P. Lovecraft* (Creation Books, 1994), a farrago of fiction (much of it not very Lovecraftian) whose existence is justified only by its inclusion of Coulthart's evocative adaptation of "The Call of Cthulhu." Other adaptations can be found in *The Worlds of H. P. Lovecraft* (Caliber Comics, 1993), *H. P. Lovecraft's Cthulhu* (Millennium, 1993), and *The Dream-Quest of Unknown Kadath* (Mockman Press, 1995–97), among others.

In 2005, the Library of America—a publisher that had been established in the early 1980s to publish the major (or, in some cases, the complete) works of canonical American authors—published a volume of Lovecraft's *Tales.* My corrected texts were used, with my authorisation; but because the Library of America wished at this time to have "name" editors, Peter Straub was chosen to edit the volume.

It is manifest that my three Penguin Classics editions paved the way for this edition; but nonetheless, it constitutes Lovecraft's definitive accession to the canon of American literature. The volume did not appear without controversy. Stephen Schwartz, writing in the conservative periodical *New Criterion* (May 2005), expressed high disdain at Lovecraft's inclusion in the series. But numerous other critics, among them Michael Dirda (*Weekly Standard,* 7 March 2005), Daniel Handler (*New York Times Book Review,* 17 April 2005), John J. Miller (*Wall Street Journal,* 15 March 2005), and Michael Saler (*Times Literary Supplement,* 4 March 2005) were largely or wholly enthusiastic. The book was also reviewed in the *San Francisco Chronicle, Seattle Times,* and other major newspapers.

The book was also received with great popular acclaim, selling 25,000 copies in the first few months of publication—the fastest seller in the Library of America's history up to that point. And there is a further pungent irony: the very concept of a Library of America had been the brainchild of Edmund Wilson, but Lovecraft beat him into the series by two years.

Another, smaller, and less prestigious publication along the same lines was *At the Mountains of Madness: The Definitive Edition* (Modern Library, 2005), with an introduction by China Miéville. It is unclear what that subtitle could mean, since I have expounded at length that my own corrected text of the novel (which the Modern Library used) can itself only be regarded as provisional, in the absence of the actual typescript that Lovecraft submitted to *Astounding Stories* in 1935 (where he clearly made revisions that do not appear on the surviving typescript at the John Hay Library). The book also included "Supernatural Horror in Literature." But the mere fact of the book's appearance, sixty years after Lovecraft's inclusion in the Wise/Fraser *Great Tales of Terror and the Supernatural,* is notable.

IX. Dissemination and Controversy (2006–2020)

Lovecraft's work continued to be widely disseminated throughout the world. There is no need to take account of the almost incalculable shoddy editions issued by print-on-demand publishers, most of them using corrupt texts. Some important editions appeared that both allowed Lovecraft's major fiction to reach new audiences and attained an impressive degree of scholarly rigour.

In 2008, Barnes & Noble issued *H. P. Lovecraft: The Fiction,* an omnibus of the totality of Lovecraft's original fiction, with the addition of "Supernatural Horror in Literature." I was involved in the preparation of the edition but was not listed as editor. I did write an introduction and brief headnotes to all the stories. Unfortunately, because of a proofreading snafu the first printing was full of errors; but these were corrected in printings beginning in 2011, thanks in large part to the diligent and meticulous work of Swedish scholar Martin Andersson. Also regrettable is the fact that, because it was widely assumed that Barnes & Noble was merely printing public domain material, the edition was pirated by a number of unscrupulous publishers, including Chartwell Books. Barnes & Noble itself repackaged the edition in smaller units under various titles, including *Great Tales of Horror* (2012), *The Complete Cthulhu Mythos Tales* (2013), and others.

Two important annotated editions appeared. The University

of Tampa Press commissioned me to prepare an edition of *The Case of Charles Dexter Ward* (2010), with exhaustive notes as well as photographs of Providence sites supplied by Donovan K. Loucks. My two-volume edition of Lovecraft's *Annotated Revisions and Collaborations* (Arcane Wisdom, 2011–12) was the first attempt to supply commentary on this body of work; but the minuscule print run caused the edition to reach very few readers. Hippocampus Press issued a second edition of *The Ancient Track* (2013) in a trade paperback edition. It contained a few more poems that had been overlooked in the original edition of 2001.

Leslie S. Klinger, better known as an authority on Sherlock Holmes, edited the impressive-looking *New Annotated H. P. Lovecraft* (Liveright, 2014), a large and lavishly illustrated hardcover volume. The great majority of the research in the volume was derived from previous scholarship. Klinger followed it up with *The New Annotated H. P. Lovecraft: Beyond Arkham* (Liveright, 2019). If nothing else, the books gave even greater visibility to Lovecraft, as they were widely distributed and reviewed.

But the most significant work of this period was the issuance of Lovecraft's letters in unabridged and annotated editions, edited by David E. Schultz and myself and mostly published by Hippocampus. The stage was set by the University of Tampa Press's edition of *O Fortunate Floridian: H. P. Lovecraft's Letters to R. H. Barlow* (2007), one of the richest and most valuable batches of correspondence in existence. A year later Hippocampus began its Letters of H. P. Lovecraft project with a two-volume edition, *Essential Solitude: The Letters of H. P. Lovecraft and August Derleth*. Lovecraft's letters to Derleth are not as vital as those to many other correspondents, but their sheer bulk gives them some importance, all apart from Derleth's later role as Lovecraft's publisher. This edition was followed by another two-volume set, *A Means to Freedom: The Letters of H. P. Lovecraft and Robert H. Barlow* (2009), where Howard's letters actually exceed Lovecraft's in volume (in part because some of Lovecraft's letters—which exist only in the Arkham House Transcripts—do not survive).

From this point onward, Schultz and myself issued volume after volume, including the letters to James F. Morton (2011), Robert Bloch and others (2015), C. L. Moore and others (2017), Maurice W. Moe (2018), and, at long last, *Dawnward Spire: The Letters of H. P. Lovecraft and Clark Ashton Smith* (2017), an 800-page hardcover edition of one of the most valuable joint correspondences in existence. Down to the end of 2020 Hippocampus had issued eighteen volumes of the proposed twenty-six-volume set, including an immense two-volume edition of the *Letters to Family and Family Friends* (2020), a compilation of Lovecraft's invaluable letters to his aunts among others.

This set the stage for my four-volume *Complete Fiction: A Variorum Edition* (2015–17), in which I printed all the stories and revisions with exhaustive notes charting textual variants in all relevant texts from manuscript to the (uncorrected) Arkham House editions. Volume 4 (2017), containing the revisions and collaborations, was incomplete because a copyright dispute prevented the publication of the four stories that Lovecraft revised for C. M. Eddy, Jr.; these stories were included in a hardcover reprint of the volume after 2021, when the stories went into the public domain.

Hippocampus then issued *Fungi from Yuggoth: An Annotated Edition* (2017), prepared by David E. Schultz. This is an edition on which Schultz had been working off and on for roughly forty years, and his exhaustive notes are wondrously illuminating, as is his extensive introduction. It is probably the most impressive annotated edition of Lovecraft ever published. It also contains facsimiles of the handwritten manuscript and much other interesting matter.

Other publishers now attempted to capitalise on Lovecraft's growing popularity. Wordsworth Editions, an English firm that published inexpensive paperback editions of material that was largely in the public domain (although in some instances it appeared to violate copyright by reprinting compilations for which it did not secure permission), issued a four-volume edition of Lovecraft (2007–13), one volume of which consisted of some of his revisions. Uncorrected texts were used in the edition. It was not at all comprehensive but did get wide distribution. In England, Gollancz issued two hardcover omnibuses edited by Stephen Jones, *Necronomicon* (2008) and *Eldritch Tales* (2011).

Superficially more prestigious was Roger Luckhurst's edition of Lovecraft's *Classic Horror Stories* (Oxford University Press, 2013), in the publisher's World's Classics series. But Luckhurst committed the gaffe of attempting to prepare his own text of Lovecraft's tales without examination of manuscripts or early printed editions, with the result that his texts largely reproduce the Arkham House editions prior to my corrected printings. His notes to the stories are not well researched, and overall the book reveals a regrettable lack of editorial oversight.

Some publishers issued expensive limited editions, including Easton Press's *The Dunwich Horror and Others* (1993) and *At the Mountains of Madness* (2006), a Centipede Press omnibus in its Masters of the Weird Tale series (2007; 2 vols.), and the Folio Society's *The Call of Cthulhu and Other Weird Stories* (2017; a reprint of the Penguin Classics edition). In 2014 Centipede Press issued a new omnibus of Lovecraft's work as part of a new series, the Centipede Press Library of Weird Fiction, under my editorship. The publisher promised to keep this and other volumes in the series perennially in print, but has failed to do so.

In 2014 the English small press PS Publishing began an extensive series of hardcover volumes, sometimes reprinting single stories and in other cases groups of stories, all illustrated by Pete Von Sholly. Seventeen volumes were issued down to 2018, with corrected texts and introductions provided by me. Von Sholly may not be the ideal illustrator for Lovecraft, as his flamboyant and cartoonish style does not harmonise well with the subtlety and restraint of Lovecraft's overall work; but on occasion his depictions are vivid and effective.

Another small press, Sporting Gentleman, issued my compilation, *H. P. Lovecraft: Against Religion* (2010), a collection of his essays and letters on atheism, Christianity, and related issues. The publishers were able to secure a foreword by the noted atheist Christopher Hitchens. The volume was subsequently translated into German and Italian. Lovecraft's emergence as a kind of patron saint of atheism had begun at least a decade or so earlier, when I included Lovecraft's letter to Maurice W. Moe (May 15, 1918) in my anthology *Atheism: A Reader* (Prometheus Books, 2000). Hitchens apparently borrowed this and other items for his own compilation, *The Portable Atheist* (Da Capo Press, 2007).

Not to be overlooked is an audiobook recording the complete original fiction of Lovecraft, issued in 2019 by the H. P. Lovecraft Historical Society. The "book" is actually a thumbdrive, and the stories are expertly and evocatively read (using my corrected texts) by Andrew Leman.

Hippocampus Press took the lead in scholarship on Lovecraft, chiefly by the establishment of the *Lovecraft Annual,* beginning in 2007. When it became obvious that Necronomicon Press' *Lovecraft Studies* was defunct, Hippocampus stepped in with the new annual, edited by me, and containing on average about 80,000 words of text. Advances in desktop publishing allowed for the reproduction of interesting illustrations of various sorts, but the chief features of the issues were of course the articles themselves, many of them embodying pioneering research.

It would be cumbrous to do more than single out a few items, but it is difficult to bypass such contributions as T. R. Livesey's 85-page article on the role of astronomy in Lovecraft's work (2008)[1] or J.-M. Rajala's 88-page article on Lovecraft's "lost" stories (2011). Robert H. Waugh continued his penetrating if discursive articles on Lovecraft, which were later collected in two volumes of essays (see below). Canadian scholar James Goho contributed several valuable essays; these were later gathered in *Journeys into Darkness* (Rowman & Littlefield, 2014). Phillip A. Ellis, Manuel Pérez-Campos, J. D. Worthington, and Cecelia Hopkins-Drewer, commenting on various poems by Lovecraft, added significantly to our understanding of this still neglected aspect of his work.

From a biographical perspective, Kenneth W. Faig, Jr. continued his remarkable output of incisive essays, writing on the names in Lovecraft's 1937 diary (2012),[2] his travelogues of Foster, R.I. (2013), his residence at 66 College Street (2015), Lovecraft's paternal ancestors (2015), and several others. David E. Schultz added nuances to Lovecraft's submissions to the *Argosy* (2017) and, even more notably, his interactions with book publishers (2018).

Needless to say, the issue of Lovecraft and race received at-

1. See also Fred S. Lubnow's "The Lovecraftian Solar System" in the 2019 issue.

2. David Haden added a supplement to this essay in the 2013 issue. Haden runs an informative blog on HPL-related issues (tentaclii.wordpress.com) and has published several volumes of essays titled *Lovecraft in Historical Context*. By far the most important, comprehensive, and accurate website devoted to HPL is Donovan K. Loucks's "The H. P. Lovecraft Archive" (www.hplovecraft.com).

tention. Among the most astute articles was César Guarde Paz's "Race and War in the Lovecraft Mythos" (2012). My own brief article "Why Michel Houellebecq Is Wrong about Lovecraft's Racism" (2018) pointed out errors and misconstruals in Houellebecq's 1991 book. Alison Sperling wrote incisively on "H. P. Lovecraft's Weird Body" (2016), on the theme of body horror in his work.

The *Annual* regularly published small batches of letters by Lovecraft, among them those to Lee McBride White (2007), Carl Ferdinand Strauch (2010), Farnsworth Wright (2014), Marian F. Bonner (2015)

An illuminating article on Lovecraft's recognition was Brendan Whyte's "The Thing (Flung Daily) on the Doorstep: Lovecraft in the Antipedean Press, 1903–2007" (2015), a canvassing of responses to Lovecraft in the Australian press. Another Australian, Duncan Norris, began writing insightful articles on various subjects beginning with the 2016 issue, among them an analysis of Lovecraft's use of Egypt in his fiction (2016), his use of Greek myth (2017), and several articles on Lovecraft's influence on contemporary films and television shows. Two articles, by Matt Cardin and John Langan respectively (2007), probed Lovecraft's influence on Thomas Ligotti.

In a class by themselves are the musical settings of "The Ancient Track" (for four-part choir and piano) by Jonathan Adams (2010) and my setting of "Sunset" (for four-part *a cappella* choir) (2019).

Hippocampus also published a number of monographs or essay collections by leading Lovecraft scholars. Among the most notable were two volumes by Robert H. Waugh, *The Monster in the Mirror: Looking for H. P. Lovecraft* (2006) and *A Monster of Voices: Speaking for H. P. Lovecraft* (2011). These substantial treatises contain a wealth of insights, even if at times the overall thrust of the essays is not always clear. Steven J. Mariconda's *H. P. Lovecraft: Art, Artifact, and Reality* (2013) is a volume of his collected essays on Lovecraft, substantially augmented from the Necronomicon Press booklet of 1995. Donald R. Burleson's *Lovecraft—An American Allegory* (2015) is a long-overdue assemblage of this pioneering critic's best essays on Lovecraft.

Kenneth W. Faig, Jr.'s *The Unknown Lovecraft* (2009) gathers up the recent work of a scholar who remains Lovecraft's premier biographer. Christopher M. O'Brien and J.-M. Rajala prepared Faig's still valuable early volume *Lovecraftian Voyages* for publication (2017). David Goudsward's *H. P. Lovecraft in the Merrimack Valley* (2013) is a slim but valuable monograph on Lovecraft's involvement with C. W. Smith and the general topography of Haverhill, Newburyport, and related locales in Massachusetts and New Hampshire. A volume spanning both biography and criticism was Bobby Derie's *Sex and the Cthulhu Mythos* (2014), which studied the subject from the perspective of Lovecraft's life, his work, and the work of his successors.

Hippocampus did a service by publishing the full version of my biography, with some small updates, as *I Am Providence: The Life and Times of H. P. Lovecraft* (2010), in two large hardcover volumes (subsequently reprinted in paperback and ebook). As the most comprehensive biography of Lovecraft ever written, it provides an abundant resource for researchers of all aspects of Lovecraft's life, work, and thought. And the press indulged me by publishing my *Lovecraft and a World in Transition* (2014), a large volume of my collected essays on Lovecraft. It also published an augmented version of my The *Rise and Fall of the Cthulhu Mythos* (Mythos Books, 2008), as *The Rise, Fall, and Rise of the Cthulhu Mythos* (2015). Another indulgence was the publication of my *What Is Anything? Memoirs of a Life in Lovecraft* (2018), which supplies a more personal interpretation of many of the events chronicled in this treatise.

Hippocampus also reprinted the Joshi/Schultz *Lovecraft Encyclopedia* (2004) in a convenient paperback edition;[3] it also reprinted the critical anthology *An Epicure in the Terrible* (2011) and two revised versions of the *Lovecraft's Library* compilation (2012, 2017). My compilation *A Weird Writer in Our Midst: Early Criticism of H. P. Lovecraft* (2010) reprinted, among other things, the comments on Lovecraft's stories from the letter column of *Weird Tales* (not available since their appearance in *H. P. Lovecraft in "The Eyrie"* [1979]) and *Astounding Stories,* along with early reviews of Arkham House books and much other matter.

Not to be overlooked—and a clear indication of how Lovecraft's colleagues and associates were becoming celebrated in their own right, or at least were basking in his reflected glory—was *Lovecraft's New York Circle: The Kalem Club, 1924–1927* (2006), edited by Mara Kirk Hart (the daughter of George Kirk, Lovecraft's friend in the Kalem Club) and myself. The volume largely consists of letters by George Kirk to his fiancée, Lucile Dvorak, that Hart had recently discovered; they provide fascinating glimpses of Lovecraft and the other Kalems during the period in question, confirming and augmenting our understanding of this difficult time in Lovecraft's life as revealed by his own letters. Supplementary material by the various members of the Kalem Club round out the volume.

An indication of how Lovecraft had become a touchstone for the entire realm of weird fiction was a series of books in the Lovecraft's Library series, consisting of reprints (some of them containing a pair of novels in the old Ace Double format) of

---

3. Hippocampus also published Dan Clore's *Weird Words: A Lovecraftian Lexicon* (2009), although the title is somewhat of a misnomer, as the book is really an exhaustively annotated dictionary of words used by weird writers generally. But it is an heroic compilation well worthy of deep study.

weird works that Lovecraft read or was influenced by. In this way, such obscure novels as Henri Béraud's *Lazarus* (2007), Barry Pain's *An Exchange of Souls* (2007), Leland Hall's *Sinister House* (2008), R. E. Spencer's *The Lady Who Came to Stay* (2009), H. B. Drake's *The Shadowy Thing* (2010), and several others were made available to a new readership.

After a nearly two-decade hiatus, Necronomicon Press sprang back into action around 2018. One of the chief fruits of its revival was its publication of *Ave atque Vale: Reminiscences of H. P. Lovecraft* 2018), edited by David E. Schultz and myself. With Cannon's *Lovecraft Remembered* long out of print, it was felt that these valuable documents needed to be made available for a new generation that seemed to be increasingly unaware of the impression Lovecraft made upon his own contemporaries. The book was not, of course, merely a reprint of *Lovecraft Remembered;* the editors decided to use the original version of Sonia Davis's memoir (*The Private Life of H. P. Lovecraft*), and a number of other additions—to say nothing of a reorganisation of the material so that it approximated the chronology of Lovecraft's life—made the book distinctive. The editors also annotated the articles, pointing out errors or other points that needed to be addressed.

Necronomicon Press also revived *Crypt of Cthulhu* under Robert M. Price's editorship, although the frequency of its issuance was far more sporadic than in its heyday.

My 1981 bibliography was exhaustively revised and reorganised as *H. P. Lovecraft: A Comprehensive Bibliography* (University of Tampa Press, 2009), containing material on Lovecraft's publications in English and other languages, as well as criticism (now divided into thematic categories for ease of reference), down to 2007.

* * *

Other publishers—including a number of academic presses—fostered the growth of Lovecraft criticism, although in some cases their products left much to be desired. Over the last several decades, academic criticism had passed through a succession of fads that proved relatively short-lived: semiotics, structuralism, poststructuralism, deconstruction, and so on. The current fad seems to be a relentless focus on "race, class, and gender"—in spite of the fact that most academic literary critics are singularly ill-equipped to address these issues in any incisive or informed manner, leaving aside the broader issue of whether such work really constitutes literary criticism or is merely amateur sociology. And the fact that Lovecraft was now being caricatured as an unrepentant racist (and, in the view of some, misogynist) who happened to write weird fiction made his work provided a ripe field for such amateurs.

Gavin Callaghan's *H. P. Lovecraft's Dark Arcadia* (2013) is symptomatic, although in large part it is an exemplification of Callaghan's idiosyncratic outlook. In his view, previous Lovecraft scholarship has gotten it all wrong: Lovecraft was not in fact a writer of "cosmic horror," but merely manipulated conventional horror tropes; his racism, far from being tangential to his fictional work, is central to it. Moreover, Lovecraft's political conversion from extreme conservatism to moderate socialism was really no great shakes, since "fascism" was the element that connected the two positions. Finally, in Callaghan's view much of Lovecraft's work is marred by "sadism" (by which, apparently, he means overt physical horror—as if this has not been a core element in the length and breadth of weird fiction from the beginning).

The strange thing is that Callaghan, who announces these principles with dogmatic certainty in his introduction, does not make any effort to establish their veracity in the rest of his book. At one point he states: "Lovecraft's uniqueness as a horror writer

[lay] not in his supposed cosmicism, which . . . was certainly not an invention of Lovecraft's, and which in any case is actually very sparse in Lovecraft's mainly mundane weird canon" (57). (The clunky prose is characteristic of the entire book.) But if Lovecraft's work is as Callaghan declares, it becomes a fearsome puzzle how he could have become such a central figure in weird fiction, inspiring hundreds of authors after him, and also a key transitional figure in science fiction as well.

But, as I say, Callaghan doesn't argue for these bold (and implausible) positions. The bulk of his book is devoted to a relentless attempt to claim that Lovecraft's work is systematically inspired by his early readings in Graeco-Roman mythology, literature, and history. The problem with this view is that, as Callaghan (who is nothing if not a diligent researcher) should have known, there were a multiplicity of influences working on Lovecraft, all apart from the intellectual and aesthetic dynamism of his own imagination; so that harping on this single strain of influence quickly becomes an exercise in straining after gnats, to say nothing of leading Callaghan into embarrassing blunders.[4] Not every mention of "sylvan" in Lovecraft refers directly to the Greek notion of Arcadia; not every use of "mysterious paternity, magical gifts, battles with monsters, and heroic quests" (70) can be traced to the Theseus myth.

The other line of reasoning in Callaghan's book is that much of Lovecraft's symbolism and imagery is drawn from his con-

4. For example, Callaghan sees the influence of the myth of Procrustes and his bed in "In the Vault" (70), apparently unaware that the plot of that story was provided by HPL's friend C. W. Smith. Elsewhere, Callaghan makes the curious error of believing that Obed Marsh in "The Shadow over Innsmouth" made a pact with the "Devil" (53), by which he actually means the Christian Devil; then he compounds his error by chiding "Lovecraft's most ardent admirers (and apologists)" for not recognising that this brings HPL into line with seventeenth-century Puritan theologians.

flicted relationships with his parents and other family members. But here again his tunnel vision leads him to overlook other influences that are far more likely in the cases he puts forth; and, predictably, in this context he sees sexual imagery where probably none was intended. As a result, Callaghan's book, while having some illuminating insights, is overall a misfire.

David Simmons's anthology *New Critical Essays on H. P. Lovecraft* (Palgrave Macmillan, 2013), featuring the work of mostly British scholars, is quite a mixed bag. If one can get past the predictable jargon-laden and poorly researched articles on Lovecraft's attitude to race (David Simmons), women (Gina Wisker, Sara Williams), and other dreary topics, to say nothing of J. S. Mackley's sober analysis of Derleth's *The Trail of Cthulhu,* one comes upon some illuminating material. Most notable is an article by Chris Murray and Kevin Corstophine on Lovecraft's presence in comic books from the 1940s onward. Joseph Norman contributes an interesting article on Lovecraft's influence on "extreme" metal rock bands, while Mark Jones discusses Lovecraft's place in popular culture in a more general fashion.

More creditable is Robert H. Waugh's critical anthology *Lovecraft and Influence* (Scarecrow Press, 2013), which includes essays tracing influences on Lovecraft as well as his influence upon later writers. Among the more noteworthy items are J. D. Worthington's essay on the role of the Augustan poets in shaping Lovecraft's poetry; James Goho's essay placing Lovecraft within the realm of American Gothic; Waugh's groundbreaking piece on Lovecraft's influence on a trilogy of science fiction writers (Arthur C. Clarke, Fritz Leiber, and Philip K. Dick); Michael Cisco's rumination on Lovecraft and William S. Burroughs; and John Langan's treatment of Lovecraft and Stephen King.

The Age of Lovecraft, edited by Carl H. Sederholm and Jeffrey

Andrew Weinstock (University of Minnesota Press, 2016), is, sadly, chock full of the kind of impenetrable, jargon-laden articles that give academics a bad name. Lovecraft is treated from a multitude of perspectives, ranging from philosophical to cultural to (inevitably) racial; but little genuine light is cast on his work, since many of the authors make the fundamental critical error of abstracting Lovecraft's views solely from a reading of the fiction, without reference to his essays and letters.[5] The one genuinely insightful piece is Isabella van Elferen's essay on weird sounds in Lovecraft's fiction.

Considerably more impressive are two critical anthologies edited by Sean Moreland, a Canadian scholar, each of which contain perspicacious essays on various aspects of Lovecraft's work and thought. *The Lovecraftian Poe* (Lehigh University Press, 2017) features a baker's dozen articles on the interrelations between these two titans of weird fiction, ranging from studies of cosmic horror in the two writers (Michael Cisco), the influence of the earlier writer upon the later one (Brian Johnson, Dan Clinton, Robert H. Waugh, etc.), and the influence of the two writers on later work (Alissa Burger, Sean Moreland, John Langan). Of particular value are two articles on Lovecraft's poetry and the influence of Poe's theory and practice of poetry upon it (Sławomir Studniarz, Miles Tuttle).

Moreland's somewhat awkwardly titled *New Directions in Supernatural Horror Literature* (Palgrave Macmillan, 2018) takes "Supernatural Horror in Literature" as a springboard for a dozen or more articles either assessing Lovecraft's own evaluations of

---

5. And for a volume that purports to deal extensively with HPL as a philosopher, it is noteworthy that not a single contributor cites my philosophical study, *H. P. Lovecraft: The Decline of the West,* or Timo Airaksinen's *The Philosophy of H. P. Lovecraft.* Several discuss Harman's *Weird Realism* and other works of the same sort.

the writers he discusses in that treatise (Sharon Packer, S. T. Joshi, John Glover), or discussing work that Lovecraft neglected to treat, such as weirdness in mediaeval writing (Helen Marshall), or taking a more theoretical approach to the genre (Michael Cisco). There are, of course. the predictable excursions into gender studies (Gina Wisker) and queer studies (Brian Johnson); but Vivian Ralickas provides a keen analysis of the figure of the "dandy" in his critical and fictional work.

Then there is Scott Cutler Shershow and Scott Michaelsen's *The Love of Ruins: Letters on Lovecraft* (State University of New York Press, 2017). This is one of the most pretentious, bombastic, and just plain silly treatises on Lovecraft ever written. It demonstrates conclusively why so much academic criticism has become a parody of itself: based on inadequate research, full of impenetrably opaque conclusions and puffed up with authorial preening, it unwittingly provides more illumination on the authors' own biases and presuppositions than on the literary work it purports to be analysing.

The authors—whose book consists of a series of letters back and forth to each other—repeatedly stress their "love" of Lovecraft, and their enthusiasm does shine through at random moments. But there is reason to doubt their credentials in writing a book of this sort, however unorthodox its structure. Both are professors of English, but Shershow has published a book on the "right-to-die debate" and Michaelsen has co-written one on anthropology. Neither of them seems particularly well versed in the history of weird fiction before and during Lovecraft's lifetime, and they do not even appear to be familiar with the totality of Lovecraft's literary texts (fiction, poetry, essays).

I suppose it was to be expected that *The Love of Ruins* harps on Lovecraft's racism, although it at least does not use this issue to denigrate Lovecraft's achievement. Like Michel Houellebecq and others, these two Scotts seem at times to regard racism as central to Lovecraft's literary work; but they can only make this argument by ambiguity, conjecture, and equivocation. And yet, in the end they at last gain a semblance of sanity and conclude that the horrors in Lovecraft affect the entire human race.

The year 2013 saw the revival of the NecronomiCon under entirely new management. This incarnation of the event was considerably more scholarly than its predecessor, and it featured an entire track of papers given by academics or independent scholars, which had been selected by the convention committee as the best of those it had received. The convention was held in 2013, 2015, 2017, and 2019, and four volumes of papers (usually augmented from their oral presentation) have been published under the title *Lovecraftian Proceedings*. It is difficult to single out specific contributions in these three volumes, but the first does contain interesting pieces on Milton and Lovecraft (Marcello C. Ricciardi), Lovecraft's travelogues (Kenneth W. Lai), humour in Lovecraft (Stephen Walker), and Lovecraft's fiction analysed from an ecocritical perspective (Cory Willard); the second volume features a study of Lucretius' influence on Lovecraft (Sean Moreland), Lovecraft's architectural writings (Connor Pitetti), and the intriguing idea of Lovecraft as an optimist (Matthew Beach); the third volume has studies of Lovecraft and the Antarctic (Ian Fetters), Lovecraft and Mars (Edward Guimont), Lovecraft and detective fiction (Heather Poirier), Lovecraft and Egypt (Troy Rondinone), and other interesting papers.

Smaller-scale academic treatments appeared in a number of venues. My two-volume treatise *Unutterable Horror: A History of Supernatural Fiction* (PS Publishing, 2012) began with *Gilgamesh* and continued up to the present day. There is a lengthy chapter on "Lovecraft and His Influence," with later discussions of Lovecraft's influence on contemporary writers. Michael Saler's *As If: Modern Enchantment and the Literary Prehistory of Virtual Reality* (Oxford University Press, 2012) has an intriguing chapter on Lovecraft's imaginary topographies. Lovecraft is discussed all through the critical anthology *The Unique Legacy of* Weird Tales, edited by Justin Everett and Jeffrey H. Shanks (Rowman & Littlefield, 2015).

Perhaps the most distinctive—and in many ways the most brilliant—book ever written on Lovecraft is Graham Harman's *Weird Realism: Lovecraft and Philosophy* (2012). Harman, a professor of philosophy at American University in Cairo, finds Lovecraft a sort of trump card for his own brand of philosophy, which he calls "object-oriented ontology." Regrettably, Harman's use of Lovecraft's fiction—which he admires in part because "Lovecraft writes stories about the essence of *philosophy*" (33; Harman's emphasis)—is based on a fallacy that severely damages, if it does not altogether undermine, his central thesis.[6]

But this error takes away nothing from Harman's analysis of Lovecraft's stories from a stylistic and rhetorical perspective. He repeatedly takes issue with Edmund Wilson and his ilk for disdaining Lovecraft's prose as overwritten or careless, proving by

---

6. What Harman wishes to maintain is that "No reality can be immediately translated into representations [i.e., descriptive statements] of any sort. Reality itself is weird because reality itself is incommensurable with any attempt to represent or measure it" (51). He repeatedly condemns David Hume and other empiricists (probably including Bertrand Russell—admired by HPL—although Harman never mentions him), caricaturing them as believing that objects can be described satisfactorily as "a bundle of qualities." But what Harman, incredibly, overlooks is that HPL is writing fiction—and, specifically, *weird* fiction, which is inherently non-realistic. It is a severe category error to criticise philosophers (who are commenting on the real world) by means of a series of texts that are fictional and non-representational. It is as if one were to criticise the idea that rabbits can't talk by appealing to *Alice in Wonderland.*

example after example that it is so meticulously written as to convey exactly what Lovecraft wishes to convey by the best means necessary. This leads to some remarkable assertions. It is not simply that, in Harman's view, Lovecraft is "one of the greatest [writers] of the twentieth century," and that "the greatness of Lovecraft even pertains to more than the literary world, since it brushes against several of the most crucial philosophical themes of our time" (10); there is even more: "The idea that Lovecraft is outclassed as a stylist by the likes of Proust or Joyce (two of [Edmund] Wilson's favorites) is not an idea to which I can assent. The opposite claim seems closer to the truth" (145).

Whatever one may think of Harman's high opinion of Lovecraft, his dissection of individual passages from Lovecraft's "great tales" is almost unfailingly acute, although with a few curious slips and a failure to understand that such tales as *At the Mountains of Madness* and "The Shadow out of Time" are not simple "weird tales" but are what Lovecraft himself explicitly declared to be "non-supernatural cosmic art," and therefore the meticulous descriptions of the alien species in those tales is a central and compelling feature of the texts rather than a boring or inessential aside. Aside from such small blunders, it could well be said that Harman's book is the most penetrating study of what might be called Lovecraft's narratology—the ways in which his use of language effectively fosters his philosophical and literary goals—ever written. (Steven J. Mariconda's various papers remain pioneering in their study of Lovecraft as prose stylist and rhetorician.)

The number of shorter academic papers on Lovecraft (in both print and online venues), as well as theses and dissertations, have now become so extensive that it is difficult even to keep track of them, let alone analyse them. How many of these works actually advance our knowledge of Lovecraft is greatly open to debate; but I cite one major work only because it approaches

Lovecraft and his work from an entirely new and innovative direction. Andrew Gipe-Lazarou's Ph.D. dissertation, "Marvellous Marblehead: The Architecture of Weird Fiction" (National Technical University of Athens), examines Marblehead and New York City as the opposite poles of Lovecraft's imagination—not merely in terms of pure architecture but also from many other perspectives. The result is a breathtakingly penetrating examination that sheds new light on many aspects of Lovecraft's life, work, and thought.[7]

From a less academic perspective, several titles appeared. The value of these books is also significantly in doubt, and at best they testify to Lovecraft's increasing popularity among a growing body of readers—whether they be devotees of weird fiction, occultists, or general readers.

Kenneth Hite's *Tour de Lovecraft: The Tales* (Atomic Overmind Press, 2008) is a breathless treatise that, in 102 pages of text, purports to discuss 51 of Lovecraft's original tales (only those, curiously enough, in my three Penguin editions, ignoring some interesting specimens—such as three of Lovecraft's four prose-poems—found elsewhere). This averages to 2 pages per story; sometimes a story is covered in one page or less; on only one occasion ("The Dunwich Horror") do we get an analysis that goes on for six pages. All this is strange for more than one reason. Given that this casual, flippant, slang-ridden treatise began its life on the Internet, where space is not exactly at a premium, there seems no rationale for this kind of parsimony, aside from the disturbing possibility that Hite really doesn't have much of interest or substance to say about Lovecraft. Several of his analyses of individual tales are merely fragmentary notes or

7. A modified version of one chapter appeared in the *Lovecraft Annual* No. 14 (2020).

jottings, as if he read the story in question and just wrote down the first thing that entered his head.

The brutal fact is that *Tour de Lovecraft* was written about thirty years too late. The most charitable thing that can be said of it is that it is a fairly interesting example of "fan" criticism. Had it been published, say, around 1973, it might have engendered some fruitful discussion among other fans of the period. But given the enormous quantity of sound, substantial, and sophisticated criticism that has been published in the last several decades, a book like Hite's is, in the most literal and painful sense of the term, supernumerary. It has no reason for existence.

Some attempts at writing "popular" biographies of Lovecraft can be discussed. Paul Roland, a British writer, in *The Curious Case of H. P. Lovecraft* (2014) writes that he had begun "planning a biography of H. P. Lovecraft in the mid-nineties" (9). Alas! his dilatoriness has caused him to be left behind by scholarship, so that his book is almost entirely a regurgitation of previous biographers' work, sprinkled with errors and fleshed out with liberal quotations from Lovecraft and others.[8] At several points he suggests, plausibly enough, that some of Lovecraft's behaviours are indicative of a mild case of Asperger's syndrome, but doesn't follow up on the idea.[9] Aside from fleeting forays toward an occultist interpretation of Lovecraft and ventures into literary criticism that are cringingly inept, there is very little to be said about this book.

Two other books focus on Lovecraft's connexions with the

---

8. Roland seems to fancy that he has "rediscovered" Sonia Davis's memoir of HPL, having gone to the effort of securing it from the files of the *Providence Journal* and printing it complete in an appendix. Readers of this book need not be told how many times this version, as well as the complete version, have been reprinted.

9. On this subject see Gary Myers and Jennifer McIlwee Myers, *Lovecraft's Syndrome: An Asperger's Appraisal of the Writer's Life* (n.p.: CreateSpace, 2015).

occult. Donald Tyson's *The Dream World of H. P. Lovecraft* (2010) is on the whole a straightforward biography, but seizes upon Lovecraft's dreams as a kind of counterweight to the atheistic materialism of his avowed philosophy. Tyson himself is apparently a practising occultist who has written several books about the *Necronomicon* containing spells that he maintains are actually efficacious, along with all manner of other books on the Western esoteric tradition.

The problem with Tyson's approach is, first, that his study of Lovecraft's dreams is necessarily an inexact psychoanalysis of a dead man; and second, because of Tyson's bias toward the occult, he can't help reading vast esoteric significance in what can more plausibly be accounted for in a more rational manner. In discussing the apparent paradox of why Lovecraft was so fixated on weird fiction even though he was a materialist, Tyson makes the remarkable assertion that

> [Lovecraft] never seriously asked himself why he was devoting his life to something his conscious mind regarded as of no real value. Had he been able to confront this conundrum, he might have achieved a fusion between the two sides of his nature, the scientific with the psychic, the rational with the spiritual, but he could not conceive how two such seemingly contradictory viewpoints could coexist. (79–80)

Tyson's reading of Lovecraft's letters must be very selective. Since his point of view is widespread, even among non-occultists, it may be well to give a compact answer here. What Lovecraft was hoping to achieve through weird fiction was a sense of imaginative liberation; moreover, the "gods" or monsters he created in his fiction were not to be taken literally but as symbols for the philosophical conceptions he sought to convey. A key discussion occurs in a letter to James F. Morton in 1930. He begins by asserting that "Reality is all right enough so far as it goes . . . The only trouble is *that it doesn't go far enough* for a guy with extreme sensitiveness." He continues:

> It gives me no kick at all to emulate the idealist or religionist & invent false conditions & significances which actually deny reality. . . . For me, then, is . . . the consciously artificial manipulation of the theogonist's & myth-maker's privilege in manner of the eighteenth Baron Dunsany . . . that is, the deliberate exercise of the human instinct for space, reach, adventure, & cosmic identification through the weaving of fantastick aesthetic suggestions *as such*, and *not* as intellectual denials of objective reality. If you get what I mean, I like to *supplement*, rather than *contradict*, reality. I get no kick at all from *postulating what isn't so*, as religionists & idealists do. . . . My big kick comes from *taking reality just as it is*—accepting all the limitations of the most orthodox science—& then permitting my symbolising faculty to *build outward* from the existing facts; rearing a structure of *indefinite promise & possibility* whose topless towers are in no cosmos or dimension penetrable by the contradicting-power of the tyrannous & inexorable intellect. But the whole secret of the kick is *that I know damn well it isn't so*. ([1 April 1930]; *Letters to James F. Morton* 225–27)

Overall, however, Tyson's book has its merits, if one can overlook his crotchets. And much can be forgiven this author in light of his superb Lovecraftian fiction, whether it be the compelling novel *Alhazred* (2006) or the many stories he has written on Lovecraftian themes, some collected in *The Skinless Face* (2019).

John L. Steadman's *H. P. Lovecraft: The Master of Horror's Influence on Modern Occultism* (2015) is not a biography at all but a well-researched investigation of how Lovecraft's work has been seized by occultists of various stripes to promote their own specific interests. Steadman appears to be one of their number, if his sober first chapter ("The Purposes and Methodologies of Black Magick") is any guide; but he manages to restrain his tendency toward regarding Lovecraft's "gods" as actually existing—as Peter Levenda in *The Dark Lord: H. P. Lovecraft, Kenneth Grant and the Typhonian Tradition in Magic* (2013) does not—and provides straightforward discussions of the several different

Necronomicons that have been published over the decades, the embrace of Lovecraft by "vodou cults," Wiccans, Kenneth Grant and his disciples, Anton LaVey's Church of Satan, and others. It is all very engaging, even if most Lovecraft devotees will be repeatedly scratching their heads at the misuse and misconstrual of Lovecraft's work and thought by these strange folk.

W. Scott Poole's *In the Mountains of Madness: The Life and Extraordinary Afterlife of H. P. Lovecraft* (2016) is written by a professor who makes bold claims for his work: "I'm writing this unorthodox biography of Lovecraft as a historian" (14). But in fact, the book is largely a fairly straightforward biography—heavily borrowing from previous scholarship—with a certain amount of added opinionation by the author and scattered discussions of Lovecraft's wacky fans (and, it appears, scholars), and is further marred by a supercilious and arrogant tone that is quite off-putting. As Darrell Schweitzer wrote in a pungent review, "As history, his book isn't much. It doesn't do a very good job setting Lovecraft in the context of the United States of the early twentieth century, and as biography it is sufficiently skimpy (amid meandering digressions) that only by consideration of what is left out do we really have any sense of the intellectual richness of Lovecraft's life and thought."[10] Poole, indeed, makes inexplicable errors in the very area of his expertise—i.e., history.[11]

It also would have helped if Poole had boned up a bit more on the principles of literary criticism. He regards it as axiomatic, based on a reading of Lovecraft's fiction, that Lovecraft was a

---

10. Darrell Schweitzer, [Review of *In the Mouth of Madness*], *Lovecraft Annual* No. 11 (2017): 187.

11. He has a seriously erroneous understanding of HPL's late conversion to "fascistic socialism," by which he simply meant (a) a limitation of the suffrage, and (b) a distribution of economic wealth to the many. These views were espoused by a number of political theorists of the time. Indeed, that first point would seem to have greater utility in our own time than in HPL's.

misogynist and a misanthrope (thereby falling into the cardinal error of attributing fictional characters' views to their author). And as for Lovecraft's racism, he ridicules the much-maligned "man of his time" argument by the convenient expedient of making it mindlessly simplistic ("Everyone was racist then!"); but this elementary straw-man argument has little effect on sophisticated discussions of the personal, regional, intellectual, cultural, political, and other tendencies in Lovecraft's lifetime that led him to such a stance. Toward the end he grudgingly allows that "at least a few of those who have damned Lovecraft for his racial attitudes . . . are using concepts they haven't examined" (265).

Even the final section of Poole's book, dealing with Lovecraft's "extraordinary afterlife," where one might have expected some level of originality and insight, is superficial and uncoordinated, randomly dealing with Lovecraft pastiches, films, comic books, fake *Necronomicons,* and the like. There is not the slightest attempt at a history of Lovecraft's critical reception (so far as I can tell—in the absence of an index—neither Edmund Wilson nor Colin Wilson is ever mentioned in the book), but only a cursory survey of Lovecraft's effect on popular culture—just about what one would expect from a man who has written a book on Vampira.

Not of direct relevance to Lovecraft, in spite of its title, is Jack Koblas's *The Lovecraft Circle and Others as I Remember Them* (Battered Silicon Dispatch Box, 2012), which is chiefly concerned with Lovecraft fandom—specifically, the many fans (as well as professionals, among them Robert Bloch, E. Hoffmann Price, and Donald Wandrei) whom Koblas, a longtime fan who died in 2013, had known. Even so, the book is a mine of information that could and should be used by biographers to fill in gaps in our knowledge of the figures it discusses.

And it was perhaps inevitable that at this time some actual

coffee-table books on Lovecraft would appear. I was commission to write such a book, published under the not very apposite title *H. P. Lovecraft: Nightmare Countries* (Metro Books, 2012), sold exclusively through the Barnes & Noble bookstore chain. Although consisting of only 40,000 words of text,[12] its chief feature is a wealth of illustrations—ranging from photographs of Lovecraft and his colleagues, reproductions of manuscripts, images of Providence and other locales, and so on—that more than adequately displayed Lovecraft and his times.

Another book of the same sort is Charlotte Montague's *H. P. Lovecraft: The Mysterious Man Behind the Darkness* (Chartwell Books, 2015). There is of course no original research in this volume, as Montague is entirely reliant on previous biographical and critical work on Lovecraft for her account; but the wealth of images—photographs of Lovecraft and his colleagues, illustrations of his stories, covers of *Weird Tales,* and so on—make the book appealing, even if its multitude of sidebars and other distracting elements of design sometimes make for difficult reading.

In England, Sammy Maine assembled a book entitled *Gothic Dreams: Necronomicon: Dark Fantasy, Digital Art & H. P. Lovecraft* (Flame Tree Publishing, 2013). This exquisitely produced book features all manner of illustrations purporting to depict the monsters in the *Necronomicon.* Every page (or, rather, two-page spread) vividly evokes terror, awe, and wonder. As a collector's item, it ranks very high.

Translations of Lovecraft into other languages continued at their torrid pace throughout this period. It is impossible to take note of more than a few of the more notable items.

In France, older editions of Lovecraft issued by Denoël, J'ai

12. I later reprinted the text under the title *H. P. Lovecraft: A Short Biography* (Sarnath Press, 2018).

Lu, and other publishers continued to be reprinted into the 2010s. More indicative of a newer, more sophisticated appreciation of Lovecraft was the work of François Bon, who prepared numerous small volumes of one or two Lovecraft stories for the publisher Tiers Livre, with annotations; but his most significant venture was an edition of the *Commonplace Book* (2016), exhaustively annotated. Luc Deborde translated three volumes of Lovecraft—*L'Ombre du temps et autres nouvelles* (2013), *Je suis d'ailleurs et autres nouvelles* (2015), *Le Monstre sur le seuil et autres nouvelles* (2015)—with the publisher Éditions Humanis. The Paris publisher Bragelonne issued many Lovecraft-related volumes, including a two-volume set, *Cthulhu: Le mythe* (2012).

But the most significant French project was a series of new translations by David Camus, who had long recognised the inadequacy of Jacques Papy's translations of the 1950s. His work was embodied in three volumes published by Mnémos: *Les Montagnes hallucinées et autres récits d'exploration* (2013), *Kadath: Quatre quêtes oniriques de la cité inconnue* (2016), and *La Clé d'argent des contrées du rêve* (2017), the last translated by other hands. Mnémos is now scheduled to issue a seven-volume edition of Camus's translations of Lovecraft's complete fiction, with the addition of some poetry, essays, letters, and the commonplace book.

In Germany, the German publisher Festa Verlag, established by Frank Festa, undertook an extensive project to publish Lovecraft and other authors of weird fiction in new translations. The series "H. P. Lovecrafts Bibliothek des Schreckens" (H. P. Lovecraft's Library of Horror) began publication as early as 2000 and now spans nearly fifty volumes. New translations of Lovecraft's stories were made by Andreas Diesel, Felix F. Frey, A. F. Fischer, Festa himself, and others. Interestingly, several of these translations were subsequently recorded on CDs.

Suhrkamp published a selection of its various Lovecraft volumes as *Horror Stories* (2008), reaching all the way back to the translations of H. C. Artmann. Artmann's volume (*Cthulhu: Geistergeschichten,* 1968) continued to be in print as late as 2010. My annotated edition of *Supernatural Horror in Literature* (2000) was translated as *Das übernaturlich Grauen in Literatur* (Golkonda Verlag, 2014), while my annotated edition of *The Case of Charles Dexter Ward* (2010) was translated as *Der Fall Charles Dexter Ward* (Golkonda Verlag, 2016). Florian F. Marzin edited Lovecraft's *Die besten Geschichten* (Anaconda, 2016).

In Italy, publishers continued to repackage their previous editions of Lovecraft's works in ever more creative forms, such as Gianni Pilo's *I racconti del "Necronomicon"* (Newton Compton, 2015). Giuseppe Lippi's edition, *Tutti i racconti,* was reprinted in an enormous one-volume edition (Mondadori, 2017). Pietro Guarriello began editing an occasional journal of scholarship, *Studi Lovecraftiani* (2005f.), that continues to be issued down to the present day.

Gianfranco de Turris and Sebastiano Fusco prepared a slim edition of fifty letters by Lovecraft in politics, society, and philosophy, *L'orrore della realtà* (Edizioni Mediterranee, 2007). Fusco edited a bilingual edition of *Fungi from Yuggoth,* titled *Gli orrori di Yuggoth* (Barbera Editore, 2007). Another small volume of letters was *Lovecraft, l'età adulta è l'inferno* (L'Orma Editore, 2018), edited and translated by Marco Peano. (The title is a translation of Lovecraft's comment in a letter, "Adulthood is hell.") The Necronomicon Press edition of Lovecraft's *Autobiographical Writings* was translated as *Parola di Lovecraft* (Società Editrice La Torre, 2012).

Sergio Alteri edited an interesting volume of Lovecraft stories about dreams, *Il profeta dell'incubo* (Feltrinelli, 2016). Pietro Guarriello did something similar in a more comprehensive fashion, *Oniricon: Sogni, incubi e fantasticherie* (Bietti, 2017). The Milan publisher RCS MediaGroup published a number of bilingual editions of individual Lovecraft stories.

Dissemination of Lovecraft's work in Spanish-speaking countries became a veritable tidal wave in this period. Valdemar, EDAF, Alianza, and other publishers continued to reprint their editions of Lovecraft. Edgardo C. Lois edited what he believed was a three-volume set of Lovecraft's "complete works," *Obras completas,* for the Buenos Aires publisher Díada (2009). A Mexican publisher attempted to do the same in a three-volume set, *Obras fondamontales* (Stonehenge Books, 2012). Another Mexican publisher, Editores Mexicanos Unidos, released an enormous volume of Lovecraft's *Obras maestras* (2015).

Roberto Ignazio Díaz prepared a bilingual edition of an extensive selection of Lovecraft's poetry, *Poemas* (Andrómeda, 2009). A new translation of "Supernatural Horror in Literature" by Gabriela Ellena Castellotti, *El terror en la literatura,* was first published by the Barcelona publisher Backlist (2010) and subsequently reprinted by Austral (2017). Another translation of the same work, *Horror y fiction* (Promoteo Libros, 2013), was edited by Marcelo G. Burello. Óscar Mariscal prepared an edition of some of Lovecraft's essays, including some of his political writings, as *Confesiones de un incrédulo y otros ensayos escogidos* (El Paseo, 2018). A piquant volume is a slim selection of Lovecraft stories adapted for reading by "fearless kids" (*niños que no tengan miedo*), *Cuentos de horror contados para niños* (Ediciones Lea, 2016).

Francisco Arellano compiled a volume, *H. P. Lovecraft: La vida privada* (La Biblioteca del Laberinto, 2017), an extensive selection of essays, letters, and other documents by Lovecraft that illuminate key aspects of his life and work. The book was announced as the first of a multi-volume set, but so far no further volumes have appeared.

There were many editions in Portuguese, most of them in Brazil. Seven of them were edited and translated by Guilherme da Silva Braga, all for the São Paolo publisher Hedra. Several of them consisted of a single novella or short novel; but one of them, translated by Braga but edited by Luis Dolhnikoff, appeared in 2014 as *Os melhores contos* (Hedra, 2014). Hedra also published a translation of *A Dreamer and a Visionary* as *A vida de H. P. Lovecraft* (2014). Bruno Costa edited a large volume of collected tales, *Contos reunidos* (Editora Ex Machina, 2017). Another publisher, Saída de Emergência, issued a six-volume collected edition of stories (2009–17), translated by José Manuel Lopes.

In Catalan, four different editions appeared, two of them edited and translated by Emili Olcina. Not to be overlooked is a translation of *At the Mountains of Madness* into Basque (*Eromenaren mendietan* [2016]). And, incredibly, a trilingual volume of Lovecraft's poetry in English, French, and Corsican (*H. P. Lovecraft in puesia* [Materia Scritta, 2015]) is the only known book of Lovecraft in Corsican.

In the Netherlands, Pierre De Keyser translated at least three volumes of Lovecraft's tales (Voltaire, 2006–10), arranged chronologically. A five-volume Czech edition prepared by Ondřej Müller (Plus, 2010–13) presented Lovecraft's fiction from 1917 to 1935 in chronological sequence. A bilingual edition of *Fungi from Yuggoth* (*Houby z Yuggothu* [Volvox Globator, 2019]) also appeared in Czech. A volume of Lovecraft's poetry came out in Hungarian, *As ősi út és a hírnök versei* (Attraktor, 2018).

In Poland, the publisher Zysk i S-ka continued to issue Lovecraft's work, mostly in translations of such American volumes as *Bloodcurdling Tales of Horror and the Macabre* (2007),

The Dream Cycle of H. P. Lovecraft (2007), and the two Dell editions of *Annotated H. P. Lovecraft* (2008). The publisher Vesper issued an immense volume of Lovecraft's tales, *Zgroza w Dunwich* (2012), with illustrations by John Coulthart. The same publisher issued a volume, *Przyszła na Sarnath zagłada* (2016), that contained stories as well as "Supernatural Horror in Literature." Mateusz Kopacs, the leading Polish Lovecraft scholar, prepared an edition of Lovecraft's letters, *Koszmary i fantazje* (Sine Qua Non, 2013), and poetry, *Nemezis i inne utwory poetyckie* (Vesper, 2018).

Romanian editions continued to appear, including a translation of *The Call of Cthulhu and Other Weird Stories* (Leda, 2009). Six volumes appeared in Serbian, including a volume, *Šaptač u tami* (Orfelin, 2015), with an extensive biographical appendix by Dejan Ognjanovič. Three Croatian volumes were published, including a large volume, *Nekronomikon* (Everest Media, 2012), that also has some biographical material. Three Estonian editions appeared, including one that contained a translation of "Supernatural Horror in Literature," *Vari aja sügavusest* (Fantaasia, 2013). *Cthulhu kutse* (Viking, 2015) is a large volume that includes most of Lovecraft's major tales. Two large volumes of Lovecraft's stories appeared in Bulgarian (2012, 2013), as did two editions in Slovenian (2007, 2008).

In Denmark, five editions appeared, including a volume, *Ved vanviddets bjerge samt noveller* (AnTennA, 2013), that contained a biographical and critical appendix by Jakob Friis Andersen. In Finland, after a twenty-year interval, a new volume of Lovecraft stories appeared in 2009, *Kuiskaus pimeässä ja muita kertomuksia*. This was the first of six volumes of Lovecraft's tales issued by the publisher Jalava down to 2014. Another publisher issued a translation of "Supernatural Horror in Literature," *Yliluonnollinen kauhu kirjallisuudessa* (Savukeidas, 2013).

Swedish editions continued apace. Matthias Fyhr, a leading scholar in that nation, prepared an edition of "The Shadow over Innsmouth" (*Skuggan över Innsmouth* [Alastor Press, 2008]), with ancillary texts, all translated by Arthur Isfelt. Fyhr also edited (with Jonas Ellerström) Lovecraft's commonplace book (*Anteckningsbok* [Ellerström, 2009]), while Ellerström edited a volume of Lovecraft's autobiographical writings (*Självbiografiskt* [Ellerström, 2011]). Martin Andersson edited a volume of some of Lovecraft's Dreamworld stories (*Sarnaths Undergång och andra noveller* [Bakhäll, 2011]), a translation of *The H. P. Lovecraft Dream Book* (*H. P. Lovecraft mardrömsboken* [Hastur, 2012]), and a translation of the Lovecraft/Zealia Bishop stories (*Medusas hår och andra skräckberättelser* [Hastur, 2013]); he also wrote a foreword to a translation of "Supernatural Horror in Literature" (*Om övernaturlig skräck i literaturen* [H:ström, 2011]).

An edition of "Supernatural Horror in Literature" translated into modern Greek appeared as *Yperphysikos tromos stē logotechnia* (Aiolos, 2008). The publisher Brainfood began a planned fifteen-volume edition of Lovecraft's fiction in 2019. In Turkey, Hasan Fehmi Nemli edited and translated a seven-volume edition of Lovecraft's collected tales (2014–15): separate volumes for each of his three short novels as well as for "The Shadow over Innsmouth," and three volumes of miscellaneous stories. Dost Körpe translated a volume of tales, *Cthulhu'nun çağrisi* (2015).

Russian publishers also continued to issue Lovecraft's works, including such firms as Izd-vo AST (*Gipnos,* 2007), Azbuka-Klassika (*Drugiye bogi,* 2010), Azbuka-Attikus (*Inye bogi i drugie istorii,* 2013), and others. In *Nekronomikon* (Enigma, 2011), Nina Bavina has translated "History of the 'Necronomicon'" and included commentary by other Russian critics about the imaginary tome. A volume of Lovecraft's poetry appeared in 2020.

In Ukrainian, at least three volumes of a "Complete Prose Works" series appeared around 2017–18. An earlier volume, published in 1992, had included a Lovecraft story among two tales by other authors.

Chinese editions proliferated. *The Call of Cthulhu and Other Weird Stories* appeared in 2016; it is unclear whether my notes were also translated. A volume, *Kesulu shen hua* (2016; *Cthulhu Mythos*), contained several major tales, although also a few non-Mythos tales, such as "From Beyond" and "The Hound." An enormous volume of Lovecraft's tales came out as *Kesulu shen hua he ji* (2017). An even larger volume, exceeding 1000 pages, came out as *Si ling zhi shu* (2018). "Supernatural Horror in Literature" came out in a Chinese translation in 2014.

In Japan, the publisher Kokusho-Kankohkai continued to keep its multi-volume edition of Lovecraft, published in the 1980s, in print into the 2010s. It also issued an eight-volume edition of Cthulhu Mythos stories by various writers (2007–09). Another publisher, Aozura Bunko, began an extensive line of Lovecraft volumes in 2015. Keisuke Otaki prepared an edition of "Supernatural Horror in Literature," *Bungaku ni okeru choshizen no kyofu* (Gakken, 2009).

Several Korean editions appeared, including a four-volume edition of what appears to be Lovecraft's complete stories, *Lŏbŭ K'ŭraep'ŭt'ŭ chŏnjip* (2009–12). "Supernatural Horror in Literature" appeared as *Gongpo munhag-ui maehog* (2012).

Two more Hebrew editions appeared, one translating "The Shadow over Innsmouth" (2013) and the other "The Call of Cthulhu" (2013). And Lovecraft would no doubt be tickled that an edition of his work appeared in Arabic (2019), as an ebook.

My *H. P. Lovecraft: A Life* was translated by Mateusz Kopacs in an enormous hardcover volume, *H. P. Lovecraft: Biografia* (Zisk I S-ka, 2010). This book of course emerged exactly at the time the full version of my biography, *I Am Providence,* appeared. It took some time for that work to appear in other languages, but later in the decade translations into German (*H. P. Lovecraft: Leben und Werk,* tr. Andreas Fliedner [Golkonda Verlag, 2017–20; 2 vols.]), French (*Je suis Providence,* with a translation supervised by Christophe Thill [Editions ActuSF, 2019; 2 vols.]), and Italian (*Io sono Provdence,* with a translation edited by Giacomo Ortolani [Providence Press, 2019—the first of a planned three-volume edition]) appeared. Frank Belknap Long's *Dreamer on the Nightside* appeared in Italian as *H. P. Lovecraft e le ombre* (Profondo Rosso, 2010).

Alessandro Bottero and others prepared a volume of tributes to Lovecraft on the seventieth anniversary of his death, *Da Arkham alle stelle* (Bottero Edizioni, 2007), consisting of stories, essays, comics, and other material. Antonio Tentori and others prepared a volume, *Lovecraft e il cinema* (Profondo Rosso, 2014), assessing film adaptations of Lovecraft over the years. Along the same lines, Gianluca Di Fratta wrote *Lovecraft e il Giappone* (La Torre, 2018), studying Japanese adaptations of Lovecraft in film, manga, and anime. Claudio Foti wrote several books, including *I segreti del Necronomicon* (Enigma, 2016) and a short biography, *Misteri e curiosità di H. P. Lovecraft* (Weird Book, 2018). Daniele Corradi's *Il linguaggio di Cthulhu* (Jouvence, 2019) is a formidable philosophical study of Lovecraft. Massimo Guzzinati's *Lovecraft oltre la soglia* (Lulu, 2010) is a psychological study of Lovecraft's life and work. *Il luoghi di Lovecraft* by Michele Mingrone and others (NPE, 2018) is a guide to Lovecraft's fictional topography.

The number of film adaptations of Lovecraft's tales now reached epic proportions: for this period IMDb.com lists 135 films and television shows, including a dozen or more announced or in post-production as of this writing. Most are short and of little account (we even find one film adaptation of "The Beast in the Cave"), but several are of note.

By far the most distinguished—and perhaps the best film adaptation of a Lovecraft story ever made—is *Die Farbe* (2010), an extraordinarily faithful and evocative interpretation of "The Colour out of Space." Although the film is a German production, its director is Vietnamese. Huan Vu has done a splendid job in writing and directing this film, which is set in post–World War II Germany but otherwise follows the story accurately. Its black-and-white ambiance (except when the "colour" manifests itself toward the end) and its sense of cumulative horror are impeccable. The film did not receive wide distribution, but can be secured by the diligent devotee. Huan Vu has announced a live-action version of a film set in Lovecraft's Dreamlands, but it appears far from completion.

A more recent adaptation of the same story—*Color out of Space* (2019) by the Australian director Richard Stanley—received far more press upon its release, but is largely a disappointment. It departs radically from the story in numerous particulars; very few of them are improvements to the original. And Stanley inexplicably leaves out scenes from the original story (such as the dying speech of Nahum Gardner as he crumbles to dust) that would have been highly effective on screen. There are some nice special effects here and there, but overall this is simply an updated B-movie not a great deal superior to the 1970 *Dunwich Horror* film.

The H. P. Lovecraft Historical Society attempted a full-length black-and-white film of *The Whisperer in Darkness* (2011); but here too the departures from the story—evidently the writer and director, Andrew Leman and Sean Branney, did not find the "face and hands" conclusion to the story sufficiently dramatic—spoil the fine atmosphere of Lovecraftian horror established in the early parts of the film.

Cthulhu (2007), directed by Dan Gildark with a screenplay by Grant Cogswell, is an able and atmospheric film, although it evoked controversy upon its release because of its gay subtext (an element handled quite ably). It is not an explicit adaptation of any single work by Lovecraft, but includes elements from "The Call of Cthulhu," "The Shadow over Innsmouth," and other tales. Set on the West Coast, and mostly filmed in the historic town of Astoria, Oregon, it manages to convey the sense of the cosmic that filmmakers seem to have difficulty depicting on screen.

Aside from these films, the record of Lovecraftian films in this period is pretty weak. Why Jeffrey Combs and Dean Stockwell allowed themselves to be resurrected into a remake of *The Dunwich Horror* (2009), directed by Leigh Scott, can only be left to the imagination. Other films of this era are so wretched that they do not deserve individual citation.

Let it not be assumed that only Anglophone filmmakers are involved in adapting Lovecraft's work. We have such things as a French television series, *L'Appel de Cthulhu,* that has extended to at least three seasons (2015–17); *La noche del océano* (2015), a short film adapting the Lovecraft–Barlow collaboration "The Night Ocean"; a short Swedish film, *Skuggan över Innfyr* (2017), inspired by Lovecraft; and much else besides. As with the translation of his work, Lovecraft has become a worldwide phenomenon in film and television.

And, as we saw in the previous chapter, some of the more interesting media items do not adapt a specific Lovecraft story but still convey Lovecraftian elements. Most notable perhaps is Guillermo del Toro's *The Shape of Water* (2017), which won the Academy Award for best picture (as del Toro won the award for best director); its debt to "The Shadow over Innsmouth" is manifest. Like several recent literary treatments of the same idea, del Toro extends sympathy toward the hybrid entity at the centre of the film, and it features the elegance and panache we expect from the director of *Pan's Labyrinth.*

One of course must lament the failure of del Toro to fulfil his long dream to film *At the Mountains of Madness,* for if there is any director with both the artistic sensibility and the prestige to engender an effective adaptation of this difficult story, it is del Toro. He was denied funding by Universal Studios when he asked for a budget of $150 million for an R-rated film; subsequently, he decided that Ridley Scott's film *Prometheus* (2012)—which broaches the idea that the human race was created by an alien species—had stolen his thunder. But of late del Toro has stated that his plans are not entirely dead, so perhaps we can have hope for a major Lovecraftian film from him in the future.

The HBO miniseries *Lovecraft Country* (2020), based on the 2016 novel by Matt Ruff, was co-produced by Jordan Peele, the celebrated African American director; but the actual Lovecraftian content of this program was minimal. It largely consisted of conventional supernatural tropes that resembled Stephen King far more than they resembled Lovecraft, along with relentless episodes of racism. Even if the show gave further publicity to Lovecraft, the implication that Lovecraft is nothing more than a racist who wrote horror stories (or a horror writer who was a racist) is regrettable.

And we can hardly ignore such things as the episode of the animated TV series *The Simpsons* in which the *Necronomicon* is featured (6 January 2002). Cthulhu is occasionally mentioned on the show, especially in some of the "Treehouse of Horror" Halloween episodes. Cthulhu also figures in an episode of the animated TV show *South Park* (10 November 2010). More seriously, Frank H. Woodward directed an able documentary on Lovecraft, *Lovecraft: Fear of the Unknown* (2008), that spanned the entirety of Lovecraft's life and focused on his posthumous recognition.

Tom Pomplun edited a volume of Lovecraft comic adaptations in *Graphic Classics, Volume 4* (Eureka, 2007), featuring a range of artists and adapting even such obscure works as "Sweet Ermengarde." Mark Ellis issued two volumes of adaptations under the collective title *The Miskatonic Project* (Millennium Concepts, 2008–09). Also of note are the five adaptations of Lovecraft stories in Steven Philip Jones's *The Worlds of H. P. Lovecraft* (Transfuzion, 2009).

Dan Lockwood edited two volumes of various comic artists' renderings of Lovecraft stories, *The Lovecraft Anthology* (Self-MadeHero, 2011–12). This set was subsequently translated into Italian and Spanish. Several such volumes appeared in Italian: Erik Kriek's *Da altrove e altri racconti* (Eris, 2014), *Alle montagne della follia* by Giovanni Masi and others (Star Comics, 2015), *Nyarlathotep* by Rotomago and others (NPE, 2016), and *Incubi* by Michele Penco (NPE, 2019).

Pat Harrigan and Brian Wood edited a volume entitled *The Art of H. P. Lovecraft's Cthulhu Mythos* (Fantasy Flight Publishing, 2006), containing illustrations from works by Lovecraft and many of his disciples and successors; the images were largely taken from publications by the gaming publishers Chaosium and Fantasy Flight Gaming. The book was subsequently translated into Japanese (2013).

But nothing can top *A Lovecraft Retrospective: Artists Inspired by H. P. Lovecraft* (Centipede Press, 2008), a stunningly lavish book (presumably assembled by the publisher of Centipede Press, Jerad Walters) that presents an entire history of Lovecraftian illustration from the pulp magazines all the way to the present day, and including the work of dozens of artists from Virgil Finlay to Lee Brown Coye to Les Edwards to Bob Eggleton to

Jason C. Eckhardt and many others.

Speaking of Eckhardt, he teamed up with Sam Gafford to produce a splendid graphic novel biography, *Some Notes on a Nonentity: The Life of H. P. Lovecraft* (PS Publishing, 2017), a work that boils down the essence of Lovecraft's life into 128 pages, all meticulously illustrated by Eckhardt. The premise of the work is that Lovecraft himself is speaking in a lecture hall about the salient features of his life. The overall execution is impeccable, and one only wishes there were more of it.

It is impossible to speak of Lovecraft and comics without discussing the work of Alan Moore. This British comics artist has been active since the 1970s, but of late he has turned his attention to Lovecraftian themes in a striking manner. *Neonomicon* was first published (2010) a four-issue comic written by Moore and illustrated by Jacen Burrows, then as a book (2011). This work, full of aberrant sex and generally set in the Lovecraftian realms of Red Hook and Salem, also features fishmen and the imminent birth of a child named Cthulhu. Moore has stated that in this work he has sought to make explicit the highly covert and unspoken racial and sexual elements inherent in some of Lovecraft's tales. Some of the threads of this comic draw upon Moore's earlier comic, *The Courtyard* (2003), which is itself elaborated from a short story that Moore published in the *Starry Wisdom* anthology of 1994.

Still more quintessentially Lovecraftian is *Providence,* also written by Moore and illustrated by Burrows, issued as a twelve-issue comic (2015–17) and then in a three-volume limited hardcover edition (2016–17). Moore asserts unequivocally that this work is a grand summation of his understanding and appreciation of Lovecraft. Set in 1919, it features occult books, nightgaunts, minimally altered Lovecraftian characters such as Thomas Malone, Robert Wheatley, Walter Race (see Walter Rice in

"The Dunwich Horror"), Randall Carver (i.e., Randolph Carter), Henry Annesley (the original name of Crawford Tillinghast in "From Beyond"), and actual individuals such as Whipple Phillips and S. T. Joshi. The scholarship is impressive: at one point the Boston Police Strike of 1919 (the inspiration for "The Street"—something that Moore would have learned only from my biography) is featured. Overall, this lavish work is one of the most impressive tributes to Lovecraft's imagination ever published.

The *Call of Cthulhu* role-playing game from Chaosium continued to issue supplements in the decades after its initial release, among the latest being *Cthulhu Rising* (2008) and *Atomic-Age Cthulhu* (2013). Over the past twenty years at least a dozen further games on Lovecraftian themes have been issued, including *Cthulhu Dark* (2010) and *Eldritch Rising* (2012). There is also a plethora of Lovecraftian board games, card games, and video games.

Some efforts have been made to chart the bewildering array of Lovecraft-related media, but the coverage has been inadequate and, in the case of published works, out-of-date the moment the book is published. This is the problem with Don G. Smith's *H. P. Lovecraft in Popular Culture* (2006), a somewhat mechanical and superficial attempt to cover films, television, comics, music, and games.

Quite a bit better, although perhaps also a bit out of date, is Gary Hill's *The Strange Sound of Cthulhu* (2006), an exhaustive study of Lovecraft's influence on rock music. Here the focus is on psychedelic rock (the 1960s band H. P. Lovecraft, among others), heavy metal (Metallica, Rage, Manilla Road, and numerous other bands in Europe), Goth (Fields of the Nephilim, Nox Arcana), and much else, with a specific focus on The Darkest of the Hillside Thickets as well as a discussion of passing references to Lovecraft in the music of such bands as Black Sabbath and Blue Öyster Cult. I have not had the energy to research further use of Lovecraftian motifs in rock music subsequent to the book's appearance.

It should by now be evident that Lovecraft had become a monumental figure in both popular and high culture. It is difficult to trace the multifarious ways in which his celebrity is displayed, beyond what has been said above; but one indication is the ongoing use of Lovecraft as a fictional character, both in print and in other media.

My own novel *The Assaults of Chaos* (Hippocampus Press, 2013) is a whimsy in which Lovecraft ventures to England and meets up with his literary idols (Arthur Machen, Lord Dunsany, Algernon Blackwood, and others) to battle Nyarlathotep. Much more serious, and poignant, is Jacqueline Baker's *The Broken Hours* (Talos Press, 2016), which takes place in the final months of Lovecraft's life at 66 College Street. Even if at times the portrayal of Lovecraft is not historically accurate and can even be considered defamatory (one character refers to him as a "monster"), the overall atmosphere of the book is one of deep sadness; and in the end, Lovecraft emerges as a tragic figure who has failed to realise the promise of his youthful precocity.

Less commendable is Paul La Farge's *The Night Ocean* (Penguin Press, 2017), whose premise is that Lovecraft may have had a homosexual relationship with the young R. H. Barlow. While written with some panache, the novel is littered with all manner of needless factual errors, and overall its characterisation of Lovecraft simply does not ring true.

One cannot discuss Lovecraft's own burgeoning worldwide reputation without referring to his role in the attention being given to other writers in the weird tradition—either those who influenced him (Arthur Machen, Lord Dunsany, Algernon Blackwood, M. R. James, Ambrose Bierce, etc.), or who were his own colleagues (Clark Ashton Smith, Frank Belknap Long, Robert E. Howard, August Derleth, Donald Wandrei, Robert Bloch, Fritz Leiber, Henry Kuttner, C. L. Moore, etc.), or who were influenced by him (Ramsey Campbell, Brian Lumley, Gary Myers, William Browning Spencer, Michael Shea, Jonathan Thomas, Caitlín R. Kiernan, etc.). It is undeniable that the extensive reprinting of the work of nineteenth- and twentieth-century weird writers—including virtually every author or work mentioned, however briefly, in "Supernatural Horror in Literature"—owes something to Lovecraft's interest in them.

This point is underscored by the several volumes that have emerged over the decades in which stories by famous or obscure writers whom Lovecraft claimed to enjoy were collected. The first such volume appears to have been *H. P. Lovecraft's Book of Horror* (1994), edited by Stephen Jones and Dave Carson. Later compilations, such as Douglas A. Anderson's *H. P. Lovecraft's Favorite Weird Tales* (2005) and my own two-volume series (H. P. Lovecraft's Favorite Horror Stories), *The Ghost of Fear and Others* and *The Dead Valley and Others* (both 2012), also have interesting material and surprisingly little overlap.

Foreign publishers also joined the bandwagon, as exemplified by the Dutch volume *Kosmische angst: de 10 beste griezelverhalen volgens H. P. Lovecraft,* edited by Pierre De Keyser (Voltaire, 2006).

And one supposes it was just a matter of time before Lovecraft's work entered the realm of children's literature. Tro Rex wrote *Littlest Lovecraft Presents: The Call of Cthulhu* (2013), with illustrations by Eyona Bella. The publisher's blurb warns that "Content may be difficult or disturbing to children under the age of 9." Let's hope so! Jason Ciaramella wrote *C Is for Cthulhu*

(2014), illustrated by Greg Murphy. A similar book is R. J. Ivankovich's *H. P. Lovecraft's The Call of Cthulhu for Beginning Readers* (2017). Ciaramella has also produced something called *Sweet Dreams Cthulhu: A Lovecraftian Bedtime Book* (2017), with illustrations by Murphy. Charles Gilman has written four volumes of a *Tales from Lovecraft Middle School* series of supernatural adventure stories (2012–13), some volumes of which have been translated into French, Italian, Swedish, Hungarian, and Turkish. And one can scarcely ignore *The Necronomicon Pop-Up Book* (Poposition Press, 2017), which presents images from five major Lovecraft stories. The design and illustration was by Skinner, a flamboyant artist who has also expressed devotion to Clark Ashton Smith.

But Lovecraft's reach into popular culture extends far beyond print or even media, and has now ventured into actual merchandising. "Cthulhu for President" bumper stickers are visible, as are metal Cthulhu emblems that parody the Christian fish symbols placed on the rear of automobiles. In 2013 Toy Vault marketed a Cthulhu plush doll that has proven to be very popular, however much it makes something cute and cuddly out of that which was originally designed to be cosmically terrifying. Archie McPhee put out an "Inflatable Cthulhu Beard" and an "Inflatable Cthulhu Arm" (i.e., a tentacle). There are reports of Lovecraftian Christmas tree ornaments.

Some of these products may have the effect of sentimentalising or parodying the dark, misanthropic horror of Lovecraft's stories, but at a minimum they indicate that his celebrity is manifest in both high and low venues—a singular distinction in an author, especially one who never had a book of his stories published in his lifetime. And it is safe to say that, if Lovecraft had lived to profit off of all this merchandising, he would be a very rich man today.

* * *

I am forced to conclude this book with a discussion of the numerous recent kerfuffles about Lovecraft's racism. In discussing this whole issue I am irreverently reminded of the old joke about the Christian and the Jew:

A Christian meets a Jew and beats him up. The Jew says, "What did you do that for?" The Christian says, "Because your people killed Christ!" The Jew says, "Wasn't that a long time ago?" The Christian says, "Yes, but I only just heard about it!"

Awareness of Lovecraft's racism is not exactly breaking news. It was known since at least the 1950s; it received a fair amount of air time in the 1960s, when the first two volumes of *Selected Letters* made his views on the subject abundantly clear; and, as we have seen, it was widely discussed in de Camp's 1975 biography and in the extensive discussion that book received in the fan press.

So the question becomes: Why are we (or some people) so agitated about the issue *now?*

One does not wish to ascribe base motives for the level of indignation that certain individuals feel on the matter, but one cannot help feeling that there is a liberal dose of virtue signalling going on here, among other features even less flattering.

The current furore appears to have begun with an online article, "H. P. Lovecraft's Madness," posted on May 3, 2013, by Phenderson Djèli Clark, the pseudonym of an African American science fiction writer.[13] The post did little except point to various instances of Lovecraft's racial views—in the poem "On the Creation of Niggers," in the stories "The Street" and "The Horror at Red Hook," and in his private correspondence—and essentially say, "What a horrible racist Lovecraft was!" There was not the slightest attempt to place Lovecraft in historical, intellectual, and cultural perspective; instead, Clark sets up a straw man by assert-

13. See disgruntledharadrim.com/2013/05/03/hp-lovecrafts-madness/.

ing that Lovecraft's apologists try to excuse Lovecraft's racism by appealing to his "isolated upbringing"—an argument I do not recall anyone making. Clark makes no reference to my extensive work on the issue.

Clark acknowledges that Lovecraft "is without doubt one of the 'greats,'" but takes umbrage when others attempt to explain to him the sources for Lovecraft's views. It appears he feels he has nothing more to learn on the issue: "Lovecraft spoke loud and clear. If you can't hear him, you're just not listening." It doesn't occur to Clark that perhaps *he* is not listening to well-reasoned arguments (a) that Lovecraft's racism was far more nuanced that he is prepared to admit, and (b) that it does not in fact significantly taint the great majority of his literary work or his philosophical thought.

But in these troubled times, this was an argument that was difficult to convey: it was so much more satisfying to condemn Lovecraft root and branch. From this point on the number of people of various stripes who jumped on Lovecraft became so great that it became a fool's errand to correct them or to suggest that their thunderous fulminations were not very well argued.[14]

Some of these individuals were opportunistic in their attacks. In the summer of 2014 Daniel José Older, a young writer of Puerto Rican descent, launched a rather awkwardly worded broadside against Lovecraft, specifically aimed at the Lovecraft bust that represented the World Fantasy Award. It is true that Nnedi Okorafor, an American writer of Nigerian descent, had expressed reservations about the award when she received it in 2011; but she appeared genuinely conflicted about the award. Not so China Miéville, a lily-white liberal who also received the

14. For my sins, I attempted to do so; see various sections of my book *Lovecraft and Weird Fiction: Selected Blog Posts, 2009–2017* (Seattle: Sarnath Press, 2017).

award and expressed this opinion: "I put it [the WFA] out of sight, where only I can see it, and I have turned it to face the wall. So I am punishing the little fucker for the malevolent clown he was. I can look at it and remember the honour, and above all I am writing behind Lovecraft's back."[15] This, in my humble view, does not seem to be the action of a sane and rational person.

But Older began lobbying unrelentingly for the replacement of the award. He went so far as to suggest the recently deceased Octavia Butler as his preferred choice for a replacement bust, even though Butler, an undeniably fine writer, did not work at all in the field of weird fiction; moreover, it was painfully obvious that Older was putting her forward largely or solely because she was an African-American woman. He gave the game away, however, by his comment that Lovecraft was a "terrible wordsmith" (this from someone whose own struggles with the English language are painfully evident in his writing).

It becomes clear that Older simply doesn't like Lovecraft as a writer, and has seized upon this one flaw in his character to take him down. Regrettably, Older's fanatical crusade was successful, as the World Fantasy Committee, in a craven act of cowardice, banished the Lovecraft bust in 2015. But the last laugh may have been at the convention's expense; for the controversy stirred up by its actions in this matter, as well as the tediously political and "woke" nature of the programming it began to institute, caused a massive reduction in its attendance—well before the COVID pandemic caused it and other events to terminate altogether.

The most breathtakingly vicious attack came from Charles Baxter, a (white) professor and novelist who seems to know nothing about Lovecraft, but who was inexplicably assigned to

---

15. Cited in nnedi.blogspot.com/2011/12/lovecrafts-racism-world-fantasy-award.html.

review Leslie Klinger's *New Annotated H. P. Lovecraft* for the *New York Review of Books* (December 4, 2014). Aside from bewildering personal attacks on Lovecraft (he was a "stranger to joy"; he had "the timid shut-in's phobia of difference, variety, and diversity") and crude mischaracterisations of his work (it is suited only for "adolescents"), he predictably refers to Lovecraft as a "pathological racist."[16]

One of the most galling features of the whole controversy is the alacrity in which certain figures who have benefited from Lovecraft's popularity—and the popularity of weird fiction that he has helped to engender—are prepared to kick Lovecraft posthumously while continuing to profit from their own Lovecraftian writings. I have stated at the beginning that I am not treating in this volume the incredible proliferation of Cthulhu Mythos writing (to say nothing of its infusion into media and other areas), although that has undeniably had a significant influence upon Lovecraft's own ascending reputation. Over the past half-century such writers as Stephen King, Neil Gaiman, Peter Straub, Anne Rice, Ramsey Campbell, Caitlín R. Kiernan, Jonathan Thomas, and numerous others have written explicitly Lovecraftian works or works clearly influenced by Lovecraft.

But the controversy over Lovecraft's racism led several popular or highly regarded writers and editors—from Laird Barron to Paula Guran to Jeff VanderMeer to Scott Nicolay (who professed a desire to urinate on Lovecraft's grave)—to condemn Lovecraft. Guran, in her introduction to *The Mammoth Book of Cthulhu* (2016), picked up on one of Charles Baxter's more egregious claims—that Lovecraft was a misogynist—by declaring, "He may not have hated women (misogyny), but he does seem to have feared them (gynophobia)." It is hardly worth

---

16. See my rebuttal, "Charles Baxter on Lovecraft," in *Lovecraft and Weird Fiction* 63–76.

pointing out that Guran presents no evidence for this startling assertion, to say nothing of ignoring mountains of evidence that contradicts it.

The most stunningly hypocritical example, in this regard, is noted editor Ellen Datlow, who was happy to cash in on three different anthologies of Lovecraftian stories but who was also instrumental in influencing the World Fantasy Committee to discard the Lovecraft bust (and then lied about her role in the matter) and regularly disparaging Lovecraft as a person, about whom she appears to know little.

The amusing thing is that, as can be seen from my discussion earlier in this chapter, this obsessive focus on Lovecraft's racism has had virtually no effect on his continuing popularity and critical esteem. His work continues to be disseminated worldwide; indeed, critics, editors, and publishers in the non-Anglophone community—the very ones you would think would be most perturbed about the issue—simply don't care about it, and they frequently wonder about our own single-minded fixation on it.[17] The HBO miniseries *Lovecraft Country* had the regrettable effect of conveying the misleading idea that Lovecraft was nothing but a racist who wrote horror stories, but its influence was fleeting.

For a sane counter-example, consider the words of Maurice Lévy. His *Lovecraft ou du fantastique* (1972), let us recall, began as a dissertation for the Sorbonne in 1969—not exactly a time of sociopolitical tranquillity in the West. But, while discussing Lovecraft's racism frankly, and quoting liberally from some of the more outrageous passages in his letters (especially those written after his first visit to New York in 1922), Lévy wisely concludes that these passages "suffice . . . in showing how Lovecraft *dreamed his repugnances* and with what verbal richness he ranted

17. See my recent article, "H. P. Lovecraft: Racism and Recognition," *Truth Seeker* No. 147 (September–December 2020): 23–27.

from purely sensory data. In him, art was nourished by neurosis—it furnished him with his materials; but that art allowed him to sublimate the horror, to extract from it its quintessence, and through it, perhaps, to cure his neurosis."[18]

The current obsession with Lovecraft's racial views is itself a "product of our times"—a result of a multitude of historical and cultural factors that has led some of us to focus single-mindedly on this one element of Lovecraft's life, work, and thought to the exclusion of nearly all others. I daresay it will pass when (or if) our society becomes a little less polarised. One can only hope that, at that time, the full range of Lovecraft's achievement will be appreciated without the current tunnel vision and with a proper understanding of the place of racism—as well as atheism, aesthetic integrity, political rumination, travel, and countless other facets of Lovecraft's personality—in the totality of his work.

---

18. Maurice Lévy, *Lovecraft: A Study in the Fantastic,* tr. S. T. Joshi (Detroit: Wayne State University Press, 1988), 29.

Epilogue

As should be evident, Lovecraft's popularity worldwide has never been greater. Translations continue to proliferate, and his work continues to be studied, adapted, and imitated in a wide variety of media. In the Anglophone community, in spite of the recent controversy over his racism, the same situation largely holds, and there is no shortage of editions of his work, scholarship and criticism, and adaptations in all manner of media.

So where does Lovecraft go from here?

In terms of the dissemination of his work, virtually every extant text he wrote has been published or will soon be published. The Hippocampus Press edition of his collected correspondence is expected to conclude around 2023, in twenty-five or twenty-six volumes. At that point, all that will remain unpublished are his juvenile scientific writings—the *Scientific Gazette,* the *Rhode Island Journal of Astronomy,* and a number of separate booklets—and the logistical and technical difficulties in a facsimile reproduction of these documents are formidable. They are, however, available online through the Brown Digital Repository.

The analysis of his work, and the assessment of his character and temperament, will always be an ongoing enterprise. Every generation will need to express its judgment on these issues, and those judgments are likely to vary widely from what has been said of him in the past because of inevitable changes in cultural outlook, intellectual progress (or regress), and countless other factors.

That his work *will* endure seems certain. Even if some academicians and other figures refuse to accept his canonisation, and a small but vocal minority indignantly declare that he should not be read at all, the readership for Lovecraft's works seems destined to be ever-increasing, because the core of his work speaks to us in ways that much of the writing of his generation—ranging from the mainstream work of Sinclair Lewis (now largely restricted to sporadic academic interest) to the pulp hackwork of Seabury Quinn, E. Hoffmann Price, and others, which will never reach a wide or universal audience in spite of the most valiant efforts of its few partisans—does not.

The physical and spiritual loneliness of humanity in the universe; the potential nebulosity of the human body in the wake of technological advance; the terrors of heredity, of isolation, of the untenanted wilderness, of the teeming clangour of cities—these and other elements in Lovecraft's fiction have greater relevance today than they did when they were written, and their expression is untainted either by his much-documented racism or by specific cultural references to their own time that might otherwise make them resonate less intensely to today's and tomorrow's readership.

And the profound, complex, and flexible character revealed by Lovecraft's letters, as well as the core of philosophical depth found in his atheism, his devotion to aesthetic integrity, his measured respect for the cultural heritage of the past, his acknowledgment of science as the arbiter of truth accompanied by his realisation that emotion and imagination must also play a key role in any well-ordered human temperament, will provide succeeding generations endless fodder for debate as to exactly what elements—personal, regional, cultural, intellectual, social, political, economic—went into the making of the person we know as H. P. Lovecraft.

His life and work have been dissected with the rigorous minuteness of biblical texts; his relations with his family, his friends, his fellow writers, and his literary predecessors and successors continue to be weighed. The enormous paper trail he left behind, especially in terms of letters, will generate mountains of further research and analysis as all these documents are assessed for the light they shed on him and his work.

But it is transcendently brilliant fiction that will remain the essence of his work and the touchstone of his enduring fascination to future generations. That fiction is a flawed but towering monument of literary achievement that will continue to engage us as long as human beings are capable of absorbing its inexpressible fusion of terror, wonder, and awe. H. P. Lovecraft has proven himself a man and writer of the ages. His fame has expanded so far beyond what he could have imagined as itself to constitute a "weird tale" of the most spectacularly bizarre sort.

Bibliography

A. Primary Texts

Collected Essays. Ed. S. T. Joshi. New York: Hippocampus Press, 2004–06. 5 vols.

Collected Fiction: A Variorum Edition. Ed. S. T. Joshi. New York: Hippocampus Press, 2015–17. 4 vols.

Dawnward Spire, Lonely Hill: The Letters of H. P. Lovecraft and Clark Ashton Smith. Ed. David E. Schultz and S. T. Joshi. New York: Hippocampus Press, 2017.

The Dunwich Horror and Others. Ed. August Derleth. Sauk City, WI: Arkham House, 1963.

Essential Solitude: The Letters of H. P. Lovecraft and August Derleth. Ed. David E. Schultz and S. T. Joshi. New York: Hippocampus Press, 2008. 2 vols.

Letters to C. L. Moore and Others. Ed. David E. Schultz and S. T. Joshi. New York: Hippocampus Press, 2017.

Letters to Family and Family Friends. Ed. S. T. Joshi and David E. Schultz. New York: Hippocampus Press, 2020. 2 vols.

Letters to J. Vernon Shea, Carl F. Strauch, and Lee McBride White. Ed. S. T. Joshi and David E. Schultz. New York: Hippocampus Press, 2016.

Letters to James F. Morton. Ed. David E. Schultz and S. T. Joshi. New York: Hippocampus Press, 2011.

Letters to Maurice W. Moe and Others. Ed. David E. Schultz and S. T. Joshi. New York: Hippocampus Press, 2018.

Letters to Rheinhart Kleiner and Others. Ed. S. T. Joshi and David E. Schultz. New York: Hippocampus Press, 2020.

Letters to Wilfred B. Talman and Helen V. and Genevieve Sully. Ed. David E. Schultz and S. T. Joshi. New York: Hippocampus Press, 2019.

Letters to Woodburn Harris and Others. Ed. David E. Schultz and S. T. Joshi. New York: Hippocampus Press, 2022.

Letters with Donald and Howard Wandrei and to Emil Petaja. Ed. S. T. Joshi and David E. Schultz. New York: Hippocampus Press, 2019.

Marginalia. Ed. August Derleth. Sauk City, WI: Arkham House, 1944.

O Fortunate Floridian: H. P. Lovecraft's Letters to R. H. Barlow. Ed. S. T. Joshi and David E. Schultz. Tampa, FL: University of Tampa Press, 2007.

Something about Cats and Other Pieces. Ed. August Derleth. Sauk City, WI: Arkham House, 1949.

B. Secondary Texts

Airaksinen, Timo. *The Philosophy of H. P. Lovecraft.* New York: Peter Lang, 1999.

Callaghan, Gavin. *H. P. Lovecraft's Dark Arcadia.* Jefferson, NC: McFarland, 2013.

Campbell, Ramsey, and August Derleth. *Letters to Arkham: The Letters of Ramsey Campbell and August Derleth, 1961–1971.* Ed. S. T. Joshi. Hornsea, UK: PS Publishing, 2014.

de Camp, L. Sprague. *Lovecraft: A Biography.* Garden City, NY: Doubleday, 1975.

Harman, Graham. *Weird Realism: Lovecraft and Philosophy.* Winchester, UK: Zero Books, 2012.

Joshi, S. T. *Eighty Years of Arkham House.* Seattle: Sarnath Press, 2019.

———. *Lovecraft and a World in Transition: Collected Essays on H. P. Lovecraft.* New York: Hippocampus Press, 2014.

———. *The Rise, Fall, and Rise of the Cthulhu Mythos.* New York: Hippocampus Press, 2015.

———. *Sixty Years of Arkham House.* Sauk City, WI: Arkham House, 1999.

———, ed. *H. P. Lovecraft in the Argosy: Collected Correspondence from the Munsey Magazines.* West Warwick, RI: Necronomicon Press, 1994.

———, ed. *A Weird Writer in Our Midst: Early Criticism of H. P. Lovecraft.* New York: Hippocampus Press, 2010.

———, and David E. Schultz, ed. *Ave atque Vale: Reminiscences of H. P. Lovecraft.* West Warwick, RI: Necronomicon Press, 2018.

King, Stephen. *Danse Macabre.* 1979. New York: Berkley, 1982.

Loveman, Samuel. *Out of the Immortal Night: Selected Works of Samuel Loveman.* Ed. S. T. Joshi and David E. Schultz. Rev. ed. New York: Hippocampus Press, 2021.

Mosig, Dirk W. *Mosig at Last: A Psychologist Looks at H. P. Lovecraft.* West Warwick, RI: Necronomicon Press, 1997.

Poole, W. Scott. *In the Mountains of Madness: The Life and Extraordinary Afterlife of H. P. Lovecraft.* Berkeley, CA: Soft Skull Press, 2016.

Roland. Paul. *The Curious Case of H. P. Lovecraft.* London: Plexus, 2014.

Tyson, Donald. *The Dream World of H. P. Lovecraft.* Woodbury, MN: Llewellyn, 2010.

Wilson, Colin. *The Strength to Dream: Literature and the Imagination.* 1961. Boston: Houghton Mifflin, 1962.

Index

www.ingramcontent.com/pod-product-compliance
Lightning Source LLC
LaVergne TN
LVHW020529100826
845148LV00010B/1400

9781614983453